BETSY COWLES PARTRIDGE: MOUNTAINEER

For Sue,
With Much Affection,
Jan Robertson

BETSY COWLES PARTRIDGE
MOUNTAINEER

Janet Robertson

UNIVERSITY PRESS OF COLORADO

Copyright © 1998 by the University Press of Colorado

International Standard Book Number 0-87081-480-x

Published by the University Press of Colorado
P.O. Box 849
Niwot, Colorado 80544

The University Press of Colorado is a cooperative publishing enterprise supported, in part, by Adams State College, Colorado State University, Fort Lewis College, Mesa State College, Metropolitan State College of Denver, University of Colorado, University of Northern Colorado, University of Southern Colorado, and Western State College of Colorado.

The paper used in this publication meets the minimum requirements of the American National Standard for Information Sciences — Permanence of Paper for Printed Library Materials. ANSI Z39.48–1984

Library of Congress Cataloging-in-Publication Data

Robertson, Janet, 1935–
    Betsy Cowles Partridge : mountaineer / Janet Robertson.
        p.   cm.
    Includes bibliographical references (p.   ) and index.
    ISBN 0-87081-480-X (hardcover : alk. paper)
    1. Cowles Partridge, Betsy, 1902–1974.   2. Mountaineers—United States—Biography.   I. Title.
    GV199.92.C69R63   1998
    796.52'2'092—dc21
        [B]   97-48725
                                                                                     CIP

This book was designed
and typeset in ITC Cheltenham
by Stephen Adams

10   9   8   6   5   4   3   2   1

To Kay Graber with gratitude

Contents

Illustrations   ix

Acknowledgments   xi

Prologue   1

CHAPTER ONE   The Early Years   5

CHAPTER TWO   Marriage to Bob Cowles   15

CHAPTER THREE   Betsy Becomes a Mountain Climber   41

CHAPTER FOUR   "The Tetons to Me"   53

CHAPTER FIVE   First Ascents in Colombia   69

CHAPTER SIX   A Fragmented Decade: The 1940s After the
Santa Martas   89

CHAPTER SEVEN   "The Trip of a Lifetime"   101

CHAPTER EIGHT   To Tengboche   121

CHAPTER NINE   "Sceneries All Round"   143

CHAPTER TEN   "America's Foremost Woman Mountaineer"   165

Epilogue   187

Mountain Trips of Betsy Strong Cowles
Partridge, 1933–1970   197

Bibliography   201

Index   203

Illustrations

Photographs

(*Cover*)   Betsy Cowles on the Jungfrau, 1937.

1.1   The three Strong siblings, circa 1910.   7

2.1   Colorado Springs house party, 1932.   17

2.2   Portrait of Bob Cowles in 1932.   19

2.3   Betsy Cowles and her father, John Strong, circa 1935.   26

2.4   Josef Georges on the Dent Blanche.   29

3.1   Paul Petzoldt on Mount Owen in 1940.   45

3.2   Betsy Cowles, circa 1935.   48

3.3   Gottfried Fenz on the summit of the Jungfrau.   50

4.1   Unnamed person on Mont Blanc in 1937.   55

4.2   The Wetterhorn in Switzerland.   56

4.3   Climbers on Mount Owen in the Tetons, 1940.   61

4.4   Bill House on Nez Perce, Wyoming.   64

5.1   La Reina, Colombia.   70

5.2   The summit of La Reina.   83

6.1   Betsy Cowles and Paul Petzoldt, circa 1941.   90

6.2   Dinner party in the late 1950s.   94

7.1   "Tears in a Katmandu Street," 1950.   109

7.2   Nell Houston in Kathmandu, 1950.   110

7.3   The Maharajah's palace in Kathmandu in 1950.   112

ix

7.4   Kathmandu's wind sock and dirt airstrip of 1950.   115

8.1   "Our Sherpas."   122

8.2   The main street of Dhankuta in 1950.   125

8.3   Bill Tilman, 1950.   129

8.4   "The Three Musketeers": Sherpas near Phedi in 1950.   133

8.5   Charles Houston on bamboo bridge, 1950.   134

8.6   Mani stone in Nepal, 1950.   136

8.7   Namche Bazar, the Sherpa trade center of the Khumbu,
      in 1950.   138

9.1   The stone house on the grounds of the Tengboche
      gompa in 1950.   144

9.2   The Tengboche gompa in 1950.   145

9.3   Oscar Houston and the young Tengboche lamas.   146

9.4   The sixteen-year-old Rimpoche at the Tengboche
      gompa in 1950.   148

9.5   The practice dances for the 1950 Mani-Rimdu festival
      at the Tengboche.   152

9.6   The Houston party of 1950 in front of the
      Tengboche gompa.   155

9.7   The head man of Namche Bazar.   157

9.8   Ferris-wheel-like swings at the annual festival of Tihaar,
      in 1950.   159

9.9   Betsy arranging flowers in 1950.   161

10.1 Betsy Cowles at home, circa 1956.   169

10.2 Betsy Cowles Partridge and her husband, General Earle
      (Pat) Partridge, USAF, circa 1958.   175

11.1 The Rimpoche of Tengboche in 1993.   193

Maps

1.   India and Nepal.   105

2.   The 1950 Houston party route.   124

Acknowledgments

Without the patience, kindnesses, and help of the following people, I would never have been able to write Betsy Cowles Partridge's biography. Thank you all.

First and foremost, I am grateful to the staff of the American Heritage Center in Laramie, Wyoming. Gene Gressley, formerly its director, was instrumental in persuading Betsy to donate many of her papers, trip diaries, scrapbooks of articles about her and by her, 35mm slides, and black-and-white prints to the University of Wyoming archives. I'm also grateful to Nora Quinlan, formerly curator of the Special Collections at the University of Colorado's Norlin Library. She permitted me to look through Betsy's personal library of mountaineering books when they first arrived in Boulder, just after they had been unboxed and before they were catalogued. The authors of many volumes had personally inscribed them to Betsy, obviously having sent them to her as gifts. Seeing the library in its entirety gave me a sense of just how many famous climbers Betsy knew.

Kay Partridge granted me permission to use all the Cowles Partridge materials in the Heritage Center. She also provided some wonderful details about Betsy and her second husband, the late General Earle E. ("Pat") Partridge.

To write about Betsy, though, I needed more than a paper trail. So I am most indebted to Betsy's beloved sister, Emilie Strong Smith, and Emilie's late husband, Judge Macauley Smith. They filled me in on family history I could not have found out from anyone else. In between anecdotes, they offered me fine Kentucky bourbon and tours of Louisville. Em and Mac were extraordinarily hospitable to me as well as informative and generous with their time. Em loaned me photographs of Betsy's early days and permitted me to draw on the many letters that Betsy wrote to the famous pianist, Miecio Horszowski. Betsy's nephew, John, added vivid accounts of his remarkable aunt. He also loaned me what has become my favorite photograph of Betsy; it shows her and Paul Petzoldt sitting on the ground close to a clutch of empty beer bottles, devouring watermelon.

The following people were responsible for my discovering Betsy's urban life: Elena Bertozzi, Dorothy Bryson, Stuart Dodge, Jack Hettinger, Vi Ryder Nicholson, Virginia Ryder, William Ryder, M.D., and Marka Webb Stewart. Thanks to Dodge, Nicholson, Ryder, and Ryder, I obtained yet more photographs of Betsy and her relatives.

I interviewed the following climbers who helped me fill in the blanks about Betsy's mountain life: Stan Boucher, Stu Dodge, the late Elinor Davis Ehrman, Laney House, and her late husband, Bill, the late Bob Ormes, and Dorothy Teague Swartz. In addition, I am grateful to Sallie Greenwood for permitting me to use her taped interview with Paul Petzoldt. I thank my good luck for meeting Julia Robinson, who put me in touch with Betsy's godson, Hugh Cheney. Through letters from Andrews Black, Robert C. Black, Thomas D. Cabot, Robert Dodson, Glenn Exum, Maynard Miller, and Dee Molenaar, I added yet more details.

Had it not been for Al Ossinger, I would never have discovered Ben Hammett, who provided invaluable information about Betsy's first husband, Alfred Cowles III. Dona Hildebrand and Duane Reed helped me track down a photo of Betsy's second husband, General Pat Partridge.

I have a large debt to many for enabling me to write knowledgeably about Betsy's historic 1950 trek in eastern Nepal to the Khumbu. In the fall of 1993, a month after I had undergone arthroscopic surgery on my right knee, I set out to retrace her footsteps. (I hadn't realized beforehand that the Nepalese don't do switchbacks.) A few days into the trip, I would have bailed out if I could have found any practical way to do so. By the narrowest of margins I persisted, encouraged by my trekking companions, Louise Bradley, Kim and Nancy Malville, Cal Whitehall, and my dear husband, David. Every day at least one staff member of the Sagarmatha Trekking Company lagged far behind the rest of our party to assist me down endless steep stone steps. Jangbu Sherpa, Dawa Sherpa, and Dawa Tamang (not to mention our cheerful cook, Duti) were simply wonderful, and I made it to Tengboche.

It was my great good fortune to be able to interview two members of the Houston party of 1950: Dr. Charles Houston in Burlington, Vermont; and Father Anderson Bakewell, S.J., in Santa Fe, New Mexico. In addition, Dr. Houston made helpful comments and corrections to the manuscript. Others who provided details about some aspect of Nepal and/or the Houston party's trek are: Professor Jana Everett, the late Dr. Edwin L. Licht, Tim Madge, Dawa Sherpa, Jangbu Sherpa, and Dr. Shi-Kuei Wu. I was privileged to meet and talk to (via an interpreter) His Holiness Nawang Tensing Jangpo, the Reincarnate Lama of the Tengboche gompa. My husband, David, as always helpful and supportive *and* a computer whiz, made the maps showing Betsy's journeys in India and Nepal.

Finally, I bless Rick Ewig and John Hanks of the American Heritage Center, who patiently assisted me on many occasions when I pored over Betsy's papers and photographs.

Dingbuzy [Dingboche near Mount Everest] has nothing but sceneries and sceneries all round.... I wish I were a man and not a woman to accompany you to these darling places to see with my own eyes those hills where we often played a childish hide and seek game with much frolics....

—Letter from Ang Yang Tsen, wife of Ang Tharkay, Sherpas both,
to H. W. Tilman, October 20, 1950

Prologue

When Betsy (Elizabeth) Strong Cowles took up mountain climbing in the early 1930s, she stunned her old college friends because at Vassar she had never shown the "slightest interest in or aptitude for athletics of any kind."[1] It was her Baptist minister father who introduced Betsy to the sport in Switzerland. Two years later, she became the first female to traverse the rugged Grand Teton in Wyoming. In 1940 she wrote a climbing friend that she'd "just about decided to make mountaineering [her] Calling."[2] A year later, Betsy, as a member of a small party led by Paul Petzoldt, made three first ascents in the Santa Marta Range of Colombia. For more than thirty years she climbed mountains in the United States, Canada, Switzerland, Italy, Germany, Wales, and East Africa.

However, Betsy regarded a trek she made in 1950, rather than any of her climbs, as "the trip of a lifetime." Betsy was the only woman in a party of five, the first Westerners ever to visit the Everest region of Nepal. After reaching the Tengboche *gompa* (monastery), two members of the party went on to make the first mountaineering reconnaissance of Everest in the Khumbu Glacier area, the side by which it was eventually first ascended.

As the group's official photographer, Betsy took both 35mm slides and black-and-white photographs of the journey. She kept a detailed diary while sightseeing in India and Kathmandu and while making the difficult trek up the Arun River valley, across the grain of the land to the trade center of Namche Bazar and, finally, to the Tengboche gompa. Betsy reported that she, Oscar Houston, who organized the trip, and his wife, Nell, were the seventy-fifth, seventy-sixth, and seventy-seventh Westerners to visit Kathmandu. To reach Nepal's fabled capitol, Betsy and the Houstons rode ponies—and

1

sometimes walked—on the historic high road over the Sisagarhi and Chandragari Passes. However, they were able to return to India by plane on the second-ever commercial flight to leave Kathmandu.

Sir Edmund Hillary once wrote Betsy, "You were always renowned for your energy." The famous Swiss guide Otto Furrer called her "one of the best lady mountain climbers he had ever had." Glenn Exum, founder of the Exum Mountain Guide Service and the School of American Mountaineering in Jackson Hole, Wyoming, rated Betsy as "the most outstanding and best woman climber in North America" of her era. Dave Brower, a famous environmental activist and a pioneer climber himself, described her as "one of the country's foremost women mountaineers."[3]

Betsy Cowles was tough and quite willing to "put on the hair shirt" when necessary. However, she always carried a lipstick in her pack and wore color-coordinated climbing attire. Once she commented to a reporter that it had never been her view that the rough life became more delightful the worse one looked.[4]

Her sister recalls that Betsy attracted men like a honeypot. Chubby as a child, she metamorphosed into a slender young woman. Although in repose her face was almost plain, the nose slightly too large, Betsy's vivacity and responsiveness transformed her. During a conversation, she directed her attention totally to the other person as though no one else were in the room.[5] Her godson recalls that she had an "uncanny sense of how to read people and how to draw out the best in them."[6] Friends, especially men, describe Betsy as being very good-looking, "a true lady," or "a strikingly attractive captivating, articulate, witty, a raconteur, a charming and unforgettable person."[7] But women warmed to her as well.

Betsy's nephew, John Smith, fondly remembers that while hiking on a trail,

Betsy had her own "call," a cheery melodious two-note signature that she sounded whenever she wanted to avoid words but wanted to communicate "hello dearie" or "I'm here, where are you?" or "aren't we having fun!" She would call when she first caught sight of you, or when you passed each other on a switchback or any other time she wanted to make contact. The first note was higher than the second and the combination was magical. When you heard the call, you answered with the same notes. It was a musical bond.

John thinks it likely that "everyone who ever met Betsy fell a little bit in love with her, and maybe she did the same with them." As a young boy he sometimes went into a restaurant with his Aunt Betsy; it was a memorable experience. He would watch as she struck up a conversation with the waiter or waitress. "By the end of the meal she would know their history, their goals, their hopes and fears and when she left it was as if she was saying goodbye to an old friend." Betsy sometimes directed her interest to the people or food in the next booth "and it was not unusual to find her sampling the desserts that were being served nearby." Her smile was "dazzling" and her enthusiasm "infectious." The dining room was always "a different place after she had been there."[8]

Betsy had a magical, quicksilver quality that pervades her writing. She knew how to charm the reader by making mountain climbing sound like fun and by telling stories on herself. Her published articles never dwelled on illness or fatigue unless for humorous effect. She deplored chronicles that abounded in "lacerating details" of weariness and praised ones that described mountaineering so that it made sense. Betsy added high spirits and playfulness to a genre frequently burdened by what she called the "grim white-tower attitude,"[9] referring to the macho attitudes of climbers in James Ramsey Ullman's then-popular novel, *The White Tower.*

It is no accident that Betsy was charming *and* an American woman mountain climber of the 1930s and 1940s. Had she been lackluster and unfeminine, it is unlikely that she would have been invited along to browse the unclimbed summits of the Santa Martas in 1941 or to tackle Nepal's *terra incognita* in 1950. Betsy was climbing in an era when male climbers, especially American ones, called the shots. And because most of those males were well-educated Easterners, they felt at home with someone like Betsy, whose background was similar.

Although this book is mostly about Betsy and the fascinating paradoxes in her personality, it also offers a peep at the sport of mountaineering as it was emerging in the United States after World War I. Colorado mountaineer Robert Ormes has pointed out that, in those days, mountain climbers were a novelty and more in the limelight than they are now.[10] Betsy's writing reflects the enthusiasm of an acolyte who has been introduced to an almost unimaginably wonderful world. It is the antithesis of "stuffy"—full of unexplored places, rock faces close to unclimbable, mercurial weather, incredible raw beauty, and people who know how to have fun. For a well-brought-up, educated woman, it is a world of freedom.

One of Betsy's friends has mentioned knowing a climber who was quite critical of her because he felt she epitomized what was wrong with the Climbing Establishment in the United States up to the 1950s. But this critic must have focused on the outward trappings of Betsy's privileged life rather than on the person herself; a host of other people who knew Betsy have remarked that many of her closest friends were climbers and that she was completely indifferent to whether they were young or old, rich or poor, famous or obscure. If they loved high hills, she drew them into her circle.

Betsy Cowles's writing reflects her genuinely deep feelings for mountains and all things to do with climbing. Because almost none of her articles ever appeared in a magazine of general interest, large portions of them are reprinted in this book. For the same reason, many of her photographs are reprinted as well; Betsy was a better-than-average photographer who took pride in printing her own black-and-whites. We have to disbelieve her once-stated preference for taking portraits of mountains rather than people, for she made compelling pictures of both.[11] Her 35mm transparency of the legendary and crusty mountaineer H. W. Tilman, caught when he looked up while kneading bread dough, is a superb candid.

Although Betsy had many interests—the Colorado Springs Symphony and the Colorado Springs Fine Arts Center, to name two—it is her passion for mountains that is most apparent to those of us who never knew her. It glows in her writing, in her photographs, and in the speeches she committed to paper, most of which, up to now, have lain undisturbed in mountaineering journals and university archives. Betsy is too good for such obscurity, both because she thrived in a male-dominated sport and because she was an articulate, sensitive advocate of mountaineering.

Notes

1. Elizabeth S. Cowles, caption for photo in "North to Everest," *Vassar Alumnae Magazine* (ca. early 1950s), Archives, American Heritage Center, University of Wyoming, Laramie.
2. Elizabeth S. Cowles, letter to Paul Petzoldt, October 13, 1940, Archives, American Heritage Center.
3. Sir Edmund Hillary, letter to Elizabeth S. (Cowles) Partridge, September 13, 1971, Archives, American Heritage Center; Christine Reid, letter to Elizabeth S. Cowles, n.d., Archives, American Heritage Center; Glenn Exum, letter to the author, February 17, 1992; Dave Brower, ed., *Going Light with Backpack or Burro: How to Get Along on Wilderness Trails (Chiefly in the West)* (San Francisco: Sierra Club, 1951).
4. "America's Most Interesting People," *American Magazine*, n.d., Archives, American Heritage Center.
5. Kay Partridge, telephone conversation with the author, 1991.
6. Hugh Cheney, letter to the author, February 21, 1996.
7. Dorothy Teague Swartz, interview with the author, January 14, 1993; Robert Dodson, letter to the author, July 11, 1992.
8. John Smith, letter to the author, December 24, 1993; corrections to the manuscript, April 1, 1996.
9. Elizabeth S. Cowles, text for a talk about mountaineering presented to a newly organized climbing club, n.d., Archives, American Heritage Center.
10. Robert M. Ormes, interview with the author, May 13, 1985.
11. Elizabeth S. Cowles, "A Camera in the Mountains," *The Villager* (November 1940), Archives, American Heritage Center.

CHAPTER ONE

The Early Years

On March 14, 1941, Betsy and her climbing companion, the guide Paul Petzoldt, set out on what turned out to be the disheartening reconnaissance of a high peak in the Santa Marta Range of Colombia. As Betsy described it:

> *We crossed three wearisome ridges, like triplets each was so identical with the other except that it got a bit higher each time. From the top of the last we saw at least five more and beyond, as unconcerned as may be, our mountain looking incredibly remote. Really, it looked further away than when we had started. We retreated like Napoleon from Moscow. When finally, in desperation, far below in the old labyrinth of cliffs and lakes, we decided to wade a last obstacle, we sank in mud up to our waists and probably would have disappeared completely and forever had we not clung by our ice axes to niches on the overhang above us. Paul declares it was the most dangerous moment of his life.*
> *I just know that it was the dirtiest of mine.[1]*

Slightly more than thirty-eight years earlier, on April 8, 1902, in New Britain, Connecticut, Betsy (christened Elizabeth) Livingston Strong was born into a genteel family which scorned dirt and had no interest whatever in mountain climbing. For many years, Betsy remained traditionally respectable. She conformed to her parents' expectations, fulfilling her mother's social aspirations, albeit sometimes unwillingly, and graduating from Vassar College. She adhered to her father's code, attending church, and, after her marriage, becoming a dutiful, faithful wife. By the time she was in her early thirties, however, she had expanded her horizons considerably.

Betsy's mother, Eliza Livingston McCreery, grew up in Pittsburgh, Pennsylvania, where she attended public schools. Eliza's father, William, who had been raised on a farm, became an extremely successful entrepreneur as well as one of Pittsburgh's most public-spirited citizens. He helped establish the area's first exclusively wholesale grain commission house, erected one of the country's largest grain elevators, became director of the Citizens' Bank, organized the Imperial Coal Company, served on the Pittsburgh Board of Trade, and conceived of and built seven railroad lines in the vicinity of Pittsburgh. A retiring man, "he [made] no display with his well earned fortune."[2]

During her senior year of high school, Eliza met a graduate of Vassar College who so impressed her that she taught herself enough Latin to gain admittance. In 1888 she graduated. Shortly afterward, her father, William McCreery, died. Grief-stricken, his widow and two daughters, Eliza and Emilie, sought solace in Europe. They spent a year in Vienna, where Eliza studied singing and her older sister studied piano under the great Polish-born piano teacher Thedor Leschetizky. On their trip home, Eliza met John Henry Strong on shipboard, and was smitten. She told her sister he was the handsomest man she had ever seen.

John was sailing back home after a year's study at the University of Munich, where he had been mulling over his future. Finally he had decided to make a career in the ministry rather than music. After he and Eliza met, they courted and became engaged. John enrolled in the Rochester Theological Seminary, graduating in 1893. A year later he and Eliza McCreery were married.

John Henry Strong was following in the footsteps of his father, the eminent Baptist minister Augustus Hopkins Strong, who was, as Emilie puts it, "an intellectual giant." John, born in Cleveland, Ohio, moved with his family to New York after his father accepted the presidency of the Rochester Theological Seminary. John became a student at the Phillips Academy in Andover, Massachusetts. After graduating Phi Beta Kappa from the University of Rochester in 1889, he earned a B.A. from Yale University. (Had his family been able to afford it, he would have attended Yale for all four undergraduate years.)

It was in Cleveland that Augustus Strong, serving as minister of the First Baptist Church, met John D. Rockefeller, a dedicated Baptist also, though a member of the Erie Street congregation.[3] (By 1905, John D. had tithed nearly $100 million to the Baptists.[4]) The two men became friends, as did their families. Augustus's oldest son, Charles, married John D's oldest daughter, Bessie. John D., Jr., was a groomsman at John and Eliza's wedding. John Henry Strong and Eliza also served as chaperons for the European tour of John, Jr., and Alta

Figure 1.1 The three Strong siblings, circa 1910; Bill (about twelve), Emilie (about two), and Betsy (about eight). (Courtesy of Emilie S. Smith.)

(who later became a Prentice), which included a trip to Russia at the time of the coronation of the last czar.

Eliza bore four children, three of whom survived to adulthood. A son, William McCreery (Bill), was four years and a day older than Betsy; he was ten years older than Emilie. In between Betsy and Emilie, another girl was born who died in infancy. While the family grew, the first twenty years or so of John's professional life included pastorates in Cincinnati and New Britain, Connecticut; a professorship of New Testament interpretation at Rochester Theological Seminary (1903–1912); and studies in Germany to gain his D.D. in Greek New Testament at three different universities—Berlin, Marburg, and Halle. John and Eliza spoke German well, which helped Betsy and her brother, Bill, to pick it up too. Emilie was too young to go to school as her elder siblings did.

In 1913, John accepted a pastorate at the Eutaw Place Baptist Church in Baltimore, which proved to be a bittersweet interlude in his life. John, a fit outdoorsman, was an imposing figure. He enjoyed leading his young church members on hikes during which he discussed spiritual matters. But the elders of his Southern Baptist church pointed out that hiking took time away from instructing youths in Scripture. It was one of many ways in which John found himself at odds with his more conservative congregation. Betsy did not help matters; she once remarked that the only reason she had never been bounced out of Sunday School was the fact that she was the minister's daughter.[5] As an adult she rarely attended church.

After eight years in Baltimore, John resigned to become a professor of Greek New Testament and homiletics at the Biblical Seminary in New York City, a position he held until his retirement in 1928.[6]

Although Eliza and John had different temperaments, they were a devoted couple and agreed that their children should receive the best education possible, that their teeth should be fixed, that Betsy should take piano lessons, and that Bill should study the violin. Eliza made "nice" dresses for Betsy, but clothes "or anything frivolous like that" were not emphasized. (Emilie wore hand-me-down dresses from her cousin, Madeline Prentice, which arrived in a big box every fall. They featured high white necks and box pleats; Emilie hated them and found out years later that Madeline did too.[7])

Certainly John Strong had a serious side. He was a Greek scholar who, in his later years, became increasingly a poet and mystic. He was also a gentle father who never laid down the law to members of his family. As Emilie remembered, "We didn't have an argument....You didn't bring things out in the open...in our family." John's zest for learning served as a potent example to his children, who were "not even faintly competitive."

But he had a playful side, too, which Betsy emulated. The unwritten rule was that one ought to engage in an activity for the sheer joy of it. In addition to composing music, John dashed off rhymes, only one of which survives. It pokes gentle fun at the then-current fad of thorough food-chewing espoused by an American dietitian, Horace Fletcher:

Fletcherism Revived

Wouldst thou be good?
Then chew thy food.
Wouldst thou be great?
Insalivate.

Wouldst thou be wise?
Then "Fletcherize"
Until thy food
In liquid lies.

Wouldst thou be strong?
Chew straight along.

Wouldst thou be smart?
Chew on with heart
Through soup, roast,
salad, fish and tart.

Wouldst thou be known?
Chew to the bone.

Wouldst thou rise high?
Chew on the sly.

Wouldst thou be great
and shine afar?
THEN RIDE UPON THE
CHEW-CHEW CAR.[8]

Betsy came to share her father's delight in words. For example, after driving through an English village called Thursby, she began calling the days of the week, "Thursby, Friby, Saturby" and so on.[9] In her writing, she tossed off such phrases as "early morning coolth," cloudiness that "makes vilibizzity of what's below rather slight," "Admirable Byrd." Betsy found it "peaceifying" to do "cruel work"; said that the combination of the great outdoors with housekeeping was the best "youthifying pursuit a woman could want"; deplored the "messitude" of trash left on mountains; and dubbed the Matterhorn the "M-horn."[10]

Betsy's mother, Eliza, was quite different from her husband. She was gregarious and talkative, thriving on family get-togethers at Christmas Cove, Maine, which Emilie remembers as "long summers…pleasure-filled." In the early years, the Strong and McCreery families went by train to Damariscotta and then by boat to Christmas Cove. Without automobiles or electricity, life slowed down. People entertained themselves. Mostly the grownups talked while drinking tea on the porch; the younger set romanced.

John Strong found the place too folksy and "all those tea parties" oppressive. He did not particularly like little children and relished solitude. Emilie recalls, only half-jokingly, that her father's favorite phrase, from a hymn, was "Peace, perfect peace with loved ones far away." Frequently he escaped the noisy sociability of his in-laws at Christmas Cove by canoeing on a Maine river (either solo or with a friend); for a time he owned a birchbark canoe. On the wall of John's study was a beautiful trout, mounted, attesting to his skill as a fly fisherman.[11]

Eliza had good business sense; John had none. "Papa was easily satisfied with the best," Emilie recalls. Incidents such as the following were typical: John might visit "old Mr. Rockefeller" at his Pocantico mansion on the Hudson River and return home telling Eliza that Mr. Rockefeller had given him $100. Eliza would be relieved, saying she could now pay the grocery bill, but John would then explain that on the way home he had purchased "that encyclopedia that I've always wanted." After John inherited money from his father, his tastes became more extravagant. Betsy's first cousin, Richard Sewall, recounts how, during the Depression:

> *John horrified the whole family (mine included) by buying a violin for $5,000! Eliza was in despair. A year later he sold it for $7,000 and bought a better one for $6,000, thus realizing a tidy profit (and a better violin), while all the relatives (canny, shrewd business types) were losing their shirts.*[12]

It was John's brother, Charles Strong, "generous to his family when things were bad," who paid off the mortgage on John and Eliza's house. Emilie speculates that during the first twenty years of her parents' marriage, almost certainly various grandparents bailed them out of financial crises.[13]

Because Betsy was so aligned with her brother and Emilie was so much younger than she, the sisters did not become good friends until they were both adults. However, Betsy and Bill were very close from childhood on, despite the fact that they were quite different. "Betsy was considerate of other people and incapable of vulgarity," whereas, as Emilie puts it, "my brother…was good and vulgar…and very funny; I'm still quoting Bill. You don't quote Betsy."

Bill thought that their mother approved of people who were "stuffy," which must have influenced Betsy to think so too. At any rate, Betsy and her mother "did not get on." Emilie remembers that Eliza was "ambitious…and pushed things that Betsy didn't like," one of which might have been a "kind of a coming out" in Baltimore. Whether or not Betsy balked at making a debut, it is certain she enjoyed dancing with her brother's classmates at Princeton proms.

Bill was anything but stuffy. Good-looking and six feet four inches tall, he was extremely talented. After his first year at Princeton, he supported himself through the rest of his college years by giving violin lessons, editing the *Nassau Lit*, writing for the *Princeton Tiger*, and putting on the Princeton Triangle show. Bill paid for a trip to Europe by putting together an orchestra composed of Princeton boys who played on the ship and at London's Savoy Hotel. After college, he worked at Batten, Barton, Durstine and Osborn, Inc., one of the early advertising firms in New York City, and somehow found time to write two books, *Photography for Fun* and *How to Travel Without Being Rich*.[14] Bill's good friend, Eric Hodgins, wrote a best-selling book, *Mr. Blandings Builds His Dream House*, that was later made into a popular movie.[15] The story concerns a naive advertising man from New York City who purchases and renovates an old house in Connecticut. Family lore says that many traits of the hapless hero, Mr. Blandings, were based on those of Bill Strong.

The year after Bill graduated from Princeton, Betsy entered Vassar College, just as her family had assumed she would from the time she was born. Her great aunt on her father's side, Belle Strong Miller, had been a member of Vassar's first graduating class in 1869. Two aunts, Kate Strong Sewall and Bessie Rockefeller Strong, were Vassar graduates, as were Betsy's mother and Betsy's cousin, Elizabeth McCreery Monroe. Later Betsy's sister, Emilie, also attended Vassar.

The gregarious Betsy revelled in her four years at college, where she made lifelong friends. She sang second soprano in the glee club and managed it in her senior year, was somewhat involved with the Christian Association, and served as vice president of the dramatic society known as the Philaletheis Association.[16] Many years later, in a speech she gave to honors students at Colorado College, Betsy summed up her college days:

> *I cannot remember one thing about trigonometry but I shall never forget the wonderful Miss Wells who taught me math (or tried to) at Vassar. [I] could not possibl[y] pass one of Professor Dickinson's music exams now but the door he opened to me in the enjoyment of music has changed my whole life. I often think of a quotation which is probably familiar to you all and seems to me to express all this: EDUCATION IS WHAT IS LEFT AFTER WE HAVE FORGOTTEN WHAT WE HAVE LEARNED.*[17]

Laura Cheney, Betsy's roommate and close friend, lived in South Manchester, Connecticut. During a college summer, Betsy was hired by Laura's family to take a white-collar job at the Cheney Brothers Silk Mills in South Manchester that required knowing how to drive a car. She met a cousin of the Cheneys, Alfred Cowles III (known as Bob), a tall, self-assured, dazzlingly handsome man with magnificent blue eyes, more than eleven years her senior.[18] He was the oldest of the four sons of Alfred Cowles II, a Chicago philanthropist who had served as a director of the *Chicago Tribune* for forty years. Alfred Cowles I, Bob's grandfather, had been the business manager and one of the principal stockholders of the *Tribune* since its founding.[19] Bob was a product of the Taft Preparatory School and Yale University, where he had been a member of the prestigious Skull and Bones society.

Bob and Betsy courted and became engaged. On May 10, 1924, a year after Betsy's graduation from Vassar, her father officiated at their marriage ceremony in New York City.[20] Bob and Betsy honeymooned at the Homestead Hot Springs of Virginia.

Eliza and John Strong rejoiced in their daughter's match—and in the beginning, Betsy did too.

Notes

1. Elizabeth S. Cowles, text for speech presented at the Colorado Springs Fine Arts Center, n.d., Archives, American Heritage Center.

2. "William M'Creery," *Magazine of Western History Illustrated* 3 (5) (March 1886): 509–13.

3. Information comes from papers provided by the American Baptist Historical Society, Valley Forge, Pennsylvania, July 1994.

4. Peter Collier and David Horowitz, *The Rockefellers: An American Dynasty* (New York: Holt, Rinehart & Winston, 1976), 4, 12, 37, 46.

5. Elizabeth S. Cowles, "Round Robin Letter #7," 1950, Archives, American Heritage Center.

6. Papers from the American Baptist Historical Society.

7. Emilie S. Smith, comments on the manuscript, March 1996.

8. John H. Strong, "Fletcherism Revived," n.d., collection of Emilie S. Smith.

9. Kay Partridge, letter to the author, April 6, 1993.

10. Viola Ryder Nicholson, interview with the author, July 17, 1995.

11. Emilie S. Smith, comments on the manuscript, April 25, 1995, and March 1996. Emilie also recalls another summer spent at Cooks Point on Canandaigua Lake south of Rochester, New York, where the young cousins surfboarded, played tennis, and romanced.

12. Richard Benson Sewall, additions to the manuscript, March 1996.

13. Smith, comments, March 1996. Unless noted otherwise, information about Betsy and her family comes from interviews by the author with Emilie S. Smith (Mrs. Macauley) in March 1992.

14. William M. Strong, *Photography for Fun* (New York: Leisure League of America, 1934); William M. Strong (with photographs by the author), *How to Travel Without Being Rich* (Garden City, N.Y.: Doubleday, Doran, 1937).

15. Eric Hodgins, *Mr. Blandings Builds His Dream House* (New York: Simon & Schuster, 1946).

16. Copies of Vassar College records, sent by the Alumnae and Alumni Association of Vassar College, September 1993.

17. Elizabeth S. Cowles, text for talk, "Peaks and Passes," n.d., Archives, American Heritage Center.

18. Emilie S. Smith, letter to the author, April 27, 1995.
19. Copies of papers sent by the Chicago Historical Society, August 1993.
20. Elizabeth Strong [Cowles] Partridge, biographical information sheet, October 31, 1968, Colorado Room of the Penrose Public Library, Colorado Springs; Emilie S. Smith, postcard to the author, August 11, 1993.

CHAPTER TWO

Marriage to Bob Cowles

Bob Cowles brought his bride to Colorado Springs. Except for a period in the late 1930s and the World War II years of the 1940s, Betsy would call it home for the rest of her life.

Although Bob had spent most of his growing-up years in Chicago, he had lived in Colorado Springs for a short time when he was a small child. His father had taken him and his younger brothers there to be close to their mother, who had tuberculosis. Since the late 1880s, Colorado Springs had been known as the "TB Mecca of the West." Tuberculars from all over the country and even from parts of Europe fled to the Springs in a last desperate attempt to regain their health. Although there was no known cure for TB, the best medical knowledge of the time indicated that sunshine and a dry climate offered some hope. Indeed, a few patients did recover—but Elizabeth Cheney Cowles was not one of them. She died in 1898, leaving her husband of eight years to cope with raising their four sons: Alfred III (Bob), Knight Cheney, John Cheney, and Thomas Hooker.

We know that Bob's father, Alfred Cowles II, supported his family well. A Yale graduate, Alfred was an enormously successful businessman in Chicago. However, family stories about the man himself are contradictory. One says that during World War I, Alfred II wrote not a single letter to his son, Knight, while he was in the trenches. A second account, however, portrays him as providing a "wholesome, cheery life" for his family in Chicago.[1]

In 1916, Bob Cowles moved to Colorado Springs from Spokane, Washington, where he had been a reporter for his uncle's newspaper. Although Bob had engaged in athletics and other activities at Yale, where he had earned a B.A. in 1913, he had become ill in Spokane. In 1914 he contracted typhoid; two years later, tuberculosis. At the famous Cragmor Sanatorium in the Springs, he became a patient of Dr. Gerald Webb, widely regarded as one of the world's leading lung specialists.[2]

After a year's convalescence, Bob recovered and moved into the home of his father's sister, Sarah Cowles Stewart ("Aunt Fannie"), and her husband, Philip ("Uncle Phil"). The house, since willed to Colorado College, is number 1228 on Wood Avenue, which was then known as "Millionaire's Row." Bob then left Colorado Springs for several years, but returned to live with his aunt and uncle before he married Betsy.

Following his marriage, he and Betsy moved into a small house at 30 Broadmoor Avenue, near the golf course close to what was, according to advertisements, the country's first "complete resort hotel." The Broadmoor Hotel was the brainchild of a transplanted Philadelphian, Spencer Penrose, who had made his money in mining. Combining the tasteful elegance and beauty of a continental hotel with the latest conveniences of a modern American one, it had opened in 1918, six years before Betsy moved to Colorado Springs. It operated year-round and attracted wealthy vacationers from the East as well as locals, many of whom had first come to Colorado Springs for their health. Opulent residences sprang up near its grounds. An entire social set gravitated toward the Broadmoor and the nearby Cheyenne Mountain Country Club, founded in 1891.

Betsy found herself immersed in a world that revolved around golf, tennis, bridge, and costume parties. She and Bob entertained often and traveled with a crowd that went to the right place at the right season. Often they spent part of the winter at Montecito in the high hills above Santa Barbara visiting some of Bob's relatives.[3] Because dressing fashionably became obligatory after her marriage, Betsy spent freely on her attire for the first time in her life. She liked clothes so much that she jokingly called herself a "dress-aholic and a hat-aholic." Being about five feet six inches tall and thin, she wore them well. Although Betsy was somewhat flat-chested, she had wide shoulders, narrow hips, and "good legs." When dressed up, she put on high heels and was always "well turned out."[4]

Shortly after her marriage, Betsy discovered that she was unable to bear children. It was a bitter blow.[5] In 1925 she and Bob went to Boston and arranged to adopt a little boy, whom they named Richard Livingston. Several years later they returned to Boston and adopted a little girl, born in 1928, whom they named Ann.[6]

Figure 2.1 Colorado Springs house party, 1932, hosted by headmaster Francis Froelicher and his wife, Elizabeth, at the Fountain Valley School near Colorado Springs. Betsy Cowles is first on the left, front row; Bob Cowles is first on the left, third row. (Courtesy of Viola Ryder Nicholson.)

At the time Betsy took up residence in Colorado Springs, its population was about 30,000. The town's founder, General William J. Palmer, had deliberately discouraged heavy industry so that wealthy tourists, riding on his railroad, would be lured to the area. Although General Palmer was long dead when Betsy arrived, his legacy lived on. In many ways Colorado Springs was an Eastern community. Tree-lined boulevards and an elegant downtown hotel, the Antlers, exuded respectability. Colorado College (CC), also downtown, was "an outpost of Boston," according to the late Marshall Sprague. New England money supported the small liberal arts college initially, New England professors taught in it, and Boston architecture inspired its appearance.[7] In the decade following Betsy's move to the Springs, the town would come to boast its own symphony orchestra, a fine arts center, and a new preparatory school for boys, again with a strong Eastern flavor.

But the setting of Colorado Springs was definitely *not* that of an Eastern town, for although it lay on the edge of the Great Plains, magnificent Pikes

Peak—all 14,110 feet of it—soared behind. This huge mountain often created its own private weather system. A blizzard might be assaulting the summit while the townspeople 7,000 feet below strolled in shirtsleeves. Or Colorado Springs might be deluged with rain while sunshine caressed the top of the peak. Light and clouds constantly played on its summit. It was hard to live in Colorado Springs and not gaze at the local mountain a couple of times a day.

And yet there is not a shred of evidence that, until 1933, Betsy ever regarded Pikes Peak as anything more than an arresting backdrop. Probably she ventured on its slopes only while riding in an automobile or on the cog railway to the top. Once, when she was a freshman at Vassar, Betsy had had an unfortunate hiking experience. In her words:

> *I'm sure that one reason I postponed becoming a mountain enthusiast until the awful age of 30 was that at 18 two fire-eating Yale boys took me up Mount Marcy in the Adirondacks. It took me 12 years to get over the memory of my agony that day, breath coming in gasps, eyeballs popping out. It's a wonder I ever wanted to climb again.*[8]

At first Bob Cowles listed himself in Polk's Directory as a "journalist," harking back to his reporting days on the Spokane *Spokesman-Review.* However, by 1932 he had established and served as president of Cowles Company, Inc., an investment firm, and the Cowles Commission for Research in Economics. His offices were in the Mining Exchange Building. The Cowles Commission offered classes through Colorado College, and its research conference held there was attended by people from all over the world. Affiliated with the Econometric Society, "an international body founded in 1930 for the advancement of economic theory in its relation to statistics and mathematics," the Cowles Commission published monographs and estab-lished two research fellowships.[9]

After the addition of their two children, the Bob Cowles family moved into a larger house at 1506 Culebra, not far from where Aunt Fannie and Uncle Phil lived. Betsy became fond of all the Stewarts, but it was Uncle Phil who become her lifelong friend and loyal supporter, even after she was technically no longer part of the Cowles family. Philip Stewart was the son of a former Republican governor from Vermont. Between his junior and senior years at Yale, Philip took a horseback riding tour in Colorado and fell in love with the country. In 1900 he moved to Colorado Springs, where he lived until his death in 1957. An avid outdoorsman, he became good friends with Teddy Roosevelt, accompanying him on hunting trips in Colorado and Montana.[10]

Figure 2.2 Portrait of
Bob Cowles when he
was president of the
Cheyenne Mountain
Country Club in 1932.
(Courtesy of the
Cheyenne Mountain
Country Club.)

Money and servants enabled Betsy to lead a life of leisure. She might play tennis or golf "at the club." Or she might visit her closest friend, Vi Ryder, often picking her up in a big La Salle to go shopping or simply to indulge in an ice-cream soda from Murray's drugstore, an early drive-in on the edge of the CC campus. Betsy and Vi talked together nearly every day, using their private vocabulary. They added "ing" to words so that "ice box" became "ice-ing box"; "knitting needles" became "knitting neenews." Betsy called Vi's daughter (also named "Vi" but known as "Vizie") Veezie Vizie, spelling the first name "VZ."[11]

Often Betsy entered the Ryder house without knocking, announcing herself by calling up to Vi's husband, who would be resting in bed, with a piercing "Chassy!" "Chassy" was known to almost everyone else, even to his wife, as "Charles" or as "Dr. Ryder." Only Betsy called him by a nickname, for he was a somewhat somber man who suffered from tuberculosis. Betsy was one of the few people he enjoyed seeing during the final stages of his illness. "She [Betsy] was just so natural...so easy."[12]

Betsy became a member of the select Tuesday Club, founded in 1895 and modeled after a similar club in the East. Members met between Thanksgiving and Easter except for Holy Week, always wore hats and gloves, and ran their meetings on a strict schedule. At 3 P.M. sharp, a designated member gave the first talk, on a serious topic preapproved by the president. Politics and religion were forbidden subjects, but anything else was fair game. The 20-minute "serious" talk was followed by a 40-minute discussion, sometimes very frank and even pointed, always articulate and often bristling with sharp wit. Then at 4 P.M., a member presented a 10-minute "light" talk followed by a 20-minute discussion. The formal tea, which began at 4:30, always included cucumber sandwiches. Although the framework of the Tuesday Club was rigid, its members were not. Their purpose was to be intellectually stimulated *and* to have fun.[13] Betsy also became a member of the Bloomer Girls, which met every Monday of the year for an informal lunch or picnic, and (probably many years later) a member of The Thinkers.[14]

A detailed account of a 1932 house party Betsy and Bob attended reveals something of their lifestyle. It took place in late July, at the Fountain Valley School near Colorado Springs, and was hosted by the school's headmaster, Francis Froelicher, and his wife, Elizabeth. The account, written by either Bob or Betsy and illustrated by twenty snapshots taken by an unidentified photographer, begins by listing the seventeen guests in two categories, "Those present and (fully) accounted for" and "those present and (partly) accounted for." It continues in this tone, archly describing the entertainment—tennis, swimming, dancing, indoor baseball, "wrestling," bridge, piano playing, ping pong, billiard golf, and "conversational pyrotechnics." There was plenty of liquor.[15]

Perhaps it was in the 1930s that Betsy acknowledged to herself that she and Bob were basically incompatible and that she found their lifestyle "stuffy." Betsy and her handsome husband had "absolutely nothing in common." She was spontaneous and impulsive, responsive to people and the arts; he was deliberate, serious, analytical, and "something of a genius with money."[16] And he was thorough, sometimes maddeningly so, in whatever he undertook. For example, after becoming fascinated with wines, Bob immersed himself in the subject, studying oenology and stocking his cellar with bottles of the finest vintage. He then insisted on serving the "right" wine with each course, not permitting exceptions even if a dinner guest happened to prefer a white to a red.

One speculation is that Bob Cowles's personality was influenced by the "rigorous regime" he endured to cure his tuberculosis.[17] Whatever the reason, his relationship with Betsy soured. "In a way, he [Bob] never quite approved of me," Betsy once confided to her sister. She could often sense his frowning at her, even across a crowded room, when she laughed too loudly.[18]

Betsy burst with physical energy; Bob was afraid of going to high altitudes and of overdoing, although he did play tennis and golf. He was, according to Emilie, "an intellectual but not imaginative." An acquaintance, who was a small boy when he first met Bob Cowles, found him "austere and forbidding."[19] Yet one of Bob's young relatives, Ben Hammett, retains a quite different impression, recalling that "Uncle Bob" always sought him out, was interested in him and responsive, and in fact became his mentor.[20]

Bob Ormes recounts a story he heard concerning a game of bridge at the Broadmoor. After a particularly disastrous hand, Betsy's partner began pointing out her mistakes. Suddenly Betsy threw the deck of cards in the air, stood up, and walked out.[21] Emilie thinks that although the story might be true, Betsy's walking out would have been a dramatic gesture, not an indication that she had lost her temper. At any rate, despite their differences, for several years Betsy apparently did not consider divorce to be an option.

In 1924, the same year that Betsy and Bob were married, Betsy's father, John Strong, took up mountain climbing. He was fifty-eight. Before beginning this new endeavor, he had consulted a highly regarded New York doctor who had warned him not to do anything energetic—not even to walk against a strong wind! After sailing to Europe, John consulted another doctor, a Swiss of fine reputation, who advised him to climb the Wildstrubel, a snowy peak above Adelboden. "Now," John later wrote, "what does one do when the doctors disagree? One obeys the doctor whose advice one likes best. I did that, took up serious and systematic climbing, and soon became convinced that many people lay off mountains just when they ought to take them on." In 1926, two years after he had climbed his first Swiss peak, John Strong joined the American Alpine Club.

He blended his devotion to mountain climbing with his religion. "Of course one must have faith," he wrote. "One must follow the inner light. There is such a thing as divine guidance. Apart from that everything is dangerous."[22] Frequently he used mountains and mountaineering as vivid symbols or metaphors in his sermons.

In 1933, John Strong invited Betsy to go to Switzerland with him to climb mountains. Perhaps he was emboldened to make such a suggestion because the previous year Betsy had had a pretty good time climbing two easy Colorado "fourteeners" (mountains over 14,000 feet high), Lincoln and Bross, with her father and Francis Froelicher.[23] Bob was fully supportive of Betsy's proposed trip to Switzerland, and so she said yes.

In mid-June, John arrived in Colorado Springs to try to get his daughter in shape. Acting as her guide, he arranged a series of progressively more difficult hikes. Sixty-six years old and coming from sea level, John benefited from the outings, too. Father and daughter began with a gentle walk over the Palmer Trail to Crystal Park, followed by climbs up some of the foothills near Colorado Springs. Then the pair worked up to a couple of high but technically easy mountains west of Colorado Springs (one of them, Mount Sherman, a four-teener). This went so well that Betsy and John then climbed Pikes Peak, a longer climb than Sherman. The climax was an ascent of Longs Peak, which is about the same height as Pikes but much rougher. It was an ambitious regimen and Betsy performed well. She even enjoyed herself.

In late July, Betsy and her father boarded a steamship. A week later, they arrived by train at the village of Champéry in Switzerland, from which they walked up to the chalet de Mettiquy where they spent the night. At 3 A.M., they arose to begin their attempt on Betsy's first "technical" mountain, meaning it was steep enough to require the protection of secured ropes while climbing. The Dents du Midi, as it was called (the Teeth of the South), was considered simple by mountaineering standards, although it was exposed, that is, it was airy and sheer. Simple or not, it launched Betsy on a pursuit that changed her life.

The following is Betsy's description of the summer of 1933. In this account and in one she wrote about a Swiss *Bergschule* (a school that teaches mountain-climbing techniques) that she attended the following year, Betsy frequently compared features in Switzerland to ones in New York City: a steep trail climbed "five times as high as the Chrysler Building" or a ledge was "no 42nd Street." Several years later, references to New York City rarely appeared in her writing.

The Dents du Midi

August 3, 1933
    4 P.M. Left Champéry (2,450 feet)
    6:15 Reached chalet de Mettiquy (5,906 feet)
    August 4
    3 A.M. Started off
    8:30 Reached the summit (10,696 feet)
    4:30 P.M. Got to Salvan (3,061 feet)

Climb: 4,790 feet (from chalet)
Time: 13½ hours

Father and I landed in Champéry for our first Swiss climb after a funny trip over from Montreux in three trains (one at a time, however). It took us half a day to go about as far as from New York to Stamford but when we finally arrived we found it was a nice town and worth the struggle. Everyone of all ages from six months up had hobnailed boots on, all the houses were chalets with pots of geraniums at the windows and from our hotel we could see mountains and mountains. It was not my first glimpse of the Dents du Midi for we had had a fine view of them across the lake from Montreux but here they looked formidable indeed and seemed to be almost toppling over on us from above. However, we understood that people were in the habit of getting to the top of them and in that spirit we started off optimistically at four in the afternoon for the chalet de Mettiquy where we were to spend the night.

Our guide, Fabian Mathay, was not as powerful looking as I could have wished, for I had no idea what he might be called upon to do to keep me on the mountain next day. But he was young and vigorous and evidently didn't feel especially apprehensive about the morrow for he laughed and joked with us. We began our Swiss career as wits that day with a success due I imagine not so much to our high grade humor as to the astonishing French we were in the habit of using. Fabian was as much fun to look at as to talk to. He seemed very Alpine with his great hobnailed boots and the climbing rope tucked through a strap in his knapsack. Everything about him had a look of honorable wear and tear and made me feel a little ashamed of the obvious newness of my mountaineering equipment. As for his ice ax, I should just like to have it in the next war!

The walk up was lovely, winding along through the wooded slopes. We kept hearing cow and goat bells in all keys and passing people who said, "Bon soir, Mademoiselle" with real French tact. In a little over two hours we reached the chalet. At seven we sat down to large bowls of onion soup into which we shaved quantities of Swiss cheese, and what with a great loaf of French bread and a pitcher of fresh milk, we dined well. That night we had quarters over livestock. All night the social life of the animals and the arrival of other climbing parties, combined with my excitement at being in Switzerland and about to become a climber, made sleep a sketchy matter. Luckily I didn't have to stay restless long; it was soon two o'clock and we began fumbling for boots and sweaters in the early morning cold. Breakfast was café au lait and bread. I could have used ham and eggs but didn't have time to become morbid about it as we were soon on our way.

It was a long dark march at first, with just one lantern for light. Luckily the going was easy over the grassy slopes and there were no trees to bump into as we were now well above timberline. Soon it was getting lighter (and steeper). After a tussle with the kind of slope where you can neither stand upright with dignity nor have the satisfaction of being on all fours, we stopped to have our second breakfast and rope up. I don't remember much about the breakfast but I will never forget my sensations at being put on my first rope! Fabian was first, Father last, and I was firmly noosed in the middle by means of knots that would have given Houdini trouble.

It was getting light enough to see where we were going, and we were certainly going somewhere. I felt as though I were on Fifth Avenue looking up at a couple of Empire State Buildings. As we got nearer it began to look more possible and soon we were scrambling up the rock by a series of couloirs that presented few hazards except the constant one of dislodging loose stones. By the time daylight had arrived, we were traversing to the right by a chain of ledges. Next we crossed two steep snow slopes where Fabian cut steps and I endeavored to stay in them, feeling that it would be extremely unwise to start coasting down that toboggan. I tried too to copy Fabian's ice ax technique: he used it in a sort of canoe-paddle fashion, putting the spike end firmly in the snow on the side toward the mountain and leaning on it for balance. After another short rock passage we were on the ridge with the summit to our left and high above us. Below us on the snow were some of our companions of the night before looking like a line of little black bugs tied to one another, while rising up on all sides were neighbor mountains we hadn't known existed in the valley below. With one eye on them and the other on the work at hand I started up on the last long pull. But it was not the kind of going that permitted one the luxury of divided attention; soon I was entirely occupied with finding the necessary hand-and-foot-holds and the view was left to itself for the time being. This was beginning to look to me like big-league work. I remember one narrow ridge where there was a tremendous drop. I had not yet reached the stage where I could happily contemplate abysses and this time I looked the other way and tried to think about something else. I was aware that my rock climbing technique was rather elementary but I adhered as best I could, using thoroughly every square inch of my anatomy. Next day my bruises counted up into the dozens!

Suddenly we were at the top. It is queer the way summits, receding and receding for hours, all at once give in when you least expect it. I looked up one minute and thought: "We will never get there," and the next we were scrambling over the last boulder. A tremendous sense of achievement swept over me. I was on my first Swiss summit! Around us was a glorious mountain panorama. There unmistakably was the Matterhorn and to the south the great dome of white was Mont Blanc of course. There were certain outstanding masses: the Grand Combin, the Dent Blanche (a sort of immense white Rock of Gibraltar) and the Weisshorn, looking somehow suspended in space. I recognized them all and thought to myself: it is lovely that we don't have to be introduced. Fabian pointed out the Arolla peaks, our next objectives. The big snowy tooth was the Pigne d'Arolla and the dark rocky ridge beyond it the Petite Dent de Veisivi. The Oberland was covered with clouds but through them emerged the summits of the Finsteraarhorn, the Aletschorn and the Jungfrau group.

We began to notice that it was very cold and if there is any place that you want to get off of fairly promptly it is a mountain top in the cold. So after we had shaken hands, taken our pictures by the summit cairn and had a last look around, we started down by the steep gravel slope at the back. After six hours of climbing, the thought of going downhill for a change seemed unbelievably luxurious. But it wasn't long before I realized that descending can have its points too. We slid and coasted down the gravel which was inconsiderately spread over tilted rock slabs. It was horrid going and we kept taking spills. My ice ax was getting a thorough breaking in, acting as combined rudder and brake and saving me countless times from disaster. But it hasn't looked quite the same since and I never again had to worry about the newness of my equipment.

The gravel dwindled out at a sandy col and here we parted from Fabian who was going back to Champéry while we went down to Salvan. Now we were on a path but it was a very steep one with unevenness that forced us to concentrate every minute on our footing and this when we were beginning to feel that we had earned the right to a little relaxation. We zigged and zagged. It was hot now that we were getting lower and our packs felt heavier by the minute. Then when the flesh was growing very weak indeed, we emerged on Alpine meadow which felt divinely soft and spongy under our weary feet. We stopped for a sketchy lunch and took naps in a field surrounded by astonished cows. After this, and some fresh milk from a neighboring chalet, we felt sufficiently bucked up to continue on our way....

Salvan provided Father and me with a shave and bath (respectively), but did not afford the consolations of strawberry ice. So the family

Figure 2.3   Betsy Cowles and her father John Strong on top of an unknown mountain, circa 1935. (Courtesy of Emilie S. Smith.)

united on two thés complets and had no regrets. Then we bought post-cards upon which we inscribed boastful comments to our friends and repaired to the railway station where we embarked for Sion and a good night's rest.

Several days later, father and daughter were at it again, this time with John Strong's favorite guide, Antoine Georges, who was also his friend. In Betsy's words:

Traverse of the Petite Dent de Veisivi

August 7, 1933
4 A.M. Started off from Arolla (6,437 feet)
11:45 Reached the Summit (10,465 feet)
6 P.M. Back in Arolla
Climb 4,428 feet
Time: 14 hours

First it should be clearly understood that there is [no]thing PETITE *[LITTLE] about this* DENT *[TOOTH]. It makes up in versatility for what it may lack in height and as far as sheer labor is concerned it is the Mount Everest of small mountains. Although this was to be Father's third time on it he was excited at the prospect because it is the kind of mountain that one enjoys having a reunion with. I was excited on general principles and also because it was to be my first experience on really high class rock.*

Not having snow conditions to consider, we started from Arolla at the comparatively luxurious hour of four A.M. The first half hour we filled with the dubious pleasure of a 500 foot descent down the valley, realizing only too well that it was going to be what Antoine would call "assez penible" [painful enough] to have to get up this piece at the end of the day. It is a pleasure to introduce our guide Antoine Georges: one of the best and most faithful of mountain companions—always patient, courteous and thoughtful, humorous and appreciative. Father and Antoine had already climbed some forty Swiss peaks in seven summer campaigns together, but though his name had been a household word in the Strong family for some time, he and I had not met in person until the day before when we arrived in Arolla from Sion.

There he was in front of me on this first climb, walking in that solid yet supple style of his, the rope slung in his knapsack and the lantern swinging by one hand. We struck across a stream and began going up the other side of the valley wall, discarding the lantern at about five o'clock. The going was uncompromisingly steep and laborious. There was altitude to be gained and we gained it without sugar coating. It took a good four hours to reach the rocks below the Col de Zarmine which lies between the Grand Dents de Veisivi and the long jagged arete of the little Dent. Here we roped up.

The first thrill came on top of the col where one had to face the fact that the rock sloped precipitously 4000 feet to the Val d'Hérens below. I soon found that a precipice is worse if you try to ignore it than when you face the fact that it is there. Next I discovered that one cannot negotiate difficult rock and have enough energy left to worry about abysses. Ten minutes on the ridge and I was completely occupied with the work at hand. And such work! It was just one first class brand of excitement after another. I no sooner felt a little at home on the sharp arete [ridge] (it had to be straddled in some places) than I was led onto a ledge: hardly had I learned to edge myself around great bulges of rock than I was faced witth the necessity of worming my way up a chimney [a crack wide enough for a person]. And I had barely gotten the knack of playing off my shoulders on one side against my knees and feet on the other when I was given a gendarme to assimilate.

A gendarme is a rock tooth blocking a ridge, and the one on the Petite Dent is very exciting. First you pull yourself up on a ledge (all arm work as there are no footholds), then you scrape your way upward with your arms doing yeoman's duty on a sharp rock spine at the right while your feet do what they can on a holdless slab on the left. This lands you puffing on a flat jumping-off place with the gendarme beside and above you. The next step is the kind you read about in books. You have to step over a three foot gap filled with nothing but air for several thousand feet up onto the big rock column beyond. When you have achieved this and worked your way up to the top of the rocky tooth you look down dizzily and may perhaps be excused for feeling a little honest pride. Descending also has its points. The step across the cleft has to be made backward and you grab the handholds for dear life while you reach with one hopeful foot for the little platform. Going down the slab is something to have gravity on your side. Trying to churn the air with your feet as little as possible, you inch your way down on your stomach, and when you get to the ledge you throw a leg over it, let yourself down by the arms and drop (amid applause). Ahead of us was a party of fellow Arollans composed of an English canon named Mr. Bell, a young Mr. Gibson and Antoine's cousin Josef as guide. They watched us come down here one by one and in my most graceful postures I will never forget hearing with dismay the snap of their combined Kodaks.

I was beginning to have a wonderful time. I discovered that the drops to right and to left weren't bothering me much any more and I felt pleased at being able to negotiate what looked to me like quite sensational passages. I didn't realize then that you are expected to be able to do anything when you have the proper holds and get little praise for it, even if the Grand Canyon is below you ten times over. The really sensational passages have a way of looking quite innocent and it is only

Figure 2.4 Josef Georges, a guide known as *"le skier"* on the Dent Blanche in Switzerland. Apparently he made the comment, *"J'ai bien travaille aujourdhui"* ("I have worked well today"). Photo by Betsy Cowles. (Courtesy of the American Heritage Center, University of Wyoming. Copyright restricted.)

when you are on one that you find ladder technique useless and discard it in favor of more heroic methods. There is this kind of rock behind the hotel at Arolla and everyone tries his hand at it at one time or another, often ending by getting hauled up like a sack of potatoes. I gave a lot of good clean fun to an audience of guides and tourists here a few days later and while I didn't manage to get up under my own steam it was a terrific struggle. The guides, going first on the rope and unprotected in the event of a fall, bear the brunt of this type of passage. By the time you get to i[t] you have the encouraging face of an Antoine above you and the consolations of several lengths of stout Manila rope.

It took us almost four hours to traverse the ridge and it was nearly twelve by the time we reached the summit where in the warm sun we ate and relaxed. Father and Mr. Bell were very jovial. I felt simply wonderful and as though this were my native land from which I had been too long away. Josef and Antoine sang Swiss songs and we all chimed in when not too much occupied with the business of eating.

Antoine told us a wonderful story about the climbing career of the Prince Consort of Holland. It seems that a few years ago Antoine and a client were about to climb the Aiguille de la Za. They had come around by the Col de Bertol and had reached the foot of the rock pitch when they noticed that on its rather limited surface a great emigration was under way. It was the Prince Consort of Holland, well past middle age and way beyond middle size, out for a day's sport. With him he had four guides and three porters and this is how they got his highness up the mountain. Two guides went first, each with a rope attached to the royal torso. Next came the Prince and below him the second pair of guides whose business it was to place the feet of their client in the proper holds. This done they would should "TIREZ!" and the upper two would pull. Inch by inch the party progressed, cheered at crucial points by champagne from the sacks of the porters. This went on for hours on a rock pitch that usually takes half an hour to climb. We wondered what the Prince got out of it. Antoine said he supposed he had said to himself: "J'ai quatre guides, j'ai trois porteurs, alors—je monte!" [I have four guides, I have three porters, therefore, I climb!] "Did you ever get up yourselves?" we asked Antoine, remembering the limited capacity of the Za. "Oh no," he said, "I said to my client, 'La montagne est occupée' ['The mountain is occupied'] and we went over and climbed the Peroc."

Everyone was feeling extremely witty at this point. We posed for pictures and Antoine and Josef sang "Marietta" and "La-haut sur la montagne." I knew this last from Father, but it was the first time I had heard it sung as it should be sung; out on a mountain top in the sun. I was bursting with pride and confidence as I looked back over the way we had come. It seemed to me that I could climb anything, anywhere. Soon lunch was over and we began to prepare for the descent. I remember going over the edge thinking to myself: "J'ai un guide, j'ai un père, alors—je descend!" [I have a guide, I have a father, therefore, I descend!] Going down the face was a lot of fun. I depended a good deal on gravity and the seat of my trousers but it seemed to work. There was one ticklish place where we had to slide down and around a granite bulge with only the sketchiest of holds. Using every finger nail and an almost mental adherence I managed to get down without the humiliation of being "on the rope." The descent seemed over in no time. Soon we had unroped below the cliffs and were striding valleywards. Once there (but it took time) we broke the painful return climb to Arolla with tea at the Hotel Victoria while a sudden downpour of rain drenched the valley. Everyone was very hungry and very jolly. Mr. Bell told us about the sign that used to hang in the hall of the Mont Collon Hotel for the benefit of its English patrons: IT IS DEFENDED TO CIRCULATE IN THE CORRIDORS THE BOOTS OF ASCENSION BEFORE SEVEN HOURS.

This convulsed us all, including Antoine and Josef who couldn't understand a word of it. Then, as it seemed about time to circulate our boots of ascension toward home, we tackled what Antoine called le dernier gendarme *[the last gendarme] and by six or so were walking up the steps of the Mont Collon.*

Betsy came to refer to the four weeks she spent in Switzerland in 1933 as being "best of all possible introductions to climbing by the best of all possible fathers." It was also on this trip that Betsy came to regard singing as an integral part of climbing.

She later advised a climber to "use as best he can such vocal cords as nature gave him." She suggested singing to forget weariness or to keep up courage but, above all, "to sing for the joy of singing on the mountain top that he has earned by his own efforts."[24] (When he lacked singing companions on a summit, John played his violin, which, in later years, Antoine Georges carried.[25] One wonders what the patient Antoine thought, for John played "abominably." Despite his abilities on piano and organ, he never got the hang of his stringed instrument. Years of lessons—and playing on a Guarneri—did not help much either.[26])

Although Betsy was absorbed by her new sport, she was under no illusions about her sometimes awkward attempts to learn climbing techniques.

She describes her ascent of the Dent de Satarma, a 120-foot tooth near the village of Satarma:

> *We watched Antoine go up, marvelling as always at his balanced and effortless climbing. There should be a reel of moving pictures to compare us! At first it wasn't so bad. I started off in fairly good style and had beginner's luck for a while. Then momentum began to grow less and less and finally I spent several minutes of completely suspended animation on the worst ten feet of rock I have ever seen. By means of infinitesimal cracks and crannies (and none too many of those) I at last managed to hoist myself up the few remaining feet and land on the summit, if you can call two square feet of rounded bulge a summit. While Antoine was bringing Mr. Bell and Father up and down, I tested my stamina by looking over the edge, overhang and all, and was pleased to discover that it did not overcome me as I had expected. I have since tried to hold this over Father's head but he reminds me that I was still roped which, he says, takes the edge off the experience. Then he adds (when I fail to show signs of being subdued) that it took him exactly three minutes to get up whereas the melancholy truth is that it took me seven.*

Betsy crossed her first glacier when she, her father, and their guide, Antoine, traversed the Pigne d'Arolla. Her first glissade (a controlled descent using an ice axe) was "short but violent." Betsy and her father each took a spill, nearly upsetting Antoine with their "contortions on the rope."

Father and daughter befriended two Englishmen. The first was Canon Bell, whom they met on the Petite Dent. He was, in Betsy's words, "the perfect type of English climbing clergyman and Father being the American version, they made a great pair." The next Sunday they collaborated in spiritual matters at a little English church where John Strong played the organ while Canon Bell conducted the services. The second was "Mr. Lloyd," with whom they shared a table at a hotel.

> *Our friendship with him had begun rather inauspiciously our first night in Arolla when he asked what we had to say about American foreign policies. It soon being evident that we had nothing authoritative to offer, a happy switch was effected to mountain topics upon which we had remained ever since.*

Canon Bell and Mr. Lloyd had climbed the big peaks, often by difficult routes, and had done so with such "greats" as George Leigh Mallory and

Geoffry Winthrop Young. On the morning of July 11, when Betsy and her father were preparing to leave for a climb of the Tête Blanche, they said goodbye to their new friends. Mr. Lloyd gave them "all sorts of jars of things to
sustain" them on the heights, guaranteeing that soup cubes and fruit tablets
would get them up anything. Mr. Bell said he could "hardly face" the Sunday
service without John Strong at the organ. They exchanged addresses and
Betsy and her father promised Bell and Lloyd first ascents if they ever came
to Colorado.

Then Betsy and John embarked on a steep trail that finally ended, "five
times as high as the Chrysler Building," at the first climbing hut Betsy had ever
stayed in, the Bertol. "Well," she wrote, "it was certainly no Waldorf-Astoria. I
saw a small, dark, den-like place, lit by one oil lamp and crowded with people. There was a terrific din and hubbub, of which 25% was probably the
sound of heavy hobnailed boots, 25% the clatter of dishes, and the remaining
half composed of equal parts of French, German and English, with the patois
of each." Betsy marveled at the *gardien* who prepared meals for each new
party over a stove she regarded as much too small. The menu consisted of tea,
soup made from Maggi tablets, cheese, bread, and chocolate. She was tired
and hungry and especially grateful for Antoine's efficiency in picking out a
place to sleep in the garret and locating hut slippers of approximately the correct size. "Antoine seemed to know everyone," she wrote, "and to be able to get
whatever he wanted, including extra blankets for me for the night." The
French and German climbers were eager to try out their English, and Betsy
and her father attempted to answer in kind. "Father achieved a mixture of all
tongues that ought to rival Esperanto."

Once settled in to sleep, Betsy found the cold counteracted by "a sort of
animal warmth, due to the fact that there were at least 20 people occupying
12 square feet of space." As soon as she would doze off, people would clatter
upstairs in their wooden shoes, or there would be loud bursts of laughter, or
someone would light a candle in the sleeping loft. Things would quiet down
again and then a new climbing party would arrive at the hut, talking loudly.
Finally, in spite of snoring, peace came—and suddenly, it was time to get up!

The climb was successful and they then descended to the Monte Rosa
Hotel in the bustling town of Zermatt, where they spent the night. Next morning, under a blue sky, John, Betsy, and Antoine began toiling back up the trail
down which they had come the day before. They hoped to climb the Matterhorn by the Zmutt ridge. As they walked, Antoine regaled them with the story
of his first ascent of the ridge. The night before his climb, the Zermatt guides had
told him the Zmutt ridge was *"quelquechose de terrible"* (something terrible)

and had declared that he was insane to take a client up it without having ever climbed it himself. All night long Antoine dreamt about ledges and chimneys. Then he looked at Betsy quite solemnly and said, "I tell you truly, Madame, there was not a passage that was not familiar to me. I had climbed them all, rock by rock, in my dreams. We did not have to pause once for the route and made the top without difficulty in eight and a half hours."

They reached the Bertol hut, where the same *gardien* was cooking meals over the same small stove. Betsy, her father, and Antoine lunched on ham and eggs. When people finished eating, they rushed outside to look at the sky and to watch two Germans who were attempting a new route up the face of the Dent d'Hérens. They had gotten stuck below a huge snow cliff. Antoine took one look and announced that it wouldn't go. He was right. The two black dots did not budge until they disappeared for a night's bivouac in a large ice crack.

By afternoon, new snow on the Matterhorn dashed all hopes of an ascent. Antoine said that in climbing it was necessary to be a philosopher and so Betsy and her father spent a pleasant evening in the hut "trying to get the German boys to tell us what they really thought of Hitler." After a stormy night they awoke to a gray and threatening sky. At breakfast Betsy noted a new man who had come in late the previous night from a difficult climb, and his guide, the famous Franz Lochmatter, a "splendid looking fellow." Only later did she realize that the famous British climber, Geoffry Winthrop Young, had called Lochmatter's 1906 ascent of the south face of the Täschhorn "the greatest mountaineering feat" he had ever witnessed.

Betsy and her companions left the hut early in the morning, soon to be passed by Lochmatter and his client. "We could see him ahead of us long enough to notice his fine physique and the deft way he moved. We were stepping right along but he passed us as though we were standing still." Two days later, Lochmatter and his client were killed descending an easy section of the Weisshorn.

While waiting for a break in the weather on the Matterhorn, the trio made a traverse of the Untergabelhorn. Then, leaving John Strong behind in Zermatt, Antoine and Betsy walked up to the Trift Hotel, singing a little two-part harmony along the way. They ate breakfast at 1:30 A.M. and were off by 2. By lantern light they forded a half-dozen streams, negotiated a ticklish rock buttress, and finally scrambled up a steep moraine to a glacier where the going was easier. When they halted for another breakfast and to watch the sun come up, a guide and his young English client caught up. The Englishman said, "We will never see anything more beautiful than this."

It was "too cold to stop long even in the interests of aesthetics," Betsy later wrote, and so Antoine and she started on. After their "first gymnastics" where the glacier met a rock wall, Betsy asked Antoine (in French) if he was afraid. "His mahogany face broke into smiles" and he replied that "No, Madame, truly," he was not afraid. As they approached precipitous slabs below the summit, they encountered the full force of the wind and a snowy film on the rocks. Soon Antoine's eyebrows and eyelashes turned white and a row of icicles hung from his woolen cap.

> *We were going up with a bang and I could see that the idea was to waste as little time as possible. Above me Antoine was climbing with the greatest care and deliberation, never making a jerky or hasty motion. At times we moved together over places that looked very difficult to me and I wavered between pride at the confidence he seemed to have in me and doubts about my ability to adhere to the cold and slippery wall up which we were making our way. We began working over to the left and now and then I was left in a state of painful isolation with Antoine completely out of sight around bulging corners of rock.*

When they reached the summit and shook hands, Betsy noticed that Antoine's hands were like ice. An Englishman whom they encountered said to her, "Your guide is sacrificing his hands to your safety," and so Betsy tried to "make speed" on the descent. The steep snow below the ridge was now very slippery; twice Antoine caught Betsy's "inadvertent glissades." Betsy described the passage as being one that "put the novice quite wholesomely into his place, lest he too quickly assume that he has become a mountaineer." Finally they attained the glacier and, after enjoying mineral water at the Trift Hotel, continued down the path where John Strong met them. Reunited with their tenor, the three began singing songs beside a glacier stream. At the Edelweiss Hotel, Betsy heard Antoine refer to her as *"une alpiniste du premier ordre"* (a female climber of the first rank) but wrote, "I like to think that the wink that accompanied this statement was observed by me alone."

Father and daughter climbed the Riffelhorn and then hung around Zermatt for a week, hoping the weather would clear. Betsy learned to rappel and to cut steps in ice. She and her father drank tea and sent postcards, having decided in the beginning that "it is only fair to one's family and friends to climb mountains that look well on post cards." Betsy oiled her ice ax to get a "mellow, weathered look" and darned socks. They visited her father's friend, the coiffeuse Marie Biener, now an old woman. Years ago, she had shaved

Edward Whymper, whose famous ascent of the Matterhorn in 1865, the first ever, had ended so tragically when four of the party had slipped to their deaths on the descent.

Then, miraculously, the weather cleared and Betsy, John, Antoine, and a second guide, Elias Perren, hiked up to the Belvedere Hotel, where they would stay for their attempt on the Matterhorn. Betsy described Elias as "a great ox of a man who looked capable of carrying us all to the summit single-handed if we couldn't get up any other way." Unfortunately, he was tone-deaf.

They arose early, hoping to be first on the mountain, "preferring to face the possibility of our dropping rocks on someone to that of having someone drop rocks on us." But two parties beat them out, "their lanterns twinkling" above on the mountain, for by 1933 the Matterhorn had become "the Niagara Falls of Swiss mountaineering." Elias and John were on the first rope, Antoine and Betsy on the second. Betsy and her party often had to wait when they wanted to climb. However, just as frequently, they had to climb when they would have preferred to rest, not wanting to lose their places in line. She observed that people varied considerably in their climbing techniques, just as guides varied in their methods of leading. For example, Elias climbed an entire pitch before sitting down and belaying her father. In contrast, Antoine and Betsy stayed closer together and often moved in unison. She felt especially sorry for a "poor puffing frau whose guide was pulling her along on the rope much as a man pulls a reluctant mule. If she paused for so much as a split second, he plucked her up bodily to a new section." Betsy thought, "There go I, but for Antoine Georges."

By now Betsy had come to truly appreciate Antoine's abilities as a guide. "He didn't overwhelm me with suggestions," she said, "and I always had a sense of his approval when I had done a passage presentably." During especially long waits, Antoine and she sang in harmony." 'La-haut sur la montagne' went awfully well that day and... 'Nos Alpes de neige.' "

For Betsy, attaining the top of the Matterhorn was a "great moment"; she had never seen such a place—"the height of it fairly screamed at one." She likened it to being on the top of an immense mast. After looking in all directions, the party was driven by cold to begin the descent and although going down was "never really difficult," it required intense concentration. At last they stopped at the Solvay Hut to rest and to eat a real lunch, their first food in ten hours. Then, fortified, they began the final tricky part down to the Belvedere Hotel. "At the choicest of passages, Elias would brighten up and say, 'Here is where Fraulein So-and-so went off...' (his hand describing a series of eloquent spirals)."

Betsy was climbing down first, the safest position for the client. "Antoine was letting me do quite a lot of route picking. It was usually rather easy to do, what with the hobnail scratches on the rock and the usual pile of empty bottles at every level resting place. When it wasn't too steep I walked bolt upright and thus increased my self-respect enormously on the ridges....A month in the Alps had taught me not to expect the equivalent of a subway strap on every rock by any means. I found myself doing wonders with a quarter of an inch of crack and cranny here and there and getting a safe balance on many a downhill lie." Then they came onto a section of loose rock:

At one place we were all given an attack of the jitters when an unattached stone eluded Father's watchfulness and caromed over the head of a guide below us. Antoine shouted, "Attention!" [and] there was [a] long agonized instant while we watched the projectile and then it bounded harmlessly away while every one heaved a sigh of relief. But it was not a pleasant experience.

They reached Zermatt at 7:15 in the evening, sixteen hours after beginning their climb, exhausted but with sufficient spirit to throw out their chests and stride along as though they had made the first ascent of Mount Everest. The next day they celebrated with tea and cakes and bade farewell to their climbing friends. As a souvenir, Antoine brought Betsy the climbing rope she had used, a gesture she found very touching. He promised to send her words and music to the mountain songs they had sung. As Betsy and her father walked to the train station, a cloud streamer was blowing south off the Matterhorn. As they boarded the train for Visp, Betsy asked her father what they should climb the next day.

"How would the Eiffel Tower be?" he replied. And they shook hands.[27]

Notes

1. Marka Webb Stewart, interview with the author, March 25, 1994; Ralph E. Dyar, *News for an Empire: The Story of the* Spokesman-Review *of Spokane, Washington, and of the Field It Serves* (Caldwell, Idaho: Caxton Printers, Ltd., 1952), 117.
2. Later Bob and several other grateful ex-Cragmor patients put up money to support Dr. Webb's Colorado Foundation for Research in Tuberculosis; Bob served on the institution's board of directors. Eventually the foundation evolved into the famous Webb-Waring Institute for Medical Research in Denver. Helen Clapesattle, *Dr. Webb of Colorado Springs* (Boulder: Colorado Associated University Press, 1984), 369, 435; Marshall Sprague, "Healers in Pikes Peak History," *Denver Westerners Brand Book* 23 (Denver, Colo.: Denver Westerners, 1968), 104.

3. Ben Hammett, Ph.D., comments on the manuscript, April 1995. These family gatherings were almost certainly at the spacious residence of Buell and Harriet Cowles Hammett, which served as the winter home of Bob's uncle, William H. Cowles. Various members of the Cowles, Cheney, Stewart, Hammett, Lambert, Buell, Thayer, Learned, and Underhill families held many reunions there until the early 1940s.

4. Emilie S. Smith, comments on the manuscript, March 1996; Dorothy Teague Swartz, interview with the author, January 14, 1993; Dorothy Bryson, interview with the author, March 25, 1994.

5. Charles S. Houston, M.D., in an interview with the author on November 22, 1991, said that he recalls Betsy telling him that after she found out that her ovaries and uterus had been damaged by tuberculosis, she had a planned hysterectomy.

6. Elizabeth Strong [Cowles] Partridge, biographical information sheet (October 31, 1968), Colorado Room of the Penrose Public Library, Colorado Springs.

7. Marshall Sprague, *Newport in the Rockies: The Life and Good Times of Colorado Springs*, 3d rev. ed. (Athens, Ohio: Sage Books, 1985), 274–81.

8. Elizabeth S. Cowles, text for talk on mountaineering before a newly organized climbing club, n.d., Archives, American Heritage Center, University of Wyoming, Laramie, Wyoming.

9. Cowles Commission Reports 1932–1941 and *Decennial Report* 1932–41 (University of Chicago), Archives, Tutt Library, Colorado College, Colorado Springs.

10. Clapesattle, *Dr. Webb of Colorado Springs*, 117–20.

11. William Ryder, M.D., interview with the author, March 24, 1994; Viola Ryder Nicholson, interview with the author, July 17, 1995.

12. Nicholson, interview.

13. Dorothy Bryson, interview; corrections to manuscript, October 4, 1994.

14. Nicholson, interview. Jack Hettinger, in a letter to the author, February 13, 1996, says, "I was never privy to what they 'thought' about, but they always seemed to have a good time together."

15. "Houseparty, July 30–31," collection of Viola Ryder Nicholson.

16. Stewart, interview; Emilie S. Smith, interview with the author, March 24, 1992.

17. Hammett, comments. Bob Cowles, whom Ben Hammett called "Uncle Bob" but who was, in fact, his mother's first cousin, underwent treatment for tuberculosis at the Cragmor Sanatorium, as did his first cousin, Harriet Cowles. Treatment consisted of lying quietly in a cold room, such as a sleeping porch, for a year "without physical or emotional stress." Ben Hammett speculates that

> the training in self-denial and asceticism may have colored Uncle Bob's subsequent personality. On the positive side, it provided him…with the ability to concentrate and put his whole mind to one thing, which evolved later into the ability to devote himself to organizing and mastering a large body of knowledge. But it may have later resulted in a problem for Betsy, as it may have been that kind of personality that was able to follow the rigorous regime to survive tuberculosis included persons who could learn to replace spontaneity and impulsiveness with seriousness, deliberateness and caution.

18. Emilie S. Smith, comments on the manuscript, April 1995.
19. Ryder, interview.
20. Hammett, comments.

> *I felt understood, accepted, respected and mentally expanded as a result of my contacts with [Bob Cowles]....The result was I sought his advice and valued him as a mentor during my formative years. I would visit him in his Chicago home and office, where I always felt welcome. I was very grateful for his giving me so much one-to-one attention. This interest and attention was all the more important to my self-esteem, for I knew how busy and important he was in the financial world. In our family he often played the devil's advocate, taking a point of view that differed to keep the discussion lively and challenging. He did this in a respectful way, often starting by accepting the value system of those espousing one point of view, but then leading them around to his view in a way that still supported their value system.*

21. Robert M. Ormes, interview with the author, May 14, 1985.
22. John H. Strong, "Mountaineering: A Solace to Sedate Old Age," *American Alpine Journal* 7 (2) (January, 1949): 165.
23. American Alpine Club Membership Book (1940).
24. Elizabeth S. Cowles, "Singing on the Summit," *American Alpine Journal* 3 (1) (1937): 65.
25. Strong, "Mountaineering," 165–68.
26. After August H. Strong died in 1921, his son, John, immediately used part of his inheritance to purchase a fine Guarneri violin. He then called up the Hungarian violist Leopold von Auer and asked whom he should study under. John's inheritance included valuable stock in the Eastman Kodak Company. John's uncle (Augustus Strong's brother), Henry Alvah Strong, had met young George Eastman when he was "fooling around with chemicals" in the basement of his mother's boarding house, where Henry and his wife were living. Henry put up $5,000 to help George get started. Subsequently, Henry became president and later chairman of the board of various Eastman Kodak companies. Henry was generous to his siblings and also encouraged them to buy their own stock in Eastman Kodak, early, which they did. Information comes from papers provided by the George Eastman House in Rochester, New York, and from an interview with Emilie S. Smith in March 1992.
27. Elizabeth S. Cowles, *Alpine Beginner* (N.p.: Privately printed, ca. 1934), Special Collections, University of Colorado Libraries, Boulder.

CHAPTER THREE

Betsy Becomes a Mountain Climber

Shortly after her return to Colorado Springs, Betsy, her father, and Francis Froelicher made a first ascent of Mount Oxford, an easy but high peak which, following a resurvey two years earlier, had been elevated to fourteener status. The three waited for each other just before the top so they could set foot on the summit simultaneously. Then, in a fit of good fellowship, they declared themselves members of the Eureka Climbing Club.[1]

That fall, Betsy set to work writing what turned out to be a forty-four-page book, *Alpine Beginner*, which she privately published (much of which was quoted in chapter 2). Although it was probably based on a diary Betsy kept, no such diary exists today. Twelve of John Strong's black-and-white photographs illustrated *Alpine Beginner*, which Betsy dedicated to him and to Antoine Georges "with many thanks." She gave copies of the "slender volume" to friends and relatives, saying it told "the simple story of an introduction to Alpine climbing."

The next summer, Betsy climbed the Grand Teton by the "ordinary" route, the Owen, undoubtedly accompanied by one or both of the famous Teton guides Glenn Exum and Paul Petzoldt. The climb must have gone well, for it inspired Betsy to return the next year, with the intent of climbing the Grand via its southwest ridge and then to become the first female to traverse the mountain (to cross it using different ascent and descent routes). However, Paul and Glenn quickly convinced her that it would be far more "glorious" to traverse the Grand via its east ridge. This route had been climbed only twice before, first by Kenneth Henderson and Robert Underhill in 1929, and then by Fritiof Fryxell and Fred Ayres in 1934. Two German climbers had been killed attempting it.

The fact that Betsy would even consider tackling such a formidable climb shows how confident she had become since her novice efforts in Switzerland two years earlier in 1933. And the fact that she pulled it off shows that her confidence was justified. Certainly she was in fine shape, having spent a month in the Canadian Rockies, where she had "summited" on Whyte, Niblock, Pope's Peak, Mitre, and Edith (which she traversed and climbed via a new route).

Betsy described her Grand Teton achievement in *Trail and Timberline*, the monthly publication of the Colorado Mountain Club, which she joined in the mid-1930s. The article is the first she ever wrote for public consumption. Always the lady (and ladies don't boast!), Betsy did not minimize how taxing the climb was for her personally. Yet she described the difficulties from the viewpoint of a real climber, which, by this time, she was. Here follows Betsy's article, "The East Ridge of the Grand Teton."[2]

A. F. Mummery, the great English climber, once remarked that all mountains appear doomed to pass through three stages: an inaccessible peak; the most difficult ascent in the Alps; an easy day for a lady. [Although Mummery is usually credited with the "three stages" comments, he was in fact paraphrasing material first written by Leslie Stephen in the first edition of his book, The Playground of Europe, *published in 1871.] In America this seems also to be the case with many of our great mountains and routes. The east ridge of the Grand Teton, for example, was first considered quite impossible and then regarded as very difficult indeed. The story I have to tell deals with its passing to the third category; an easy day for a lady.*

As one sees the ridge against the skyline from Jenny Lake it has a fine and formidable appearance and as Petzoldt pointed out the three great gendarmes and described the various maneuvers by which we would circumvent them it was apparent that an adventure of the first order was in store for us. From then on things began to move quickly and the same afternoon we were plodding up the duty path to Amphitheatre Lake where we were to bivouac.

We reached there just before sundown and established ourselves in a sheltered though roofless rock house. Below us was the quiet lake and around us were all the gnarled trees of timberline. I spent half an hour brushing up on my rappelling from the top of a giant boulder nearby and then supper was ready, after which we wrapped ourselves in our blankets and settled down for the usual bivouac night. This means that the hours until daylight are spent exchanging one uncomfortable position for another uncomfortable position. But as luck would have it, the first real sleep of the night descended upon us just in time to make our start next morning one hour later than we meant it to be so that it was all of six o'clock before we had broken camp and were off.

For several hours I went through the motions of being a mountaineer without my heart being in it. It was a beautiful morning, clear and windless. We were working our way north and westward by means of successive saddles, after each of which we had to drop into a gully beyond. The last of these drops landed us on the broad expanse of the Teton glacier which we crossed to the foot of the first rocks of our ridge. The first pitch looked as though it meant business so we got out the rope, which proved to be 120 feet of a strong and stubborn grocery store variety. All the rest of the day I felt like Laocoön struggling with its unmanageable coils! We climbed in one two three order, which works very well in this kind of semi-exploratory climbing. Paul was leading and Glenn who followed next could give him support in hard places as well as do whatever might prove necessary to get their member of the party up. So most of the day I didn't see much of Paul. By the time I had conquered a passage he was generally busy on the next bit and nothing but a pair of nailed boots scratching away high overhead, or a faraway voice shouting instructions.

This first passage kept us busy for some time. To begin with there was an almost vertical chimney of the most un-cooperative sort from which we emerged breathlessly onto smooth and slanting slabs with occasional cracks for the bootnails. Making the most of these we tacked upward to the foot of a second chimney as inhospitable as the first. Here some more back and knee work plus a stranglehold on a piece of wedged tree-trunk did the trick. After this taste of high class exercise what came next seemed quite painful; a long section of uphill plodding, too steep for comfort but not steep enough for fun. When this was finally over, directly ahead and towering over us was the first great gendarme.

This obstacle [had turned] the two previous parties…to the north, but it was Petzoldt's idea that we try the south, so with this in mind we kept bearing to the left and were soon seriously involved in climbing to a notch in its south wall. When we had reached this and emerged on the other side, we found ourselves on a small platform overlooking a steep snow-filled couloir [steep gully] which led behind the gendarme back to the main ridge. After a rather tricky descent we tackled this long gully, sometimes on its rocky sides, sometimes on the snow that lined it, and sometimes sandwiched in between the two in deep cracks. The rock was very poor and one had to climb with the greatest care to avoid starting any number of private avalanches. On the snow passages Paul had a lot of step-cutting to do and cold particles kept landing down my neck with every swing of his axe. Above us the narrowing couloir was completely blocked by a gigantic chockstone. I don't want to be in the neighborhood when that rock decides to see the world! It acted as roof to a perfect cave of snow and ice where we sat and rested, looking out toward Nez Perce and the South Teton through a fringe of icicles. In spite of being rather blown after a tussle with its last defences, we found it a bit too air-conditioned for comfort and it was a relief to be out in the warm sun again and again on our way upward. We climbed out onto the perpendicular side wall of the couloir and worked our way up with the aid of excellent holds until we were able to cross back and stand on our erstwhile roof. A few more minutes of simple scrambling and the couloir was a thing of the past; we were back on the ridge with the first great tower behind us.

Ahead of us was a smooth and unpromising wall which we scanned hopefully while pausing for a little nourishment. Its surface promised little cooperation with bootnails so we changed to sneakers to make things easier. After tossing another empty tomato juice can over the edge for the greatest trip of its life, Paul tackled the problem of getting up the almost overhanging pitch. Everything was slanting the wrong way and there wasn't the slightest purchase to be found any- where. He tried climbing up on Exum's shoulder, but higher up there didn't seem to be anything to moor to either, and no security whatever in case of a fall. At this point there was a general consultation and the use of a piton was decided on. With the rope belayed through this, a boost from Glenn and some first-class adherence, Paul disappeared over the skyline. A minute later a shout told us that he was well fixed.

We sent the sacks up on the rope (their weight greatly augmented by our three pairs of boots) and then Glenn, combining length of limb and ingenuity with a touch of the supernatural, climbed the mauvais pas *[bad place] unassisted. Not so the lady of the party. At first it wasn't so bad. I got to the piton under my own steam, hooked one fin- ger through it (this isn't done in the best climbing circles) and gave my- self a tremendous boost. This momentum landed me quite a distance up on the slab, clinging, as the classic saying goes, to "slight discolor- ations in the rock." There followed a few moments of more than merely moral support from the rope and then, thanks to a tiny unevenness*

Figure 3.1   Paul Petzoldt, who guided Betsy up many a mountain, posed "just for fun" while Betsy took his photo in 1940 on Mount Owen. (Courtesy American Heritage Center, University of Wyoming. Copyright restricted.)

*over at the left (which I suspect of having been purely imaginary), I fi-
nally succeeded in hoisting myself up. For a while I was busy reassem-
bling my breath from the four corners of the earth while Paul achieved
some fine yodelling that brought back so many echoes that it almost
seemed as though someone must be answering him.*

*To the foot of the second gendarme we had nondescript climbing
and made the first moves around this pinnacle to the north without difficulty. Here Paul started looking for trouble and was exploring far below on serious looking ledges before we discovered that a direct and
simple way lay right ahead of us. Once beyond the tower, however, we
had our hands full getting back onto the ridge. The complications included another of those specimen chimneys with which I was beginning to be familiar but without contempt. It was the old struggle
against holdlessness and perpendicularity, hard on the back and
knees but fine for the experience. When we had reached our ridge and
sat down to get our breath and change back into our climbing boots,
we felt we had earned the right to be there.*

*Above us things looked so simple by contrast that we decided to
unrope. The rock was steep but firm and I found it a great relief to be
free of my sixty-foot quota of cable. A diminishing distance above us still
was the third tower and beyond it the beginning of the long snow slope
that leads to the foot of the final rocks. Settling down to fast and steady
climbing, we had no trouble passing the last tower and were soon skirting the edge of the snow. We were keeping to the rocks on the north because it was a warm afternoon and no day for snow work. The sun had
melted its white surface into a maze of valleys and pinnacles. There
was a cornice-like edge toward us that kept getting higher and higher
till it was way above our heads, making a smooth white wall with a
gleaming border of gold where the sun shone through. To our right the
arete dropped off sharply; ahead of us were the summit rocks.*

*All day the summit had managed to remain at a vast distance in
spite of our efforts and now that we were within striking distance of it
we began to get a sort of fifth or sixth wind. At this point Paul suggested
that we try making a new route up the last rocks from the north and the
next thing I knew we were back on the rope and skirting a long ledge
overlooking the north precipice. It seemed to me that day that this face
of the Grand Teton was more of an "everlasting abyss" than any I had
ever seen. Here Glenn was in the lead. When we were directly north of
the summit cliffs he turned and choosing the least impossible looking
chimney proceeded to do a good job with it while we cheered him on
from below. As usual the rope was then attached to the sacks, axes and
other impedimenta and they were pulled up. But just then something*

happened. My knapsack somehow came loose and went hurtling through the air, narrowly missing Paul and me below. Mentally cataloguing the valuables it contained, including my aneroid and new German camera, in a most melancholy state of mind I watched it bound down till it paused miraculously at the edge of the abyss! While Paul went down to get it, I staged an uphill fight with the chimney. It was of the same exacting type as the others of the day but offered by way of variation a chockstone near the top that forced one out uncomfortably far in order to get around it. It proved to be the chimney to end chimneys however, the final effort of a splendid ascent. Above it we went through a few concluding maneuvers and then Glenn said: "Only two hours more." That, as I had learned the summer before, is the Wyoming way of telling you that you are on the top. A little way off was the bronze tablet and the familiar summit rocks. A warm sun shone on them and us and we shook hands in great contentment just ten hours and twenty minutes after we had started out.

In spite of the lateness of the hour, there was an unspoken agreement against hurrying off the top. Not a breath of wind was blowing and everything was golden in the late afternoon light. Other people may have seen it in a less hospitable mood, but for me the top of that mountain will always typify everything desirable in a summit. Below us the whole panorama of the Jackson Hole region spread itself, its lakes and forests making accents in blue and green. Amphitheatre Lake looked quite near (but we knew better!) and one could see by the clouds of dust where automobiles were passing on the main highway. Glenn was arranging all the remaining eatables on a flat rock cafeteria style, while I took a rest on another. Paul wrote our names in the mountain register with the date, August 12, 1935. Time went fast and it was almost half past five before we decided to start doing something about getting down. The sun was low over the Idaho hills as we began descending by the usual route. We didn't bother to rope but went down at a sort of climbing gallop, the only excitement being a rappel down a long, ice-filled chimney. At the cooning place we tied up, walked by on the outside, using the famous ledge as a handhold and slid around the "Belly-Roll" rock. Half an hour after leaving the top we were at the upper saddle.

As Betsy mentions in this 1935 account, she was now carrying a camera. Her taking up mountain photography had not been entirely voluntary, as she explained in an article she wrote many years later for *The Villager*.

Figure 3.2   Betsy Cowles, circa 1935. Photographer unknown. (Courtesy Viola Ryder Nicholson.)

I take pictures in the mountains because, a few years ago, my father jumped a brook in the Yosemite. This may sound like a non sequitur but it's exactly what happened. You see, Father had always been the photographer of our expeditions and Father owned a Leica, and when he jumped the brook in the Yosemite the Leica slipped out of a back pocket and was never seen again.[3]

John Strong did not replace his camera right away and began to like not having the extra weight in his pack. Betsy:

"My dear," Father said to me about this time, "Has it ever occurred to you what you miss in not taking up photography? And don't you think it's quite enough of an undertaking for a man of my age to get himself up these peaks without the added burden of having to take pictures of them?"

Shortly after John lost his Leica, he gave Betsy a Vollenda for Christmas. Initially, she only looked at it "from the outside." Then one day she opened it up, was intrigued, and "began to feel a faint flicker of interest." Finally she bought a roll of film and took her first roll; the results filled her with equal amounts of "pride and dismay." But she was hooked and, indeed, remained so for the next thirty years. Despite many "photographic growing pains," she persisted and improved, learning the importance of making sure the camera was still when she clicked the shutter so the picture would be sharp. (Holding her breath helped.) After botched exposures, Betsy purchased a Weston light meter. The hardest lesson of all, she later said, was to avoid taking images that were confusing and learning to photograph "Less and Less" rather than "More and More."

Betsy's brother, Bill, whom she regarded as an expert, contributed to her enthusiasm for photography. He had dedicated *Photography for Fun* to his wife, "E.F.S., who escaped becoming a Darkroom Widow by making pictures herself," and had no doubt also encouraged Betsy to do her own printing. Betsy valued her older sibling's photographic judgments. She told a story on herself that Bill had puzzled over one of her early black-and-white photographs, asking, "Just what is this a picture of?" She learned always to ask herself that same question before snapping the shutter.

Although Betsy said that she much preferred taking pictures of mountains to taking pictures of people, the quality of her human portraits belies this statement. Perhaps she was modeling herself after the photographer Vittorio Sella, whom she called "great," and who is generally acknowledged to be one of the world's finest mountain photographers.

Figure 3.3   Betsy snapped Gottfried Fenz on the summit of the Jungfrau, before and after he realized he was being photographed. Although Betsy said mountains were her favorite subjects, she took many fine portraits of people as well. (Courtesy American Heritage Center, University of Wyoming. Copyright restricted.)

An Italian mountaineer, Sella took magnificent, sharp panoramas of the Alps, the Caucasus, and the Karakoram. At the time Betsy took up photography, Sella was more than seventy years old. Very likely she saw his photographs for sale in European climbing villages, although there is no record that she purchased any. Perhaps she saw an exhibit of his pictures in Washington, D.C. Certainly she would have been familiar with his black-and-whites in the *National Geographic Magazine*, which had acquired an extensive collection of Sellas at the turn of the century. Betsy once said that she envied Vittorio Sella because his patron, the Duke of Abruzzi, paid for "an army of porters" to carry "his [photographic] stuff."

Another major influence on Betsy was the Colorado Springs photo-grapher Harry Standley. He would have been an ideal mentor, for he was a gentle man, quiet, modest, and meticulous in his personal grooming. Harry was self-conscious in large groups because he had only gone through the sixth grade. For most of his adult life, he lived alone at the YMCA of downtown Colorado Springs.

Whether shooting for the local Chamber of Commerce or on assignment for a national publication, Harry took hundreds of fine photographs. He chose his exposures based on a good experienced eye and a chart that he carried in his pocket. Being a patient man who knew exactly what he wanted, he sometimes visited a site four or five times before setting up his tripod. Harry's work won several awards from national magazines. One native of Colorado Springs calls Harry Standley "our Ansel Adams."[4]

Harry was the tenth person to climb all of Colorado's then-known fourteeners, and the first to photograph them. He collected a rock from the summit of each, incorporating it into a little cabin he owned at one of the Carrol Lakes northwest of Colorado Springs. (Apparently, Betsy followed his example; eventually she climbed all the fourteeners and often gave rocks she had collected from mountain tops to her sister, Emilie.[5])

Harry photographed many of Colorado's mountains, not just the highest. Bob Ormes remembered with awe climbing the precipitous Ice Mountain while "lifting Harry Standley's box of glass plates and a tripod consisting of three joined oak trees from shelf to shelf of a slippery grass slope."[6] From Harry, Betsy learned that she would have to haul her camera and light meter up any mountains that she intended to photograph.

Betsy probably met Harry Standley through the Colorado Springs chapter of the Colorado Mountain Club, which she joined in the mid-1930s. They became good hiking companions and one can imagine that after Betsy began taking pictures, the pair would have discussed photography and that she would have asked for pointers and recommendations on equipment. Almost surely Harry taught Betsy a lot about printing, a process she found engrossing. "I can remember many a day, disappearing into the darkroom with the sun shining and the sky blue and staggering out, hours later, to find it is dark night and snowing. There is a kind of binge-y quality about printing pictures—you can't stop."[7]

Obviously the high photographic standards set by Bill Strong and Harry Standley rubbed off on Betsy. After she had been taking pictures for twenty years or so, she gave a humorous talk on the subject. Of the approximately 56,798 pictures she had shot by this time, she estimated that 25 percent were "fair to middling," that 50 percent were "downright rotten," and that "24.994% comprised that astonishing group that are so hard to understand and difficult to bear: the underexposed, the overexposed and the double exposed as well as the literally hundreds of negatives that, for reasons known only to the Eastman Kodak Co., turn up with nothing on them." This left Betsy with 0.006 percent pictures that were "wonderful, really marvelous if I say so myself."[8]

Notes

1. Robert C. Black, telephone conversation with the author, July 1995.
2. Elizabeth S. Cowles, "The East Ridge of the Grand Teton," *Trail and Timberline* no. 205 (November 1935): 126–30.
3. Information comes mainly from two sources, both of which are located in the Archives of the American Heritage Center. They are: Elizabeth Strong [S.] Cowles, "A Camera in the Mountains," *The Villager* (November 1940): 32, 33, 50, 51; and Elizabeth S. Cowles, text for an untitled talk that is "against photography" (ca. the 1950s).
4. Stanley W. Boucher, interview with the author, May 1985.
5. Emilie S. Smith, telephone conversation with the author, August 2, 1994.
6. Robert Ormes with the Colorado Mountain Club, *Guide to the Colorado Mountains*, 6th rev. ed. (Chicago: Sage Books, 1973), 118.
7. In 1947, a one-man show of Harry's photographs was hung at the Colorado Springs Fine Arts Center, that institution's first-ever exhibit of black-and-whites. It can be no coincidence that at the time Betsy was a member of the Center's board. Three more shows followed after Harry's death in 1951. Much information about Harry comes from an article by Jane Koerner, "Harry Standley: A Pioneer Photographer Exposed," *Colorado Springs Magazine*, n.d., 12.
8. Many years later, when Betsy complied with the request of the curator to give her papers and photographs to the University of Wyoming's American Heritage Center, she apparently made decisions as to which of her photographs were worthy of inclusion. She did not donate a single negative and an extensive search has failed to locate any. The Heritage Center owns about 140 of her black-and-white prints and about 400 of her slides.

CHAPTER FOUR

"The Tetons to Me"

During the summer of 1936, Betsy attended a newly formed mountain school in Switzerland designed to instruct "alpine beginners" in climbing techniques on ice, snow, and rock. She thought that the man who ran it, Kaspar Grass, was "a grand person, with a great love of his Engadine country, a big hearty laugh and a sixth, seventh and eighth sense about mountains." He combined competence in the mountains with a sense of humor. "In a mist as thick as a London fog," she wrote, "I have seen him make his way unerringly across a seamed and treacherous snowfield and in the pitch dark of the early morning hours he walked as unconcernedly up a crevassed glacier as if he were on Forty-Second Street!" Kaspar admonished his students:

> *"Do not go along with your head down and your eyes on your boots;...Look up! Watch where you are going; remember the stone here, that point of rock there. When we return this way perhaps the big landmarks will be obscured; maybe I make you lead, and then,"—(his hearty laugh rang out) "maybe we all land in a great big crevasse, yes?"*

Betsy's description of the Bergschule, which appeared in *Trail and Timberline,* contains a self-deprecating humor that characterizes her writing about mountains. In the following excerpt, she tells about learning how to cut steps in ice:

> *One day we spent with the Morterasch glacier as a laboratory and schoolroom. It took us an hour or so to reach the lower ice-fall where*

on the steep patches of ice we had step-cutting drill. Kaspar was a great sight. Poised midway on the ice wall, making vicious separate one-handed blows with his axe he looked like some kind of demon on the rampage. It appeared to be simple enough; a sideways cut made the floor of the step, followed by three blows at the back and a quick scoop with the flat end of the axe to clear away debris.

It was a joy to climb up Kaspar's steps; they were roomy without being enormous and had a fine inward slant that made one feel secure on the most vertical pitch. But to make ones like his was harder than it looked. One blow and I gave up trying to swing my axe single-handed; even with two I nearly tore my arms from their sockets. Up and up in my estimation went every iceman in the world for ice I discovered is one of the hardest and toughest materials in existence. Then too it turned out to be strangely difficult to hit the place where one was aiming. I seemed either to make a huge bucket of a step in about eighty strokes or a mere chip of a step with ten. First I made them fully three feet apart and exactly in a vertical line so that it became a major problem in equilibrium to get from one to the other, and then so close together that they tended to merge alarmingly. As you can imagine from all this, it was some time before I achieved a presentable staircase with a series of neat niches (made with the flat end of the axe) for handholds at the side.[1]

Betsy skipped the rock portion of the Bergschule, not (as she carefully pointed out) because she didn't think she had a lot to learn, but rather because she and her father went on climbs different from those of the school. By the end of the summer, she had made eleven ascents of peaks new to her. A year later she returned to Switzerland and climbed the well-known Jungfrau, Monch, and Mont Blanc; traversed the Matterhorn via the Zmutt and Italian Ridges; and made a half-dozen other respectable summits.

Betsy did not make any noteworthy climbs in 1938, for by that time her personal life was in turmoil. Sometime in the early 1930s she fell in love with a prominent Colorado Springs man, a friend of hers and Bob's, who finally said he was prepared to leave his wife and children to marry her. Believing him, Betsy began divorce proceedings as discreetly as possible. Her sister, Emilie, accompanied Betsy and her daughter, Ann, to Key West, Florida, telling no one of their whereabouts except for Em's husband, Macauley. "She didn't want to hurt Bob," Em explained.

Betsy and Bob Cowles divorced in 1939.[2] Betsy moved to Bronxville, New York, where she was to remain for the duration of World War II so as to be near

Figure 4.1 Betsy took this shot of an unnamed person, likely a guide, crossing a crevasse below the Grands Mulets on Mont Blanc, Switzerland, in 1937. (Courtesy American Heritage Center, University of Wyoming. Copyright restricted.)

Figure 4.2   Betsy often included people in her climbing pictures, as in this 1937 one of the Wetterhorn in Switzerland. (Courtesy American Heritage Center, University of Wyoming. Copyright restricted.)

her children, who were attending school in the East. Betsy's paramour never did leave his family.[3]

After their marriage dissolved, Bob Cowles continued to manage Betsy's parents' investments and to support Betsy quite generously, which he did for the rest of her life.[4] In 1939 Bob moved to Chicago.[5] Betsy remained in the East, vacationing on the Maine coast for nearly the first two years and doing a little climbing in New England. But she suffered from "melancholia," for, in addition to feeling displaced, Betsy, like all Americans, was alarmed at the Germans' aggression. So, in July 1940, she headed west "to the mountains seeking comfort."[6]

Betsy and her father rented a little cabin on the Snake River near Moose, Wyoming. Although they could not escape entirely from the "rumblings of the world crisis," their lives became "bounded for the moment by the untroubled rampart of the hills, the future by…climbing plans of that day, and the next."

A special quality stamped that summer, which Betsy reminisced about many years later. Her dear father was now seventy-three, still able to climb, but for how much longer? (In fact, John climbed the Grand Teton that summer.) America was on the edge of war, with no clear-cut future. Betsy's climbing companions, including Teton guides Paul Petzoldt and Glenn Exum, were healthy males sure to be drafted if the country did enter the war. When Betsy next returned to the Tetons, she might be too old to climb them with pleasure. For all she knew, the summer of 1940 might be the last "normal" one—ever. "Oh, the Tetons!" she wrote, "those wonderful mountains—apparently designed especially for climbers by a Providence sympathetic to mountaineering!"

That summer Betsy made several first "female" ascents, that is, she was the first female to climb the route. Later she wrote articles about them, which, interestingly, conveyed more of a "woman's attitude" than her writing had previously. She spoke of a "nice little peak that might have been the offspring of these two, trailing along after its parents." Betsy commented that a *mauvais pas* "apparently had vanished and you could almost have wheeled a baby carriage over!" And she observed that "so few mountains seem to have been planned with women in mind!"

Betsy intended to start out slowly, because she had done no climbing for three years. This was not Paul Petzoldt's idea, however.

The best cure for weak muscles, according to my old friend, was to use 'em. In the twinkling of an eye, it seemed, we were on our way up Garnet Canyon to try the Middle Teton from the north. Luckily for my self esteem, I've forgotten the details of the climb. A strong impression persists, however, of having been all-fingers-and-thumbs, with brief recollections of getting myself into some weird places when Paul sent me off to reconnoiter various ledges and chimneys. And I became very very tired. But oh how fine to see the world from a height again! A warm sun shone on it and us as we ate and relaxed on the summit. Ideas and plans came suddenly into being. Let's climb Mount Wister from the west, we said, and how about the north face of Buck? What would be a good route on Mount Moran, I asked, and is the north ridge of the Grand Teton any place for a lady? How amazing it was to realize, later on, that everything we planned that day on the Middle Teton came true.

Next on the program was a warm-up trip to Hanging Canyon for two climbs in the St. John group: Symmetry Spire by the snow gully on the north and a first ascent of a little rocky tooth nobody had ever noticed before except us. Then came four days in the Buck Mt. region. What a place to get to! It took us nine hours, heavily laden, to reach our first camping place on the desolate slope above Death Canyon. Early next morning we crossed a high valley full of wildflowers and dropped over a col into the upper end of south Avalanche Canyon. Here we pitched camp about noon on a grassy promontory overlooking our future theater of operations. The cliffs of Buck Mt. walled us in on the south, while to the north a fine turreted ridge led eastward to the summit of Mount Wister. Beside us there was a nice little peak that might have been the offspring of these two, trailing along after its parents. (We'll climb that some morning before breakfast, said Paul.) Jackson Hole lay far below, beyond the deep V of converging slopes.

Buck Mountain from Wister

After a hasty lunch we went for Mount Wister hammer and tongs, traversing it by the west ridge, all pinnacles included. From the summit, while I was taking pictures, Paul gave the north face of Buck a careful study. Three narrow, deeply-etched couloirs radiated downwards from the summit ridge. Enclosing them, like leaves of a fan, spread four widening bands of rock. These were exceedingly smooth and steep, especially at the bottom where they rose precipitously from the snowslopes below. After the manner of Holmes and Watson, Paul asked me what I thought of it. Overcoming a natural inclination to say "perfectly ghastly" (with an English accent) I murmured something noncommittal. Then Paul proceeded to point out certain important clues: there appeared to be a break at the foot of the most westerly of the bands—perhaps we could get off the snow and onto the rock here; a delicate line above in-dicated a ledge that we might be able to traverse eastward on (if the first snow gully could be crossed somewhere) and in case this ledge didn't work, a faint streak higher up might offer a possible alternative. If either of the ledges went, it would land us on the face—and if the face went, we'd reach the ridge at a point somewhat west of the summit—and if the ridge went, the mountain was ours! By this time Paul was full of enthusiasm and I, like Watson, felt quite willing to leave everything to the maker of these brilliant deductions.

Buck Mountain

Next day Paul's route unrolled for us like a vertical magic carpet. Except every now and then. We got onto the rock all right and across the snow gully but ledge No. 1 petered out at a sort of lovers' leap. Ledge No. 2 however was a honey. It took us just where we wanted to go. The middle gully was now immediately to our left and beyond it lay one of the two center sections of the face (we were on the other). All the way up it kept me from feeling dissatisfied with my lot by look-ing even less inviting than where we were.

I was beginning to have a wonderful time. The rock was splen-did, with real style and dash. It was as if, glad to have someone climb-ing here at last, our mountain was determined we should enjoy ourselves. Paul's face wore the absorbed expression of a musician ex-ecuting a complex cadenza. We scarcely exchanged a word except when he would look surprised and say, "What, you here?" when I emerged after a headline passage. On the upper part of the face the angle steepened; the rock became smoother here, more slabby. Then we surmounted an exposed corner and found ourselves on the ridge. We were on a secondary summit, it appeared. Between us and the main one the ridge made a sharp drop and then resumed its upward course with a thumping overhang. (Holy Smoke! said Paul.)

After a brief zero-hour meal for which all appetite seemed sud-denly to have vanished, we climbed down to investigate. The arete was whittled down to knife-thinness here and while Paul prepared for a try at the overhang, I had to be parked out of sight in a little pocket over the edge. I heard faint mutterings for a while, then the sound of a piton being hammered in. After that there seemed to be a lifetime of silence until finally the rope began running out rapidly and a faraway yodel told me Paul had made it. Now it was up to me. I climbed out and took a look. On either side of the mauvais pas *the mountain fell away so astoundingly that there was obviously nothing for it but to take the obstacle headon. A small ledge below the point of greatest bulge appeared to be the only way to begin but the distance between it and me was vast. So few mountains seem to have been planned with women in mind! Using a sliver of rock for a springboard, I landed uneasily on the ledge with the worst of the bulge above me and balance a delicate matter. Then a miracle happened! The handhold of a lifetime appeared just where it counted most and a split second later my eye lit on the foothold to end footholds, all but concealed by a triumph of protective coloration. (There is a Santa Claus, I thought.) Gathering myself for the effort, I swing out, up and over.*

Nothing more about this superlative day need be related here but how often I remember it and our wonderful feelings as we saw, after the overhang, the cairn that they tell me is the biggest in the Tetons. We made it bigger still that afternoon and I left a hairpin in a conspicuous place as we couldn't seem to find a woman's name in the register. (Maybe they couldn't read or write, said Paul.)

Avalanche Canyon

Next day we polished off the region by traversing the little spire (Veiled Peak on the map) before breakfast as planned. Then after a wind-up meal that brought together some amazing combinations, we broke camp and headed down Avalanche Canyon for home. I hear the authorities are anxious to keep this a Primitive area. Well, they won't have to work very hard; it looked self-perpetuating to me. For five hours we fought our way through mazes of slide rock, fallen timber, turbulent streams and clouds of dive-bombing mosquitoes until at last we reached Taggart Lake and a path. Here we ran into some dudes on horseback who looked curiously at us and asked, "Why walk when you can ride?" I couldn't think of a thing to say. Still can't.

Betsy took a week off, making griddle cakes for breakfast every morning, swimming in a lake, fishing, horseback riding, washing clothes, and attending church in Moose. "We heard a good sermon from the pulpit," Betsy wrote, "but it couldn't compare with the one we saw, looking through that window."

She climbed Mount Owen and took a photograph of Paul doing a cross-brace in the chimney below the summit—"just for photography," as she explained. It was "wonderful picture taking weather." They lingered on top for a long time, "filled with that best-of-all-possible-worlds feeling. Terrible things were happening, but not here and not now."

Figure 4.3   Climbers belaying on the col (high mountain pass) of Mount Owen in the Tetons, 1940. Photo by Betsy Cowles. (Courtesy American Heritage Center, University of Wyoming. Copyright restricted.)

On August 1, Betsy invited friends and neighbors to celebrate Swiss Day, a tradition she probably began in the 1930s and which she continued for the rest of her life. Although in Switzerland it was customary to light a bonfire on every peak, Betsy made do with a big one in the front yard, a "gala" dinner, and a display of fireworks purchased in Jackson Hole, left over from the Fourth of July. The party was a success, Betsy wrote, but for some it invoked a certain nostalgia. Three years earlier, in the town square in Pontresina, Switzerland, a man had "called upon his countrymen for strength and unity." And now, Betsy remarked, the same things were being said in the United States, with the same urgency.

Mostly, however, the outside world did not intrude. Betsy climbed Teewinot, probably with Paul Petzoldt as her guide. She called it a failure, "[n]ot because we didn't make the top but because it wasn't any fun getting there."

In early August, more climbing partners arrived—Glenn Exum, Bob Bates, Bill House, and Macauley (Mac) Smith, the former Olympic runner and mountain-climbing lawyer/judge who was married to Betsy's sister, Emilie. Thus, contrary to Betsy's expectations, the second half of the summer turned out to be even better than the first half, which had seemed to her "just about perfect."

Betsy, plus the "high class company" of Glenn Exum, Bob Bates, Bill House, Mac Smith, and Paul Petzoldt, decided to make a second ascent of the north ridge of Mount Moran. They took a motorboat across Jackson Lake and backpacked through heavy underbrush. As Betsy later wrote:

> The climb next day was something special for me: I was leading the first rope. I can remember every handhold on that slab-hung peak even now. But going first didn't mean I was boss. All serious questions of tactics and route-finding were handled by the experts, of course. And the climbing difficulties proved to be a lot less than expected which was a break for the neophyte. A few passages that looked rather grim at first glance opened up beautifully. The worse place on the ascent— a ticklish traverse somewhere between the twin summits—never materialized at all. The whole way up Paul kept cheerfully referring to the ordeal that lay ahead. When we got there, whether by miracle or rock-fall we never knew, the mauvais pas apparently had vanished and you could almost have wheeled a baby carriage over!

The weather looked threatening and so the party hurried off the summit. But their luck continued to hold; by afternoon the weather had completely cleared. Although leading must have been a heady experience for Betsy, she wrote that there were other things she was more apt to think of when she remembered Moran:

> *like our wonderful camping place in the last of the trees, with the crags overhead and Jackson Lake shimmering far below. In tune with the scene and our fine after-the-climb feelings were Bob Bates' sourdough ballads with yodeling obligatos by Glenn and chorus-work from the ensemble. And what good mountain talk there was around the campfire! Those tales of Alaska and the Karakoram will long be remembered, especially by one who'll probably never get any nearer to either than we did there by the fire. Food was important too,—at least it was to me, being cook and rather nervous about it, like the newly employed domestic who finds she has to begin on a dinner party, right off. Everything tasted surprisingly good.*

Betsy climbed Nez Perce with Bob Bates and Bill House late in the summer. The morning air was crisp and a few high aspens were turning yellow. "This gave a sense of urgency to us who had been so relaxed before," Betsy wrote, "and a *carpe diem* feeling pervaded our climbing conferences." Their finale was to be the north ridge of the Grand Teton, climbed only four times before, by very strong parties, none of which had included a woman.

"You owe it to your sex," Paul told Betsy. And so the same six who had climbed Mount Moran backpacked up to Amphitheater Lake, where they camped.

Betsy would later refer to the north ridge of the Grand as the hardest climb of her life.[7] Typically, however, in writing about this major achievement, Betsy minimized her own abilities and instead emphasized her shortcomings in speed and technique.[8] However, we can assume that Betsy was, in fact, elated by her climb, because of a letter she wrote to Paul Petzoldt several months after the climb, and because she and Paul subsequently organized a bold expedition to pluck some virgin summits of the Sierra Nevada de Santa Marta Range in Colombia.

The North Ridge of the Grand Teton

> *Our 3:30 start next morning seemed very alpine. It took me back to Switzerland to find myself plodding along in the dark behind the lantern and to hear, after the scree approaches were over, the sound of boots and axes on the snow. I had always been a little scornful of the Teton glacier but in its upper reaches it's quite respectable and by the dim morning light we peered into some sizable crevasses....*

Figure 4.4   In 1940, Betsy took this picture of her friend Bill House, one of the finest American climbers at this time, rappelling off Nez Perce in the Tetons of Wyoming. (Courtesy American Heritage Center, University of Wyoming. Copyright restricted.)

Soon difficulties and danger petered out simultaneously and we had fast and easy going to the top of the great north shoulder. After four hours' climbing we paused here for some food and to gather our energies for the real effort which was at hand.

The ridge above us looked very short. Later I realized why. It was everywhere so steep that you could only see the pitches just ahead. We were on two ropes: Paul and I and Mac on the first, with Bill, Bob and Glenn switching leads on the second. In this order we started from the col. Paul threaded his way eastward at a dizzy tangent and was out of sight immediately. Then it was my turn. I'll spare the reader details—so many follow—but that nature had never intended this as a human thoroughfare was at once apparent. My struggle for Lebensraum that day began right here. From now on I was acutely aware of climbing at the very limit of my powers, if not somewhat beyond. Oddly enough it seemed to involve great mental effort as well. At the end of the day my mind was as tired as my muscles.

The first pitch kept me busy for quite a spell; then we moved westward and were in deep shadow for the rest of the ascent. How cold it was! The business of taking off and putting on mittens, of having to blow on icy fingers, bothered me. There was so much else to attend to. I was busy watching Paul, trying to memorize his tactics so as to do better when my turn came. And I had his rope to handle: not the faintest catch or tension could be risked that might throw him off balance on these delicate passages. Then there was the piton routine, a life work in itself. The only sounds besides climbing instructions and the wind was the jangle of karabiners [carabiners] accumulating at my belt. Mac, climbing third, had to be belayed of course, and the knapsacks hauled up on the rope when the going was too strenuous to negotiate with them on. What a three ring circus it was!

Meanwhile life continued to be fairly arduous until we struck an easy ledge. This carried us around a corner and almost to the foot of that famous bit of mountain architecture, the chockstone chimney. At first view it was rather disappointing. I wasn't nearly as impressed as I'd expected to be. There was something misleading about it in relation to the other lines and angles about. A thread of ice, steeper than it looked, led towards it. From here the chimney rose like a vertically tilted trough, shallow at first but narrowing as it went on. After fifty feet or so (all measurements being the wildest guesswork) there was a small platform. The chockstone hung out over this like a huge umbrella, completely blocking the chimney except at its outer edges. Far above the great obstacle you could see the black walls mounting as if forever. Paul skirted the ice and climbed slowly and carefully up to the little shelf, looking as dependable as the Queen Mary riding out a gale at sea. As we watched his dwindling figure from below, the amazing perpendicularity of everything became increasingly apparent. The moving form brought it all into scale. Firsthand experience did nothing to dispel this impression, I might add. I had a merry time getting up myself. In the first place I kept too far in the chimney, a common climbing error. And then (another one) I became slightly flustered. By the time I had finally landed, breathless, on the platform my faith in the future had become shaky indeed. For frequent briefing on the route had made it clear that this lower section, though troublesome, doesn't compare in difficulty with the Putsch *that comes next.*

Now Paul began to prepare for the main act by threading the rope through a rising successions of pitons. Then the fun began. He climbed far out onto the west wall where there was a meager ledge. With his right foot here and facing inward, he swung his left over onto the opposite side of the chimney, making a cross-brace. Then by an exchange of hand and foot pressures, he worked his way upward until he was level with the outside edge of the chockstone. From now on he was out of my sight, but those congregated below could follow his progress as frequent cheers indicated. When these rose to a crescendo fortissimo *I knew that Paul's difficult lead had been successfully completed.*

Next thing on the schedule was to belay Mac up the lower pitch. This done, I succeeded Paul (but at a vastly slower tempo) in the various positions just described. To say that I gave my All to this passage would be no overstatement. The effort was total. For one thing, the walls of the chimney were smooth and holdless: for another it was so wide that a cross-brace was only just barely possible for one of my dimensions. For long minutes I could make no headway at all and after each little bit of progress, I had to rest endlessly. Even resting was work! Then I'd start in again and fight for a few more inches. I have no idea of the length of time involved but for that space the absolute limits of my world were the walls of that chimney. Everything else was erased from consciousness completely. There was nothing but the Here and the Now. At long last I reached the lower edge of the chockstone. Then I saw what the next move was to be—or maybe Paul told me. He was coaching from above like the man behind the runner at third base. Over at the left there was a deep crack between the chimney wall and the side of the great wedged boulder. With vast effort I lunged for it and crammed myself in. The transfer wasn't easy to accomplish and it was a pretty tight fit in the crack but I felt mightily encouraged nevertheless. I rested for awhile and began working my way up again, this time by a kind of constricted wriggle. Somehow inch succeeded inch and a little higher up a few stones jammed into the crevice proved to be a great help. Using these and my last ounce of energy, I pulled myself up over the edge. The bleachers went wild!

Although the route thereafter continued to be spectacular, it was not as difficult. The party climbed in the "long twilight of those rock walls" and then Betsy found Paul sitting on a roomy shelf. A sliver of sunlight touched them in "brief benediction" and they shook hands.

Soon we were plugging along again. One crawled up slab after hold-less slab, tilted at the last possible angle for friction holds. A long vertical pitch was memorable. We were meeting more and more patches of snow and ice now that we were getting higher. The sky was gray and the cold intense. After some concentrated work over on the west side of the mountain, we enjoyed a glorious return to the arete where, balanced grandly over the precipice, we made use of some perfectly marvelous holds. But this was exceptional. Mostly we had to work hard to make ends meet. As we neared the summit things flattened out a little. There were chances to stand upright, to walk around. The effect on me was comical—it was all I could do to keep my feet! By this time being on all fours seemed so much more natural. I made terribly hard work of a last chimney just from the habit of looking on the dark side of things, I suppose. (What's all the fuss about? said Paul.) Next thing we were on the top. It was two-thirty, eleven hours since our start from Amphitheater Lake and seven hours since we had left the shoulder, just 1700 feet below.

After their climb, the sunshine vanished and the summit of the Grand became "bleak and forbidding." The wonderful summer weather they had enjoyed had turned. A few days later, when Betsy and her father left Jackson Hole to go back East, a cloud curtain had dropped in front of all the peaks and crags.

Notes

1. Elizabeth S. Cowles, "Bergschule," *Trail and Timberline* no. 220 (February 1937), 19–21.
2. In 1939, Robert Maynard Hutchins, president of the University of Chicago, announced that the Cowles Commission for Research in Economics would move its headquarters to the University of Chicago. In 1955, the Cowles Commission moved to Yale University, where it was renamed the Cowles Foundation for Economic Research. This information comes from a copy of an obituary of Alfred

Cowles III as it appeared in the *Chicago Tribune*, December 29, 1984, courtesy of Ben Hammett, Ph.D.

3. Emilie S. Smith, interview with the author, March 24, 1992.
4. Laney House, interview with the author, October 15, 1992.
5. On October 24, 1949, Alfred Cowles III married Louise Lamb Phelps. Information comes from the family tree of Alfred Cowles I, supplied by Ben Hammett, Ph.D.
6. Elizabeth S. Cowles, "The Tetons to Me [Part I]," *Trail and Timberline* no. 353 (May 1948), 67–70. The following account of Betsy's climbs in the Tetons is from this source.
7. "America's Interesting People," *Vassar Alumnae Magazine*, n.d., Archives, American Heritage Center.
8. Elizabeth S. Cowles, "The Tetons to Me [Part 2]," *Trail and Timberline* no. 354 (June 1948), 79–82.

CHAPTER FIVE

First Ascents in Colombia

At the time of the Santa Marta expedition of 1941, American climbers, both men and women, were generally technically less proficient than their European counterparts, although there were some notable exceptions. The sport had, after all, originated in Europe in the late 1700s. For the next century it had been practiced mostly by British men who, employing guides from the Continent, often took credit for any first ascents they garnered. The Alpine Club, based in London, was founded in 1856; the American Alpine Club, based in New York City, was founded in 1902. At the time Betsy was doing hard climbs, most Americans who called themselves mountaineers—and there weren't many—had cut their climbing teeth in Europe.

In 1941, the number of potential American female climbing companions from whom Betsy could choose was tiny. Like her, almost all of them were college graduates and of some means. Many, such as Eleanor Davis (Ehrman), Dora Keen Handy, Marjory Hurd, Elizabeth Knowlton, Helen Buck, Georgia Englehard (Cromwell), Miriam O'Brien Underhill, and Betty Woolsey, had attended or graduated from an Eastern woman's college; Christine Reid (Orcutt) had studied at the Boston Museum of Fine Arts School. The four women who were founding members of the American Alpine Club (Edwina Fay Fuller, Josephine Diebitsch Peary, Fanny Bullock Workman, and Annie Smith Peck) were well educated, although none was the product of one of the elite Seven Sisters schools.

According to two men who knew her well, Betsy Cowles had "quite a rivalry" with Georgia Engelhard Cromwell, four years her junior, who had

Figure 5.1   La Reina, 18,160 feet high, from Pico Ojeda in the Santa Marta Range of Colombia. (Courtesy American Heritage Center, University of Wyoming. Copyright restricted.)

attended, but not graduated from, Vassar College.[1] (Georgia's uncle was the photographer Alfred Stieglitz, whose second wife was the artist Georgia O'Keeffe.) Georgia Cromwell became a photographer, selling to such publications as *National Geographic, Look, Harper's Bazaar,* and *Life.*

Slim, attractive, and with boyishly short blonde hair, Georgia was extremely strong and competitive, sometimes striding up a mountain so fast that her male companions—even guides—panted to keep up. Although she made climbs in the western United States and Europe, it was in Canada that she made her firmest mark, racking up thirty-two first ascents. Georgia appeared in a movie, *She Climbs to Conquer,* and in a cartoon-style ad for which she smilingly stated, cigarette in hand, "A Camel picks me up in a few minutes and gives me the energy to push on...Get a lift with a Camel."[2]

Betsy was also jealous of Miriam O'Brien Underhill's fine climbing reputation and was critical of her autobiography, *Give Me the Hills.*[3] However, Betsy did not convey these feelings publicly; in her 1957 review of the book, she expressed only admiration for Miriam's climbing career and for her "warm, sprightly [writing] style."[4]

It would have been unrealistic for Betsy to have regarded Miriam as a serious rival, for there is little dispute among the cognoscenti that Miriam was the finest American female climber of her generation. A Bryn Mawr graduate born in 1898, four years before Betsy, she made remarkable climbs before Betsy ever got started. Frequently she led, unusual enough for an American woman of her time, but in addition Miriam frequently climbed *guideless* and—even more shocking—*manless,* as well. To her credit are the first all-female ascents of the Matterhorn and the Grépon. After she married American Robert Underhill, the two made spectacular climbs together. Typically, Robert led on snow and Miriam on rock.

Still, although the pool of American women climbers was small, Betsy found an eminently qualified woman to join her in the Santa Martas: Elizabeth Knowlton. A fellow alumna of Vassar College, she had graduated seven years earlier than Betsy, in the class of 1916. After earning a master's degree from Radcliffe, Elizabeth had taken up mountain climbing. For the next decade she had written occasional articles of a general nature for such publications as *Alantic Monthly* and *Nation,* and articles about mountain climbing, which appeared in the *American Alpine Journal.*

Unlike Betsy, Elizabeth was a veteran of high-altitude and expedition climbing; in 1932 she had reached 20,000 feet on the 8,000-meter peak Nanga Parbat, a most unusual achievement for a woman at that time. The book she wrote about the expedition, *The Naked Mountain,* had been well received.

Although she usually climbed with a male guide, in 1938 she was a member of an all-female expedition that attempted Mount Confederation in the Canadian Rockies.

Elizabeth Knowlton's climbing credentials added depth to the expedition, which was venturing into an area of South America that had been virtually unknown to climbers until 1930. In that year, Thomas (Tom) Cabot, while sailing on a Caribbean cruise ship, had finally decided that the clouds he had been watching were not clouds at all, but rather high snowy mountains not marked on any map. Incredulous, he had disembarked. For a month or so, he lived in the town of Santa Marta while exploring the area. Finally he pieced together a laborious approach to the peaks, probably the only possible one, and vowed to come back one day to climb them. Ten years later he did so, accompanied by Henry Hall, Walter Wood, Anderson Bakewell, and several other men. As Cabot and his companions made their way into the range, they were astonished to meet, coming out, a German expedition that had made a first ascent of the Central Peak, part of the main group. Undeterred, the Cabot party continued, proceeding to make a first ascent of the East Peak. They also mapped the area and took aerial photographs.[5]

Several months later, at an American Alpine Club dinner, Tom Cabot discussed his trip into the Santa Martas with Betsy.[6] A year or so after that conversation, while Betsy was chatting with several AAC members, among them Elizabeth Knowlton, she suggested in an offhand way that they go climbing during the next winter. Elizabeth replied, "ALL RIGHT." Then Henry Hall said, never thinking that Betsy or Elizabeth would take him up on it, "You better go to the Santa Marta."

So in early fall of 1940, Betsy sent Paul Petzoldt a letter in which she discussed the possibility of climbing in the Santa Marta Range.

> *The land sounds fine and so does S. America. How about next year? Can you make it all right with Bernice? [Bernice, who sometimes went by "Patricia," was Paul's wife.] When we first discussed it I was only ¹/₄ serious, now I am ¹/₂ to ³/₄ serious. How serious are you? I have just about decided to make m[ountain]eering my Calling. So don't call it off as a lifework for yourself just as I call it ON, see?*

Paul wrote his reply on the letter Betsy had sent him because, as he explained, he was in the Laramie, Wyoming, post office and had no stationery.

I am 250% serious about South America. I'll need some more pictures too. We could make the trip pay for itself if you'll back it. [Presumably Paul meant he could do this by giving lectures and selling articles illustrated with photographs.] Won't cost much. Let's do it. 1) Must make winter plans 2) let me know if you really ¾ serious and I'll start getting information. It's a great opportunity for both of us and I know you can do it. You owe it to your sex.

P.S. Bernice wants me to make the South American trip. It is my work.

The tone of these quoted letters (the only ones between Paul and Betsy that survive) is friendly and bantering and, in light of later events, ironic. Betsy began her letter by telling Paul he ought to be glad he has a client who clamors for her bill and who is at the same time willing to take the kind of back talk from him that she has put up with. "Can't think why I don't send *you* a bill." She bragged a little, saying that the November issue of *Bronx Magazine* would publish an article by her about mountains and photography, "about which I suspect you don't think I know anything. Just wait till Xmas comes and you get the PICTURES I am going to send you of yourself in the mts. I have already printed some beauties." Betsy closed with "Good luck & berg heil to you both!"

Paul bragged back. He had landed a job with National Assemblies in Hollywood, which arranged lecture circuits. He hoped to make $5,000 that year, with the possibility of renewing the contract. On his own, he had arranged to speak at several colleges. He wrote, "I've really got the stuff—I know it now."[7]

Betsy was excited about the adventure and also nervous, keenly aware that she was the least experienced of the three participants. (In 1938, Paul had reached more than 26,000 feet during an attempt of K2 in what is now Pakistan, the second-highest mountain in the world and regarded as more challenging than Everest.) She wrote:

Those of you who have been on trips like this know what it's like: worse than a bride planning a trousseau. New to expeditions, I was amazed. Think of planning what kind of soup you're going to eat for dinner on February 18 when it is December 21! planning just how many sets of long underwear you're going to need to keep mind and body together at 16,000 feet. It was amazing, fascinating, appalling. This was a different kind of business from my alpinism to date and I was prey to many misgivings. Was I the expedition type? Maybe my place was on the route ordinaire.[8]

On February 10, 1941, Elizabeth, Paul, and Betsy boarded the SS *Jamaica* in the New York City harbor. Five days later they landed in Barranquilla, Colombia, where they were met by Tom Cabot's friend, Juanacho (Juan) Ujueta, and by Max Eberli, a young Swiss working in Barranquilla. Betsy found the heat overwhelming and oppressive. The hotel beds were solid wood with no mattresses or springs.

For three days, the party managed to see a few of the local sights while changing money, purchasing last-minute supplies in the local city market, and packing. They persuaded Max Eberli to accompany them at least on the beginning of their trip, which he did. Then Paul, baby-sitting a thousand pounds of supplies, took an overnight ride on a so-called flea boat to the town of Santa Marta. Next morning he met Betsy, Elizabeth, and Max at the airport and the party caught a train. The heat continued to be blistering.

Sitting in open-air cars, they wound their way up through banana-tree country, arriving at the town of Fundación in time for lunch. They ate in what Betsy described as "a marginal restaurant along with lots of flies" and puzzled over advertisements for insecticides, which adorned the walls.[9] At Fundación they boarded a springless truck to Valledupar, where they spent the night. Betsy's and Elizabeth's mosquito-netted beds were in an open L attached to a large room with other beds and their occupants. Although not a breath of wind stirred the heat, Betsy slept soundly.

The next morning she arose and wandered around in what she called the "early coolth" taking photographs, then ate breakfast in the hotel while chickens "played tag" around their feet. Betsy commented that there was "dirt everywhere" and she imagined that soon it would be on her. One senses that Betsy was in a mild state of shock from the heat and dirt, only slightly mitigated by the "nice" cable sent by Bob Bates and Bill House. She and her friends sent a telegram to Juanacho Ujueta back in Barranquilla, expressing their gratitude for all he had done to help arrange their trip. (Ujueta, a member of the 1939 Cabot expedition, and Max Eberli had helped Betsy's party go through customs and obtain a permit for photography.)

After a wild bus ride to Salada, "deep in the jungle behind Valencia," they loaded a mule train with their gear and proceeded up a trail, gaining 3,000 feet to the Monte Grande Pass before dropping down to the town of Pueblo Bello. There they stayed in the home of a German family (the Strauches) that Max knew. Many Germans lived in Colombia. There the expedition members slept in beds all in a row in one room. For the first time since they had arrived in Colombia, it was chilly enough for sleeping bags. Betsy's natural good humor returned to the entries in her diary.

Her companions and she were made to feel welcome in Pueblo Bello and were even invited to the birthday party dinner of one Osvalde Mestre, who spoke English. The feast was called a *sancocho*, which, Betsy explained, was like Thanksgiving minus any strings attached, such as the time of year. The sancocho began in the middle of the day, and the birthday boy was definitely in a mood to celebrate.

> *Much merriment. He had a bottle, was giving everybody drinks and having quite a few himself. Then—such a meal! The food (very juicy, very strange) was dumped from a large pot onto a table, covered with shiny green banana leaves, around which the dozen or so guests clustered. From then on it was every man for himself. Things kept disappearing: what happened to that nice drumstick I'd been looking forward to? The old Spaniard two seats away was hard at work at one strangely like it.* [10]

The next day, Betsy, Paul, Elizabeth, Max, and the pack train left Pueblo Bello and climbed another 3,000 feet to the town of San Sebastian. The country became "grander and grander," Betsy wrote, and the "bug-life less and less. The air began to have that tang that means a mile high." As they walked into San Sebastian, Arahuaco Indians were observing them from every doorway and seemed to be talking about this extraordinary caravan—or so Betsy assumed. She was surprised to find out that several days before she and Elizabeth arrived in the village, the news about "two American women *in pants*" had raced ahead.

The Santa Marta party stayed at the home of the Richters, German friends of Max. Betsy, Paul, Max, and Elizabeth devoured Frau Richter's meals. They rejoiced in the cleanliness and peace of their quarters, which they shared with a German family whom Betsy liked personally although she remarked in her diary, "Schmidt's first name = Hermuth. He is a German aviator—why is he here??"

At first their stay in San Sebastian passed pleasantly. They swam in the river below the Richters' house, sunbathed on a fine rock slab, and did exercises, all to the amusement of a small group of enthralled locals. Frau Richter became fond of her American guests and began addressing them with the familiar *du*. One day Elizabeth and Betsy, wearing trousers, and the rest of the party walked to the nearby Capuchin mission. They sipped coffee "very ceremoniously" with the head padre; the nuns had fled at the sight of the women in men's attire! On the way back to the Richters', all the Indians stopped still to stare at them, motionless as if they had turned to stone.

Betsy, Paul, Elizabeth, and Max had intended to stay in San Sebastian for only a day or two. However, they could not locate any bulls to carry their supplies on the final, rugged, high-altitude stint. A man who had at first promised the use of his four bulls *mañana* could not produce them, which he had said were "just outside." Well, he said, the bulls were at his *finca* (ranch) two hours away. Then, when pressed a day later and still no bulls, well, the bulls were at Pueblo Bello. Finally he admitted that there were no bulls.

It began to rain. Max became ill. The group's morale reached such a low point that even the Demarara rum sent by Bill House and Bob Bates did little to cheer them. And then the weather cleared and Elizabeth spied the constellation of Taurus, which the group regarded as a good omen. Max's temperature rose, then began to fall. Finally, after four days in San Sebastian, the necessary bulls were located. Max felt well enough to travel and so the party set off on the steep, slippery trail up to the head of the Adurea Mena Valley, accompanied by three Arahuaco Indian men and a couple of children to manage the bulls. They left at 9 A.M. and arrived so late at night (6 P.M.) that Betsy had to fabricate supper in the pitch dark. Max looked tired and obviously felt awful.

But by the next day he felt better. The party arose at 6:30, was off by 9, and reached their destination, the village of Manancanaca, in the early afternoon. At the top of a pass they had their first close look at the peaks they wanted to climb. After bathing in stream, the party toured the village of thatched-roof huts. Then they studied their map and photographs, trying to determine the route.

On the following day, which was clear and hot, they contoured around rocky moraines and descended to the first of three lakes, where they made camp. The trip had gone reasonably well. In retrospect, Betsy thought that if they had elected to take an alternate route via the Guatapuri Valley, which was shorter but steeper, the Indians would have deserted them. However, by offering "continual presents and attention = like cigars, etc.," the Arahuacos had stayed with them, friendly and cheerful during the entire journey. Now the going would be too rough for the pack animals, and so Antonio, Ignacio, Delfine, and the two children turned around, promising to return on March 19. The Santa Marta expedition would have a little over three weeks for climbing.

For their first night alone, Betsy, Paul, Elizabeth, and Max camped in Gloomy Gulch, named by the Cabot party two years earlier when they had made the unhappy discovery that the pack animals could go no farther.

Because Betsy and her party had known this ahead of time, they did not find the gulch gloomy at all. In fact, Betsy described it as "lovely" and "peaceful," surrounded as it was by "quiet, high cliffs." She and her friends even discussed alternate names for the gulch, such as Hilarious Hollow or Riotous Ravine. However, in deference to the Cabot party they finally agreed that it should remain Gloomy Gulch.

Ever since Barranquilla, they had been taking precautions against malaria and amoebic dysentery. However, there was nothing they could take to ward off the bites of a nearly invisible insect called the *jejeune*, pronounced "hayhenny." Elizabeth and Betsy, who had worn long pants, got off relatively easily, but Paul had worn shorts one afternoon; his legs were so covered with bites that Betsy wondered if they would ever return to normal. Now, camped at 13,600 feet, they were well above the zone of pesky insects, although they did find a few fleas in their sleeping bags, probably lowland stowaways.

Max was feeling much better and finally the four could relax and joke. They agreed that after the feast in Santo Bello their favorite saint was Sancocho. After dinner, they turned in early and slept soundly.

The next day, February 25, was a Rest Day. As Betsy explained in a speech she gave several years later,

> You will probably already have noticed the frequency with which I speak of REST DAYS. We had lots of them. We meant to. We wanted to see if a leisurely tempo might eliminate or at any rate reduce the effects of altitude....Slow and Easy was our motto—and I must say it worked.

Nineteen forty-one was a generation away from the appearance of a milestone article in the *New England Journal of Medicine* that suggested the reasons people frequently became ill and/or died at high altitudes and what could be done about it. Its author would be Charles S. Houston, M.D., whom Betsy would soon meet and who would become a close friend. Climbers had long been aware that high altitudes could cause people to feel lousy and even to die, but usually victims were thought to have contracted a kind of pneumonia.

The 1941 Santa Marta expedition owed its "slow and easy" approach to the high-altitude experiences of Paul Petzoldt and Elizabeth Knowlton. In contrast, the Cabot party of 1939 had moved from sea level to 14,000 feet very quickly and had generally felt so rotten that they concluded that the valley contained "stale air" and that the Andes were especially bad in this respect.[11]

Betsy compiled a list of "What we have been doing that might explain our good health and training." In addition to "frequent rest days," she added "daily dose of salt pills [in medical disfavor today]...the understanding that each person would decide the size of the load he or she was capable of carrying, eating good food, and relaxing often by reading, sometimes aloud." Members of the party also took daily doses of vitamin tablets and never went out into the "incredible glare" without sun helmet and sunglasses. Although at first Betsy experienced a terrible thirst and a slight headache, these mild symptoms soon disappeared.

Paul chose to spend the group's first rest day by reconnoitering the next campsite. Betsy bathed in the lake beside Echo Beach. She explored a little, marveling at the scarcity of life except for a dry, highly flammable shrub called *freilejon*, a few flies, several swallows, and many of the magnificent South American condors, which had twelve- and fifteen-foot wingspans. In rummaging around camp, Betsy found a gold knife with the initials HSH and was pleased to think how surprised Henry Hall would be when she would give it to him in New York City.

After supper, members of the party sorted and classified their supplies, segregating items they would take to base camps and ones they would leave behind. The next day they began their carries.

Later, after Betsy returned to the United States, she wrote an article about her trip which appeared in the *American Alpine Journal* (the bulk of which appears in the following pages), and she gave slide talks. However, Betsy's personal diary tells the most about what she really thought. Although it does not tell us quite everything we would like to know—obviously Betsy had a strict inner code about what was appropriate to write about, even in a confidential journal—it describes more of her feelings on this trip than anything else available to us.

So we know that she found Max Eberli utterly delightful. Several days after their initial meeting in Barranquilla, Max confessed to Betsy that he had told Ujueta that he was sure she and Elizabeth would be "big, big women...with feet like this" and here he spread his hands wide apart. "That," he explained to Betsy, "is why it took me so long [to recognize you]." Of course Max's fluency in Spanish and his knowledge of the route into the Santa Martas were invaluable to the expedition. But it was his innate charm that endeared him to all. Mrs. Richter called him "Hunchen."

Max's imperfect English added to his appeal, as when, for example, he wrote Betsy, Paul, and Elizabeth a note and wished them "Good luck, real fun and big impressions and a friendly shakehand."[12] His jokes and his frequent songs and yodeling had a "Swissy flavor." When the party was carrying loads to their second campsite, Max often looked up at La Reina (The Queen), the mountain they wanted to climb next day, saying, "Reina, you are too remote." In between his little speeches to La Reina, he called on his favorite movie star, Miss Oberon, beseeching, "Merle, give me strength."

Apparently Max and Paul Petzoldt got on well together. Max's speech patterns must have sounded familiar to Paul, who had grown up hearing his German mother issue such commands as "Throw the cow over the fence some hay." Born in Creston, Iowa, and reared on a ranch near Twin Falls, Idaho, Paul had climbed in the Swiss Alps and could "yodel like a jackal." So could Max.

Betsy, ten years older than Paul, regarded him as a mentor as well as a friend. In a rare flash of candor, Betsy wrote in her diary, "Can't help but write privately here that last day before Gloomy Gulch, Paul said that he would choose me as a companion for a real mountaineering assignment. 'You have what it takes.' I was tremendously touched and pleased (and helped) by this and shall remember."

Paul was much the strongest member of their party, once carrying a 110-pound load to a camp well over 14,000 feet. He was the one who reconnoitered campsites, who got up early each morning to make breakfast for the group, who selected the climbing routes, and who did the trickier leads on the first ascents that the party achieved. "Paul is in his element here," Betsy wrote, "works hard, also adds enormously to the fun of camp life with cheerfulness and jokings." He could make fun of himself, freely admitting that as far as he was concerned, their boat had gone out of New York Harbor, turned left, and sailed north for five days. Ever since, the sun had been rising in the west and setting in the east.

One speculates that Betsy's relationship with Elizabeth Knowlton was not especially close—not because of what Betsy says, but rather because of what she does *not* say, and the fact that there is no correspondence from Elizabeth in the scrapbook of letters that Betsy kept. Her references to "E" (she rarely spelled out Elizabeth's full name, perhaps telling in itself) are always objective. They are polite, sometimes even deferential, but they are never personal.[13] Examples follow: "E & I do dinner, turn and turn about...(With the loads we now are carrying, E and I feel we can be considered in the coolie class)...[Regarding the first ascent of La Reina] I led for an hour, then E...Rest Day. We talked about articles. (E. has written many.)"

On February 28, Betsy wrote in her diary: "At night in the tent I find I have to struggle with feelings of claustrophobia at times (E & I share one of the small two-man variety). But I feel well and strong." When the nights were clear and relatively warm, Betsy slept outside.

Elizabeth was not as tough as Betsy, and one wonders if this caused hard feelings. Or perhaps the two women vied for Paul's attentions. Certainly Betsy was quite conscious of the fact that she carried a heavier load than E. Her March 2 diary entry notes that when they packed up to Sunset Lake, Paul carried 85 pounds, Max 42, Betsy 37, and Elizabeth 28. Two days later, when they carried loads to their La Reina base camp, Paul carried 40 pounds, Max and Betsy each carried 27 pounds, and apparently Elizabeth did not carry any. On March 5, Betsy carried 35 pounds to a high camp at about 16,700 feet. On March 9, Paul started out carrying 75 pounds, Max 50, Betsy 37, and Elizabeth 25. However, Max became so tired that the first two divided up his load; Paul's weight shot up to 110 and Betsy's to 45.

Elizabeth climbed La Reina and Pico Ujueta. However, she remained at Gloomy Gulch while Paul and Betsy climbed de Brette Peak, which they renamed El Guardian. Betsy made no reference as to why Elizabeth stayed behind, but presumably it was because she was not up to the demands of a third peak, which had a very difficult approach and was more than 17,000 feet.

To hear Betsy tell it, her trip to the Santa Marta Range was a lark. She made no bones about the fact that she did not regard it as a real "expedition" because the intent had been to have fun rather than to accomplish anything scientific. She described her experiences in an article titled "More about the Santa Marta." It is quintessential Betsy, full of wit, humor, and vivid descriptions.

> *The day after reaching Gloomy Gulch was a rest day for everyone but Petzoldt who went off with a gleam in his eye to reconnoiter, returning at nightfall with the good news that the route beyond opened up well and a site for our next camp lay about five hours higher up. The supplies and equipment left in a vast mound by our departing transport had then to be sorted and classified. Rations for the high camps were assembled and packed, and our first loads weighed and assigned. The next day back-packing began.*

> *After climbing the steep defile at the end of the gulch, our way led eastward. It wasn't easy country to get around in. The scenery was all chopped up into deep Vs, with a lake at the bottom of each one. These lakes, lovely in their varied color tones, led upward in ascending chains. The sides were sheer in places and we had often to make long*

detours around cliffs that afforded no convenient ledges for traversing. In plain sight now were the two peaks to which Walter Wood had introduced us months before in his office at the American Geographical Society. They had been fine to look at on the maps and in the pictures he had put so generously at our disposal, but here, face to face, they were unbelievably exciting. The higher one (triangulated at 18,160 ft.) was a splendid affair with a gleaming cataract of snow and ice pouring down its northern slope. The second, slightly lower, was a handsome rock pyramid. We hoped to establish a high camp somewhere between the two from which they could both be climbed.

These mountains seemed to belong to us from the first, and we christened them almost immediately. The higher one we called La Reina for Queen Isabella of Spain and the second Pico Ujueta after Juan Ujueta of Barranquilla, the good friend of both American expeditions and a member of the first. These names have since been approved by the Colombian government, to our great pleasure. The Colombian government would have its hands full if it bothered with all the other things we named. From the moment we struck eastward we had been in the country and, like the two peaks, we felt it to be uniquely ours. Eberli was kept busy translating our ideas into Spanish and such mellifluous titles emerged as Lago de Ciel Azule [Blue Heaven Lake], Lago de los dos Islottes [Lake of the Two Little Islands, and El Nido del Condor [The Condor's Nest], (our high camp, perched on a rock).

After two days of relaying and a day of rest, we were ready to move up to Camp 1. It is amazing what a few heavy loads do to one's whole philosophy; we became Thoreaus at once, determined to reduce to a minimum the impedimenta of living. Our last sense of expeditionary self-importance vanished forever as we surveyed the pile of things we were leaving behind, including items no bona fide explorer would dream of being without. Then heavily laden in spite of our economics, we made the trip up to our new quarters and pitched camp as the sun set. The sky colors were reflected in the narrow lake below us, with a black border around the edge made by its cliff walls. To the S. rose the snow-plastered flank of de Brette Peak, a strikingly handsome mountain in spite of its being almost 1000 ft. lower than the others.

After a day of rest here, our march upward began again. We skirted two more lovely lakes with a rock wall between down which a graceful cascade poured. We were beginning to get up in the world and the flowers, scarcer now, had become furry as if for greater warmth. The color of the second lake was all but unbelievable, reminding one of the strong bright tint of laundry bluing. Shiny black *patent-leather frogs hopped about on the water's edge, one of the rare signs of life in that strangely dead landscape. Only the sound of our bootnails scraping against the rocks broke the brooding stillness, or the hum of a condor as he drifted by, speculating perhaps on the edibility of the new arrivals.*

Blue Heaven Lake was the last in its chain; above it we climbed into a world of ice and snow. The glacier flowing between our two peaks split against a sharp rock rib and poured down its either side.

Ascending this rib to about 16,000 ft., we found a place level enough for our camp, perched above everything like the crows nest of a battleship. The late sun glimmered on Pico Ujueta, now very close. La Reina was just out of sight behind a snowy shoulder. The scene was indescribably grand but we had only time for a hasty look around as we deposited our loads and descended in double-quick time.

It took two days of relaying to stock our Condor's Nest camp and on the third day we moved up, I looking like a jalopy with the pots and pans dangling on the outside of my pack. That night we built tent platforms and cooked our first supper on the primus stove (below, withered branches of freilejon *suffice for fuel). We were in a different climate bracket here. Everyone slept in his clothes and next morning the little pool that was our water supply had frozen solid.*

We climbed our first mountain, La Reina, on March 5th. The ascent proved unexpectedly easy after we gave up an attempt on the W. ice ridge as unsafe without the crampons unwisely left behind at base camp. But it was a pleasant climb over the ripples and crevasses of the N. slope and we emerged after four hours' climbing on the snowy dome of our first Santa Marta summit. The scene was indescribable and so were our feelings at being there, the first to see the treasures of the Sierra from this place. To the N. W. lay the highest group of the range with its two summits so nearly alike in height, the one ascended by Wood and Bakewell in 1939, the other by the German party that preceded them by such a short time. The third peak in this cluster lies further W. and, of that one, more anon. These mountains were very striking with their black rock faces, dazzling white crests, and masses of whipped-cream clouds gathering around them.

The descent from La Reina was fast, uneventful and hot. The white trough down which we made our way seemed a concentration point for all the sun's rays and they played on us like searchlights while we hid as best we could under every conceivable device of scarf and handkerchief.

On March 7th we climbed Pico Ujueta. A preliminary glacier approach was followed by a few rock pitches; then we made a diagonal

Figure 5.2   March 7, 1941, on the summit of La Reina in Colombia, after the first ascent. *Left to right:* Paul Petzoldt, Max Eberli, and Elizabeth Knowlton. Photo by Betsy Cowles. (Courtesy American Heritage Center, University of Wyoming. Copyright restricted.)

traverse of a steep ice slope. At first step-cutting was necessary; then, as we went further, its surface became oddly contorted until finally it was like clambering from one statue-less niche to another. Above this rather diverting passage, a long snow incline took us to the foot of the final pyramid. Broken rock made easy climbing here and five hours after the start we were on the summit, looking over the breath-taking N. face to the smiling Caribbean below. To the S. La Reina looked like an enormous helping of vanilla ice cream ("Pass the chocolate sauce," said someone). On the other side, a ship was leaving a long streamer of smoke trailing lazily across the water. It was our finest day for color. The afternoon clouds boiled up, shot with oblique shafts of light, giving the photographers so much reason to linger that it was a wonder we ever got around to descending at all.

Early next morning we broke camp and made the descent to Sun-set Lake with heavy loads. On March 9th we returned to Gloomy Gulch, the all-time high in load carrying being made that day by Petzoldt with 102 pounds. We found base camp untouched and unbelievably luxurious. Just why no roving Arahuaco had molested our belongings we were never able to fathom. Perhaps Paul's timberwolf cry, amplified by the echo of the rock walls, had convinced the Indians that a pack of wild animals guarded the camp, even in our absence!

To celebrate this and everything else, we had our private sanco-cho *that night and stopped at nothing. If you wanted dessert first and then again at the end, you could have it; or, if seized with a longing for sardines in the middle of the meat course, you could have that too. What a sky the Sierra treated us to! Shooting stars were chasing each other across the heavens like 4th of July fireworks. As we climbed into our sleeping bags the moon came out, like a benediction on the first chapter of our Santa Marta adventures.*

Two days later Petzoldt and I started off for a try at the third peak of the highest group, travelling light as we still had a touch of back-ache. This mountain is considerably more remote than the others and the lake chains that had led in the direction of our first peaks crossed our line of march here. It made a vast difference. The better part of two days was spent struggling through a maze of wildly tangled valleys that forced us constantly off line into costly detours and retreats. Still the mountain kept its distance. Finally a shortage of time and food made it clearly unwise to go on and we retreated like Napoleon from Moscow. Back we went through the old labyrinth of cliffs and lakes, in one place sinking to our waist in mud when we decided rashly to wade a last water hazard.

It took a while to recover from the rigors of this trip; then we started off again on March 15th for de Brette Peak, hoping not to find our-selves persona non grata *to this mountain as well. That night we bivouacked at the foot of the fine S. ice slope. The weather had been threatening for the first time but the mists parted at sunset and showed, high overhead, the summit's white spire touched with gold. We made an early start next morning, up ice perfect for the crampons which, this time, we had brought along. We tacked back and forth steeply and af-ter occasional pauses for breath and photography reached the top at about 10 o'clock.*

It was a fine last summit for the Santa Martas. The familiar and well-loved places were all in sight. There was La Reina across the valley and, beyond her, Pico Ujueta shot into the sky between us and the sea. Over to the S. the parallel lines of the great Mamancanaca

moraines marched down the valley and above them hung the cres-
cent of Cungacaca Pass from which we had seen the Sierra for the
first time, weeks before.

In half the time it had taken them to go up, Paul, Elizabeth, and Betsy
made their way down to San Sebastian. (Max Eberli, who had had to get back
to work, left the group on March 11.) On March 23, they left the high country
and "plunged back into a landscape vibrating with heat," arriving in Valledupar late that night. The following evening, after a long bus ride, they arrived in
Barranquilla, where they and their sixteen pieces of "filthy baggage" were
unloaded on the terrace of the elegant Prado Hotel "to the horror and aston-
ishment of the clientèle." After picking up their mail, Betsy learned that her
brother Bill, a heavy smoker, had died of lung cancer. He was forty years old.[14]
"All so kind to me," she wrote.

All in all, Betsy's first expedition had been extremely successful. Although
she wished she had brought a shade hat and had included "more nuts, sugar
and salt, less butter and corn beef hash" and more local foods in the menus,
there were few things she would have done differently.

The Santa Marta trip expanded Betsy's cultural horizons as well as her
expeditionary ones. At first she had been overwhelmed by Colombia, partly
because she did not tolerate heat well, but even more because she was looking for the cleanliness and orderliness of America and Europe. She learned,
though. For example, on their trip into the mountains, Betsy had described a
lunch place, the Fundación restaurant, as "marginal...with lots of flies." On
the way back, however, she said that a transformation had taken place "(not
in it, in us!) It seemed the last word in comfort and elegance."

Betsy began her trip with a certain prejudice toward the local Indians, no
doubt fueled by a letter written by Nelson Rockefeller to his father, to which
she had been privy. It said, "I presume Elizabeth [meaning Betsy] knows that
the area in which she plans to climb and travel is close to that of the well-
known Motilone Indians...famous for the use of poisoned arrows and their
wild and untamed method of living." Betsy also knew that the Cabot expedition thought the Arahuaco Indians were, as she put it, "an almost degenerate
people...rendered lethargic and unambitious by the constant use of a certain
form of cocaine and distinctly unimpressive and unattractive."[15] Betsy's party
never encountered the Motilone Indians. And after getting to know the
Arahuacos, she said that on this one point she and her companions would
have to disagree with the view of the Cabot party, for they had found that after
an initial shyness almost all the Indians were responsive. "We found the

Arahuacos a genial, humorous and attractive people," she wrote, "many of them very fine looking and impressive."

It was Paul Petzoldt who taught Betsy how to break the ice with "primitive peoples" by many smiles and gestures of good will—including dispensing Life Savers. Whenever the party met an Arahuaco Indian, they went through a pantomime of opening a package of Life Savers, smiling broadly, taking one out, putting it in the mouth, and chewing it, while looking delighted and patting their stomachs. They then handed one to the onlooking Arahuaco, pointing to his or her mouth while saying, *"Bueno."* The recipient would usually eat the Life Saver, smile, and gladly accept the rest of the package.

Betsy brought back some excellent black-and-white pictures of the Santa Martas, some of the first non-aerials ever taken in the area. In 1941, photography in Colombia was forbidden because of restrictions imposed due to the war in Europe. However, Nelson Rockefeller had interceded on Betsy's behalf by writing Spruille Braden, the American ambassador in Bogota.[16] Eventually, after much "wire pulling," Betsy and her companions had obtained a permit from the Colombian minister of war, covered with stamps and signatures full of flourishes, which they pulled out even when photography was not remotely involved. It helped "no end."

Early in the trip Betsy had acknowledged "the *stupidity* of not knowing Spanish." Always, in her subsequent travels, she made an attempt to learn key words of the language, at the very least.

Although she did not know it at the time, Betsy's Santa Marta trip of 1941 was probably a key factor in her being selected to go on "the trip of a lifetime" in 1950.

Notes

1. Charles S. Houston, M.D., interview with the author, November 22, 1991; Sallie Greenwood, interview with Paul Petzoldt, October 25, 1986.
2. Cyndi Smith, *Off the Beaten Track: Women Adventurers and Mountaineers in Western Canada* (Jasper, Canada: Coyote Books, 1989), 237–57.
3. Charles S. Houston, M.D., comments on the manuscript, December 1995.
4. Elizabeth S. Cowles, "New Books," *Trail and Timberline* no. 461 (May 1957): 75.
5. Walter A. Wood, Jr., "The Sierra Nevada de Santa Marta, Colombia," *Geographical Journal* 24 (4) (1940): 22.
6. Thomas D. Cabot, letter to the author, January 30, 1992.
7. Elizabeth S. Cowles, letter to Paul Petzoldt, early October 1940, and his reply, October 13, 1940, Archives, American Heritage Center.

8. Elizabeth S. Cowles, text for a talk, "Santa Marta Range 1941," presented at the Colorado Springs Fine Arts Center Members Night, n.d., Archives, American Heritage Center.

9. *Ibid.*

10. Elizabeth S. Cowles, Santa Martas diary 1941, Archives, American Heritage Center.

11. Elizabeth S. Cowles, quoting Walter Wood, in the February 27 entry of her Santa Martas diary 1941, Archives, American Heritage Center.

12. Max Eberli, letter to members of the Santa Marta expedition, copied in Elizabeth S. Cowles's Santa Martas diary 1941, Archives, American Heritage Center.

13. Several people have indicated that Elizabeth Knowlton had a certain forbidding quality. A long-time acquaintance, Kenneth A. Henderson, stated in the *American Alpine Journal* obituary he wrote after Elizabeth Knowlton's death in 1989 that "she was a most meticulous writer and resented any editorial changes, as many an editor will testify." Tom (Thomas D.) Cabot commented in a letter to the author, "What I can remember of her [Betsy's] personality is a tribute to her charm; at least she was much more cordial to me than was her climbing companion, Elizabeth Knowlton." And, in a taped interview with the author, Dorothy Teague Swartz said that she found Elizabeth to be rather "cold," especially in contrast to Betsy, who was "warm." However, in a tribute to Betsy that appeared in the 1975 issue of the *Journal of the Ladies' Alpine Club*, Elizabeth Knowlton wrote: "Those of you who have known Betsy—in Zermatt, in London, in America—do not need to be told of the warm charm of her outstandingly attractive personality." Later on, Elizabeth referred to the expedition as "a very congenial and happy group" and called Betsy "a delightful companion for such a trip."

14. "William M. Strong, Advertising Man," *New York Times*, March 27, 1941, p. 26, col. 6.

15. Elizabeth S. Cowles, text for talk about Santa Martas.

16. Nelson Rockefeller, letter to John D. Rockefeller, Jr., January 31, 1941, Archives, American Heritage Center.

CHAPTER SIX

A Fragmented Decade: The 1940s After the Santa Martas

During the summer of 1941, Betsy and her father returned to the Tetons in what was to be a last mountain fling before the United States entered World War II. They rented a cottage on Cottonwood Creek beside a meadow of wildflowers where, in the early morning, a moose and her calf often munched beneath their window. "The national state of mind was better this year, ours included," Betsy wrote. "We knew where we were going. England had survived the Blitz and won the air battle over the channel. America was arming. All this made our respite, the last some of us had for a long time, more wonderful and more deeply appreciated."

Upstream from Betsy's cottage, the honeymooning Charles Houstons were tenting in a meadow by Cottonwood Creek. (Charley and his close friends Bob Bates and Bill House were some of the best-known climbers in the country and, along with Paul Petzoldt, had been on the 1938 American K2 expedition.) Betsy and Charley had met casually at AAC dinners, but now became much better acquainted. Often Charley and his bride, Dorcas, floated downstream on their air mattresses, arriving at Betsy's for a noontime cheese and beer. Betsy taught Dorcas how to rappel.

Figure 6.1   Betsy Cowles and Paul Petzoldt on the lower slopes of Mount Moran, "wolfing down watermelon," circa 1941. Note the beer bottles between them. Photographer unknown. (Courtesy of John M. Smith.)

Also in the Tetons that summer was John Case, a member of the American Alpine Club who would later become its president. John, Charley, Dorcas, and Betsy had "fine times in the hills" climbing South Teton, Nez Perce, and the Exum Ridge. There was one sour note. For the first time, there was a "mess" on the summit of the Grand; Betsy and her friends gathered up cans, tinfoil, bottles, and banana peels and packed them down. In outrage Betsy wrote, "How incredible...that mountaineers can be guilty of such a violation."

After Betsy's long-time climbing friend Polly Merrick arrived in Jackson Hole, the two women plus Paul Petzoldt climbed the southeast face on Mount Moran. On the descent, which involved six long rappels, Betsy and Polly "muffed" a "brute of an overhang" and "only saved the day (but not our vanity) by inventing an elaborate detour over to the west."

In August Betsy threw her annual Swiss Day party, inviting everyone in the park who was "Swiss at heart." An excellent cook, she spent the day in the kitchen stirring, tasting, cooking, and baking.[1] The dining table's center-piece was a rock in the shape of the Matterhorn on which small figures were climbing.[2] Betsy wore a dirndl, as she usually did on Swiss Day.[3] Guests, also in costume, arrived early and stayed late, dancing, dining, and giving speeches. The Houstons and John Case did not attend; they were benighted on a narrow ledge of the east ridge of the Grand Teton from which they had a fine bird's-eye view of Betsy's Swiss Day bonfire.

Betsy made what she thought was to be her last ascent of the Grand Teton. (In fact she climbed the Grand Teton two more times, in 1956 and in 1958.) Apparently it was the final climb she made with Paul Petzoldt. As she described it:

> *Of the many and varied routes on the mountain the "forgotten rib" is one of the very best.... It offers high class exercise almost the entire way, with a minimum of tedious preliminaries. And it's pleasantly short (about six hours) compared with the other deluxe routes. We were four in the party: Fred Wulsin, Paul, Polly and myself. We camped at the saddle above Garnet Canyon and spent a sheltered but rather claustrophobic night under Paul's vast and confining tarpaulin. Next morning we rose at an early hour and descended a considerable distance to the point where our rib meets the valley floor. Then we started up. The rib is both steep and exposed but not too difficult, actually, for cheerful climbing. In fact a sense of general fun and amiability is what I remember most about the day besides the delights of that airy and engrossing ridge. Freddy, second on the rope, belayed me with a constant grin and Polly, in the rear, never appeared from slab or chimney without her characteristically agreeable and humorous twinkle. Of course Paul may have been in a bad mood,—we hardly saw enough of him to tell. Mostly he was a long way off, devising our next maneuvers. Remarkable the way one landing platform after another turned up, spaced just right for roping convenience! Otherwise, things might have been rather awkward for us. We crossed a steep snow couloir gingerly in our rubber soles and continued up steep rock towards the final pyramid. An absorbing passage or two followed and a last stiff chimney. Then the rocks of that well-loved summit came into view.*
>
> *I pointed out to Freddy, to whom the scene was new, the flat stone on which I'd taken many a fine siesta and the dining table beyond where so often we'd laid out a climbers' feast. I thought of past hours in this place, of the friends with whom I'd found such fun and companionship, of the different ascents after which I had relaxed here. Thinking it very doubtful that I should ever climb this hill a seventh time, I looked about me with strong feelings at all the familiar landmarks. How wonderful to have been permitted to know a region*

so fully! My eye ran over the skyward sweeps and curves of the rocky slopes, the dark mantle of the forest, the circle of shining lakes. To these and to the great peaks towering above them, I said an affection-ate and grateful goodbye.[4]

The group named the ridge after Paul Petzoldt. Later that summer, how-ever, Betsy's friendship with Paul ruptured. She never mentioned the breach to her sister, Emilie, nor to many others. But she did refer to it in her diary of the 1950 Nepalese trek, when she wrote, "We talked a lot this morning about being victimized. About Paul. I think it is better to be a sucker now and then than always to be suspicious."[5]

One friend has said he has a vague recollection that Paul publicly humil-iated Betsy, but this has not been verified. Several people with first-hand knowledge have said that Paul did not always honor his debts; they speculate that the end of the friendship had to do with money, that probably Paul did not pay back the money Betsy had loaned him for the Santa Marta trip.[6] (We know from a letter he wrote Betsy that he suggested she stake him to the trip.)

Another possibility is that Paul Petzoldt's wife put pressure on her hus-band to break with Betsy. Bernice (Patricia) Petzoldt wrote a biography of Paul called *On Top of the World: My Adventures with My Mountain-Climbing Husband*, published in 1953, in which she made a thinly veiled reference to Betsy as a "a rich lady dude" whose sixty-eight-year-old father made a climb of the Grand Teton by the easiest route. "[S]uddenly it came to me with crashing certainty," Bernice wrote, "that she [Betsy] spent entirely too much time look-ing for Paul. Until this moment I had accepted her attentions casually enough, but now I was disturbed and a little frightened too." Bernice went on to say that Betsy (never mentioned by name in the book) had then suggested that Bernice might climb the Grand by the easiest route—a remark that Bernice considered maddeningly condescending because she had already demon-strated her climbing skills on several respectable ascents. Furious, she asked her husband what he considered the most difficult climb in the Tetons. After Paul told her it was the north face of the Grand, Bernice asked him to take her up. He did.[7]

Many years later, Paul Petzoldt told an interviewer, "We [he and Betsy] never had any physical relationship but I was in love with her.…I thought she was a great woman.…She was one of my very favorite people.…I never knew a woman with less faults than Elizabeth [Betsy]. She was a very unselfish per-son…just a great woman."[8]

After 1941, in her frequent talks about mountain climbing, Betsy sometimes mentioned Paul, referring to him as a "climbing friend." But Paul and
Betsy never mended their broken relationship.

The summer following Betsy's glorious one in the Tetons, Betsy took a
train from New York City to Colorado Springs, accompanied by her thirteen-
year-old daughter, Ann, and two friends, Frances Cook and Mary Merrick. The
four then began a bike trip on Highway 24 to Salida, eventually riding all the
way to Mesa Verde National Park and back (about 600 miles) on nearly
deserted roads. They caught rides on buses over several high passes.[9]
Mostly Betsy tried to carry on during wartime. While living in Bronxville,
New York, she trained to become a nurse's aide, a volunteer job that helped
alleviate the shortage of professional nurses due to the war. Often she worked
at the hospital on Christmas Day. "All morning long I made beds, emptied you
know what, carried trays, gave back-rubs," she recalled later. "They were the
best Christmases I can remember. The sense of the too-muchness of everything, the ghastly preoccupation with self-indulgence fell away. I was freed
from all of it and deeply involved with something outside myself."[10]
When she could, Betsy visited her brother-in-law and sister, Macauley and
Emilie Smith, who had moved first to New Jersey, then to Washington, D.C.,
during the war. All three got together with Bill House and Bob Bates, who
were also in Washington, serving in the Quartermaster Corps which was test-
ing and developing mountaineering equipment for the military.
Living in New York gave Betsy a chance to become a more visible member in the American Alpine Club, which she had joined in 1934. (The AAC has
since moved its headquarters from New York City to Golden, Colorado.) Until
she lived in Bronxville, Betsy had done little more than send in dues and
attend annual dinners. Now she came to know some members quite well; it
was probably at this time that she became friends with Oscar and Nell Houston. Betsy participated in club activities, albeit in a rather limited way
because being female was a handicap.
Outwardly, the American Alpine Club was nonsexist and had been since
its founding in 1902. Certainly, the policy of the Alpine Club in London suffered
by comparison; it made no bones about excluding women from membership
and made no exceptions for 118 years. However, AAC female members did
not, in fact, receive treatment equal to male members. From its very beginning,
AAC membership was overwhelmingly male and all important offices were
held by men. The policy had not changed by the time Betsy moved to New

Figure 6.2 Dinner party in the late 1950s. *Clockwise from lower left:* Marka Webb Bennett (later Mrs. John Wolcott Stewart), Mr. Ernest Kitson, Elizabeth S. Cowles, Mr. Clement M. Brown, Mr. Philip B. Stewart, Mrs. Charles M. Swift (Mr. Stewart's sister), Mr. Charles H. Collins, Mrs. Clement Brown. (Courtesy Stewart House Collection at Colorado College, Colorado Springs, Colorado.)

York; women were officially involved in "feminine" functions only. (It is true that in 1942 Christine Reid Orcutt served on the Training of Guides Committee, but many of the club's male members were serving in the armed forces at the time and there were probably no guides to be trained.) The AAC records show, for example, in 1942, "Mrs. Cowles" served on the club's House Committee, which helped run the club rooms; "Miss Knowlton" was a member of the Library Committee. By 1944 "Mrs. Cowles" served on the Hospitality Committee as well as the House Committee. She initiated monthly teas in the club's "small" quarters on East 46th Street, which then became very popular.[11]

After living in the New York City area for seven years, in 1945 Betsy returned to her Colorado Springs residence on quiet Culebra Avenue. Later she purchased a house on Hermosa Way, which she had remodeled.

Ensconced in Colorado once again, Betsy stepped back into her former life, although now, as a single woman, when she attended a party or reception "she popped in...she never just sat down and lounged around." Once again she became an active member of local organizations. During the next five years, at various times, she served as publicity chair for the League of Women Voters, secretary of the Unity Council, president of the Junior League, and vice president of the Colorado Springs Symphony Board; she also sat on boards of the Day Nursery, the Visiting Nurse Association, and the Halfway House.[12]

Betsy associated more with her mountain acquaintances than with her purely social ones and stated in a talk she gave, probably in the mid-1940s, "My best friends are mt. people."[13]

Shortly after Betsy's return to Colorado, Dorothy Teague (Swartz) phoned her, requesting assistance in forming a junior chapter of the Colorado Mountain Club to be based on the Colorado College campus. Dorothy was co-chair of the fledgling chapter with Stan Boucher, a rock climber whom Betsy had befriended when he was a Springs high school student. After arranging an initial meeting with Betsy, Dorothy had an intuitive flash that she had better bring along a calling card. Her friend, Walt Sweet, accompanied her and as the two were walking toward Betsy's house, Dorothy asked Walt if he had a card. He searched his wallet and finally extracted one, wrinkled and smushed, which he flattened out.

> *And sure enough, we went through the gate to the front door [of Betsy's house] and the Filipino house boy came to the front door with the little silver platter. Both of us fortunately had enough background that we knew what to do—we put our calling cards on it and waited in the hall and were ushered into her library-study which was a magnificent room. And here was Betsy—it was after dinner—and she was in a full-length challis, gorgeous bright red, at home evening dress. Beautiful. She came out from behind this...big desk with a satin finish. If she hadn't been such a gracious woman it would have been overwhelming. She was so kind to us; I suppose we spent two hours talking to her and I just thought this was the most wonderful lady I had ever met.*

Betsy served as a liaison between the college students and the older, somewhat inflexible adult members of the already existing Colorado Springs chapter of the Colorado Mountain Club. She demonstrated to Stan Boucher, a rather brash young man at the time, that tact and maneuvering behind the scenes were often more effective than confrontation. (In fact, because of Betsy, Stan amended his views of the wealthy, whom he had come to dislike during summers of caddying at the Broadmoor; they weren't all bad!)[14] Finally, after a lengthy administrative process, the Pikes Peak Junior chapter of the CMC was born.

Betsy and Dorothy, who became good friends, instructed some of the Pikes Peak Juniors in rock climbing. Dorothy, from Denver, had grown up as a member of the Denver CMC Juniors; she had learned rock climbing on her own, scrambling up without any protection on Cathedral Spires and Bishop Rock, close to her family's cabin near Wellington Lake. Dorothy marveled at how Betsy "flowed" on the rock, always moving, and at how she instinctively understood that a woman's center of gravity is different from a man's.

> *Men have a tendency to have their fannies stuck out and hands here and feet kind of close together. Well, if you're a woman in that position, you're weighted wrong so instead of holding your feet onto the rock you're actually pushing away from the rock. She [Betsy] understood this.... She didn't say it quite like that but she understood it and taught [it].*

Stan Boucher says that Betsy was a fine role model for CMC Juniors, especially for inexperienced women who tensed up from fright. She would gently talk them down a rappel, an unnerving maneuver that involves backing over a cliff.

Of course, Betsy continued to climb mountains, concentrating on fourteeners, of which Colorado has fifty-four, more than any other state, including Alaska. (In the 1940s, because of inaccurate surveys, there were thought to be only fifty two.) When Betsy polished hers off, in 1949, the local paper blazed the news on the front page in an extensive article. "Mrs. Cowles" was the twenty-sixth person to climb all the fourteeners, it said. (The article failed to mention that Dorothy (Teague) Swartz finished hers on the same day.) In the party of five that accompanied Betsy on her final summit, that of Mount Eolus, was the photographer Harry Standley.[15] She had reached her first one, Mount Lincoln, in 1932; Betsy's favorite had been Capitol, which she considered the hardest.[16]

During the same year that Betsy finished her fourteeners, she wrote an article that laid out rules for introducing women and children to roped climbing so that they would come back for more. First appearing in a 1949 *Sierra Club Bulletin*, it was later published in a book edited by Dave Brower called *Going Light with Backpack or Burro* under the title "Especially for Men."

Rule one; That sense of success is actually the whole business, the secret of everything. Never forget it for a minute! She must always feel she's doing well, that you are pleased with her and delighted at her progress. If she truly feels this, she will *do well, and she* will *make progress (and you* will *be delighted—no make-believe about it.)*

The importance of this sense-of-success cannot be over-emphasized. It is the sine qua non. Remember it especially in relation to the second commandment; Don't ever let her get scared...never dream of undertaking anything at all difficult until she's entirely at home with simple chimneys, slabs and ledges and you're dead certain she's enjoying herself. That's the vital thing to watch for: is she having a good time?[17]

After Betsy's return to Colorado Springs, she remained very involved with the AAC. In New York, she had met Maynard Miller at an AAC annual meeting where he presented a slide show about the first American ascent of Mount St. Elias in Alaska. At the time he was a graduate student in geology at Columbia University, although he has since become a well-known glaciologist. Betsy and Evelyn Runnette, each a member of the AAC *and* the CMC, invited Maynard to present the same show in Denver.

Thus began Betsy's friendship with Maynard, reinforced when the pair served on several AAC committees and Betsy vigorously supported two of his proposals. Both were eventually adopted. The first was to establish an AAC Safety Committee; it has since published an annual *Accidents in American Mountaineering Report* sold throughout the country. The second proposal was to establish regional chapters of the AAC so that its Western and Alaskan members would feel less isolated. "On these issues she [Betsy] was an allied spirit," Maynard recalls, "probably because both of us were western in our background and outlook. Her support of these concepts helped change the direction of the club in the late 1940s and 50s." Although Betsy could be "hard hitting and tough" in a discussion, she always maintained respect for other people's views, and they for hers.[18] In 1947, Betsy became a vice president of the AAC's Central Section, the first woman to hold such a high office in the organization. Later she served on the editorial board of the *American Alpine Journal.*

Middle age did not seem to slow Betsy down. She hiked and climbed with her usual energy, often with people considerably younger than she. Dorothy Teague Swartz recalls that although Betsy was more than twenty years her senior, still Betsy was faster, especially when negotiating a boulder field. Betsy's balance was so fine and her movements so graceful that she hopped from rock to rock "like a ballet dancer." And Betsy "never had to worry about a trail up a mountain—she just sensed the route and became a part of it."

Bob Ormes once called Betsy a "good" rock climber, but not a great one.[19] However, Dorothy thinks Betsy was "better than good" (although not a "great" rock climber) and that she was an extremely fine all-round mountaineer, proficient on ice, snow, and rock. Betsy had tremendous endurance, always retaining a reserve of strength even after a difficult hike or climb.

Virtually all Betsy's mountain companions say it was Betsy's exuberance and her kindness and generosity that made her such a joy to be with. Stu Dodge recalls that he and his friends eagerly accepted a chance to hike with this woman who was old enough to be their mother; they "were crazy about her as a person." She had an "almost a continuous sparkle in her eyes no matter what she was doing."[20]

Dorothy never saw Betsy lose her temper, "even when it was justified," and recalls that Betsy never said anything unkind about anyone. "And she would sing…all the wonderful mountain songs," many from the Tenth Mountain Division (World War II U.S. Army troops trained to ski and mountain climb). Dorothy: "I thought one of the nicest things that Betsy ever did was to call me 'friend.'"

Dee Molenaar, a civilian advisor for the army's Mountain and Cold Weather Training Command at Camp Hale near Leadville, Colorado (the peacetime successor to the Tenth Mountain Division), recalls that Betsy's house was a "popular gathering place for mountaineers passing through the area." Betsy invited him and his wife over during their first week in town and they became friends. Dee developed a ritual; whenever he rang the doorbell of Betsy's house, he would clasp the door knob tightly so that Betsy would know who it was. He recalls that "she always enjoyed people and 'playing' such games."[21]

The mid- and late 1940s were obviously good years for Betsy. By now she and Emilie had become very close. Sometimes they went on New York City shopping trips together. Frequently Em and her family and Betsy and her kids vacationed together; a favorite destination was the town of Redstone, Colorado, nearly deserted at that time.

The 1940s climaxed for Betsy when Oscar Houston invited her to join his party on a trek in Nepal. She jumped at the chance.

Notes

1. Dorothy Teague Swartz, interview with the author, January 14, 1993. All quotations and information attributed to Swartz come from this source.
2. Emilie S. Smith, telephone conversation with the author, August 2, 1994.
3. Kay Partridge, letter to the author, December 14, 1994. Kay recalls that on Swiss Day, August 1, each year, Betsy hung her climbing boots and ice axe on the front door. "On each mountain peak in the multitude of mountain pictures hung *everywhere* in her home, a small Swiss flag was flown."
4. Elizabeth S. Cowles, "The Tetons to Me [Part 2]," *Trail and Timberline* no. 354 (June 1948), 82–83.
5. Elizabeth S. Cowles, Nepal diary, December 2, 1950, Archives, American Heritage Center.
6. Interview by the author with Charles S. Houston, M.D., October 11, 1991, and with William House, October 15, 1992.
7. Patricia Petzoldt, *On Top of the World: My Adventures with my Mountain-Climbing Husband* (New York: Thomas W. Crowell, 1953), 206.
8. Paul Petzoldt, interview with Sallie Greenwood, October 25, 1986.
9. Elizabeth S. Cowles, newspaper clipping, Archives, American Heritage Center.
10. Elizabeth S. Cowles, text for a talk, "Against Christmas," presented to the Tuesday Club, n.d., Archives, American Heritage Center.
11. *American Alpine Journal* (1930s and 1940s). At the end of the war, when she left to go back to Colorado Springs, Betsy extended an invitation to her AAC friends to come west, promising to give them a "warm welcome." A few months later, twenty-five members signed a letter to Betsy saying that her absence was a "source of regret" to her AAC friends, who wished her "health and happiness." Letter from AAC members to Elizabeth S. Cowles, n.d., Archives, American Heritage Center.
12. Glad Morath, "Woman of the Week," unknown Colorado Springs newspaper, courtesy of Ben Hammett, Ph.D.
13. Information comes from an interview with William Ryder, M.D., by the author on March 24, 1994, and from a speech by Elizabeth S. Cowles, untitled and undated, probably presented before the newly formed group of the CMC Juniors, in the Archives, American Heritage Center.
14. Stanley W. Boucher, interview with the author, May 1985.
15. In "Men and Women Who Climbed Them All," *Trail and Timberline* no. 590 (February 1968): 35, Betsy's final peak was listed (one assumes erroneously) as Wetterhorn.
16. "Springs Woman Mountaineer Newest Member of 52 Club," *Colorado Springs Gazette Telegraph*, September 13, 1949, Penrose Library, Colorado Springs.
17. Elizabeth S. Cowles, "Have You a Mountain Widow in Your Home?" *Sierra Club Bulletin* no. 6 (June 1949): 17–21. Reprinted in Dave Brower, ed., *Going Light with Backpack or Burro: How to Get Along on Wilderness Trails (Chiefly in the West)* (San Francisco: Sierra Club, 1951).
18. Maynard M. Miller, letter to the author, April 8, 1992.
19. Robert M. Ormes, interview with the author, May 13, 1985.

20. Stuart Dodge, interview with the author, October 29, 1994. "Betsy was a whole person in so many ways.... If you were walking along the trail with her and she saw the first anemone in spring you would stop and really enjoy it. And when you were with her you got more enjoyment than if you were walking along by yourself."
21. Dee Molenaar, letter to the author, January 20, 1992. In this letter, Dee also mentions that he credits Betsy for his becoming a member of Charles Houston's 1953 expedition to K2. Houston discounts this as a factor.

CHAPTER SEVEN

"The Trip of a Lifetime"

Originally the Nepal trip had been scheduled to take place in the fall of 1949. But permissions could not be obtained and so it had been postponed. "Mrs. Cowles contented herself by spending the winter on Bimini Isle in the Bahamas," a newspaper article said, "substituting deep sea fishing for the [trek]." In May, Mrs. Cowles would attend the Bach Festival in Prades, France. After climbing in the Pyrenees, she would go to Switzerland for more climbing and visiting guides and friends.[1]

Of course Betsy wanted to be physically tough enough to enjoy the Nepalese trek. But there was probably another reason for her preconditioning: in 1950, being the only female in a mountain party of men was almost unheard of and carried an enormous pressure to perform. Had the trip been an official American Alpine Club trip rather than a private one of friends, it is almost certain that Betsy would not have been invited.

Dorothy Teague Swartz says that for many years women were not even considered for expeditions because "they might get pregnant." Finally, in the 1950s, an "important" member of the AAC—a man—began compiling a list of women who were deemed competent enough to go on expeditions. He put Dorothy and her good friend Dolores La Chapelle on the list. Dorothy doubted it would do any good, but still, to increase her chances of being invited on an expedition, she described herself as an "expert high altitude alpine cook," which "was a lie!"[2]

Dorothy, a generation younger than Betsy and fully confident of her ability to lead rock climbs, keenly felt the injustices toward American female climbers. In contrast, Betsy appeared to accept the status quo as simply "the way it was." The one time she did lead the first rope of a difficult climb (the second ascent of the north ridge of Mount Moran), she made no bones about the fact that she was not the boss. In her words, "All serious questions of tactics and route finding were handled by the experts of course."[3]

Once Betsy made the comment that if Mount Everest was ever climbed, it would not be by middle-aged women or men or by younger women, but rather by "young men in perfect condition." "I'm not one of those who believes a woman can do anything a man can do," Betsy said. "But I believe a woman can be as good a trouble-shooter on an expedition as she is around the house."[4]

However, there was a crack in Betsy's unfailing acceptance that male climbers should be boss; it appeared in the text of a speech she gave to the Tuesday Club titled "Men Against Women." Although not dated, references to the Cold War, Lilly Daché, and Dior indicate that it was presented after the end of World War II. Like Betsy's other "Against" speeches (Against Christmas—Travel—Exercise—Reading), it criticized subjects that Betsy enjoyed immensely. Apparently the tongue-in-cheek device enabled Betsy to voice her real convictions while maintaining a polite facade.

In "Men Against Women" Betsy articulated the major arguments of today's feminists. She objected to a "campaign of innuendos…which belittle women such as assumptions that they are gossips…extravagant, inconsistent…vain…always nagging…changing their minds…pre-sented in the guise of jokes." Betsy thought it unfair that women were barred from men's clubs, men's bars, and men's lunch places. She lamented the fact that competent business women could aspire to no higher position than secretary and that women artists and musicians were not taken seriously.

Finally she commented about women in the mountain world:

> *Take mountain climbing, a pursuit that some people seem to enjoy. What chance has a woman got? Only by the most superhuman efforts does she get taken along on an expedition and then only when she undertakes to do all the drudgery, darn everyone's socks and provide meals equal to what one would be served at the pre-conflagration RUTHS OVEN [a fine Colorado Springs restaurant that burned down[5]]. And once en route, how difficult her position is! Everyone else can, does, get cross, tired, and messy—they can be late, make mistakes about the route, act ornery as the dickens and all grow beards—but can she? No, the future of mountaineering womanhood is at stake and she can't relax for a minute.[6]*

In late September of 1950, Betsy flew to Karachi, where she, Oscar Houston, and Oscar's wife, Nell, were met at the airport by Ambassador Warren and his wife, close friends of the Houstons. The Warrens eased the trio through customs and then escorted them in Cadillacs bedecked with U.S. flags to the American embassy, where they stayed for nearly a week.[7] Their adventure was beginning.

Charles Houston does not understand how his father obtained permission to go to Nepal. Oscar was a rather sedentary New York maritime lawyer whose firm (Bingham, Englar, Jones and Houston) had handled litigation for the *Titanic*. He was "not a [mountain] climber, but a good mountain walker," and a member of the American Alpine Club. In 1934, he had helped his son, Charles, organize a party that had made the first ascent of the formidable Mount Foraker in Alaska.[8]

Shortly before their arrival in Karachi, Oscar had learned that Walter Wood, who was to have been a member of their party, had been called into the army because of the Korean War. At the time Walter was president of the American Geographical Society and a seasoned climber who would have contributed a great deal to the party.[9] (Walter was a member of the American party that had preceded Betsy's group into the Santa Martas.) His dropping out left a party inexperienced in Himalayan travel, consisting as it did of Oscar, Betsy, and Anderson (Andy) Bakewell, an American who was living near Darjeeling at the time, studying to become a Jesuit priest. (Andy Bakewell had also been a member of the American party to the Santa Martas.) There *was* the possibility that Charley Houston, Oscar's son, could go, but it was a long shot.

In Karachi, Betsy wrote her first "circular" letter, by hand, which she then mailed to Philip Stewart (Uncle Phil) in Colorado Springs, now a widower in his eighties. He then typed the letter and mailed a copy to each of the people on a list Betsy had given him. During the course of the trip Betsy wrote seven such round-robin letters and expressed the hope that they would make "each one of you feel in touch with our adventures, as I need to have you be." The letters were mailed sporadically, depending on how much time Betsy had to write and how close she was to a reliable postal service.

In Round-Robin Letter #1, Betsy wrote that it was "hot as you-know-what" but that she was doing pretty well. Still, she said, it was hard to believe that a month ago she had had the energy "to hoof day after day in the Alps"; she declared that if the Matterhorn was plopped down in the middle of Karachi, she certainly wouldn't climb it and doubted that Whymper would have, either.

Despite the heat, Betsy marveled at her surroundings. "A steady soft wind blows through this large, high ceilinged marble-floored house," she wrote.

> *Even with your eyes shut you would know you were in a strange and faraway place—the sounds (birds and bells and distant calls in a strange tongue) and the smells (it is spicy and sandy and musty). A soft footfall makes you look up and there is a little brown bare-footed man in a white cotton suit and red fez (with the American Eagle on it) who puts down a pile of laundry on the bed, saying, "2 hankies, 2 stockings, one petticoat, one nightie, salaam" and leaves.*

Betsy and the Houstons tramped as tourists during the day, changing into formal clothes for evening parties. "Every one is terribly interested in our excursion," Betsy wrote, "and quite a few of the young attachés say 'TAKE ME ALONG.'" She concluded the letter with:

> *Dear Pets…Tomorrow we arise at 6 and go to the Mogul ruins at Tatta—will tell you about them in letter #2. Hope you don't want your money back for letter #1! Know I've been so SPEECHLESS over all that is happening as to make our correspondence hard to bear for you. But— I do love you all and feel we are in touch—now—even though only through this ill-expressed letter. Hugs to all, and so much love, Betsy.*

Betsy felt that one of the highlights of her stay with the Warrens was being able to talk freely with the Pakistanis about the challenges of building their new-born country, which had become independent from Great Britain and separated from India in 1947. But in Round Robin Letter #2 she assured her friends, "I do not (and shall not) feel that a brief stay in these countries will fit me to speak as a political expert." She was not going to fool herself into supposing that she knew "anything whatever about the incredible complexities of the political situation here."

On September 28, Betsy and the Houstons flew to New Delhi, India, to pick up the 900 pounds of food they had mailed in care of the American embassy and transfer it to their quarters at the Hotel Cecil. Then, in response to a wire they had sent to Charley Houston, they received one back: yes, he would join them on the trek. They were elated.

In between shopping sprees and an excursion to the Taj Mahal, they made final arrangements with the Indian ambassador to Nepal to visit Kathmandu before they began their trek. Nepal's capital could be reached only on foot or horseback. Nell Houston was to accompany Oscar and Betsy to Kathmandu

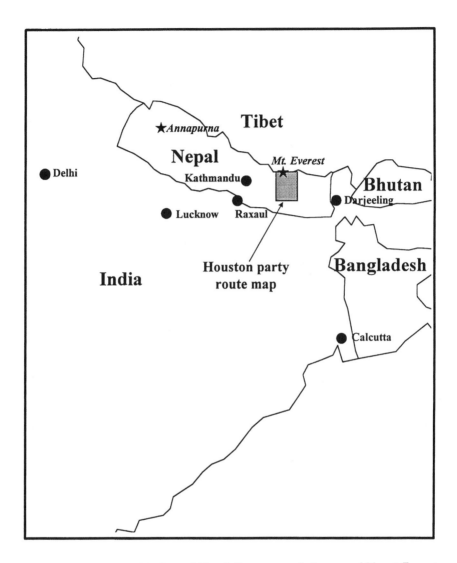

Map 1   Locator map of India and Nepal. Note rectangle in area of Mount Everest, illustrating the area shown in Map 2. (Map made by David Robertson.)

but not on their trek. On October 4, they flew from Delhi east to Lucknow, India, where they boarded a narrow-gauge train with a Pullman-style "Sahib" car. They released a DDT bomb, drank iced tea from their Thermoses, and took malaria pills. Although ceiling fans helped somewhat, their quarters were "seething with heat and humanity." The journey ended at Raxaul, India, near the border. At a Nepalese government guest house, they took cool baths in large tin tubs and ate a good dinner.

At 8 the next morning they boarded the only railroad in all of Nepal and headed north on an eighteen-mile ride that took four hours. But it had its compensations, for suddenly and unexpectedly, across rice fields, they had their first view of the Himalayas, "white and shimmering...totally unrelated to the heat-ridden country through which we were passing." Soon after, the train entered the lowland area of southern Nepal known as the Terai, which, in 1950, was almost uninhabited and densely forested with hardwoods.[10] The track ended at Amlekhgaoi, where a station wagon met the party and drove them twenty-eight miles to Bhimpedi, the first "truly Nepalese" village they saw. It was cool. Little boys were busy flying kites. Betsy's energy and morale returned.

"Ahead of us now," Betsy wrote, "was the steep mountainside leading to Sisagarhi Pass. We could see the path mounting in great zigzags. This is the beginning of the high road to Kathmandu, the historic (and the only) route to the capital city of Nepal." Betsy, Nell, and Oscar mounted little Tibetan ponies. Porters—as they are now called (Betsy called them "coolies")—carried their gear, falling into "a slow and steady pace, knees always bent a little, faces serious and tranquil under the tump-line." Most of the ponyboys and porters were barefoot.

Betsy and the Houstons stayed the night at a guest house below the Sisagarhi Pass, dining on a "curryish...chickenish" dinner and chapatties, a flat, round bread. Arising early the next day, they were underway by 8 and soon reached the 6,000-foot pass. The day was clear and they had another fine view of the high mountains, possibly including, they thought, Mount Everest. Then they lost 2,000 feet of elevation. A mechanical device that resembled a rope-tow ski lift and paralleled the trail was used to convey loads up and down to the pass.

They shared the trail with hundreds of porters carrying trunks, pottery, bales of bright cotton material, hay, wood—even a person! Women and children as well as men carried loads. "All have impressive physiques," Betsy observed. "They are small, wiry and muscular and move in perfect balance and rhythm. The mood is cheerful, too, both on the path and in the villages we go through. Smiles follow us everywhere and it is clear we have lots of comedy as well as news value."They passed an old Nepalese woman, a grand-mother perhaps; she was scolding three boys playing cards on some temple steps, probably neglecting their chores. "We understood every word," Betsy said."It could have been in Keokuk, Iowa."

Crossing a river several times, they worked their way up a valley that climbed to the Chandragari Pass, 8,000 feet high. From there they had their first view of Kathmandu, "gleaming with its turrets and towers in the golden afternoon light." Betsy got off her horse and walked down the north slope, picking some of the wildflowers along the way. At the bottom of the hill the path turned into a motor road, which was lined with crowds "whose big enter-tainment obviously came from watching" what came over the hill. Two cars were waiting for the Houstons and Betsy, who sorted the baggage and paid off the porters before being driven down a "broad avenue" to their quarters. Betsy reported that they were the seventy-fifth, seventy-sixth, and seventy-seventh Americans ever to visit Kathmandu. (Charles Houston disputes this figure, saying that many more had visited Kathmandu but had failed to sign an offi-cial register.)

Today Kathmandu's population is approximately 500,000. When Betsy vis-ited it in 1950, the population was probably closer to 100,000. Because everything had to be carried into the city, it boasted few automobiles, although bicycles were fairly common. Hence, pollution from vehicles was negligible. The smells of the city, as Betsy described them, were "marvelous," emanating as they did from "eucalyptus, mint, spice and the Far East."

At the time of Betsy's visit to Kathmandu, Nepal had been, according to historian Rishikesh Shaha, "hermetically sealed" from outside influences, especially Western ones, for nearly a century. In 1856, the prime minister of Nepal, a member of the Rana family, had, in the words of Professor Jana Ever-ett, "forced the king to become a figurehead, assumed absolute authority himself, and made his position hereditary." When the Houstons and Betsy vis-ited Kathmandu, this arrangement of "nominal rule by the king and effective rule by the Rana prime minister" was still in effect.[11] Almost certainly, Betsy was unaware of the extent of Nepal's oppressive history under the Ranas, although she did realize that it was a military government. If she had attempted to read up on Nepal prior to her visit—and almost certainly Betsy did—she would have found almost nothing on the subject.

Her diary, letters, and subsequent talks are refreshing, in that she makes no attempt to be "politically correct" (by today's standards) but simply tells it as she sees it. The Houstons and she were the guests of the Maharajah or, more accurately, of the Maharajah-Prime Minister. Being a polite guest, Betsy had nothing but kind things to say about the Maharajah and his relatives, who were members of the Rana family. And no wonder. Oscar, Nell, and Betsy were treated exceedingly well. A retinue of servants waited on them. The guest house in which they stayed was brightened with pots of geraniums, vases of fresh flowers, and new carpets. The rooms were "delightful and obviously fixed up," complete with running water, a sink, and, perhaps most astonishing of all, a Western toilet. Upon arriving, they were offered Western-style tea, English biscuits, and fruit.

Betsy unpacked and rested until servants filled a tin tub with hot water and announced that her bath was ready. At 8 P.M. she and the Houstons dined on soup, chicken, new potatoes, marrow, custard, baked apples, and potable water served in a decanter. Betsy took a big dose of salt, following the then-current belief that one needed to restore salt lost through perspiration in a hot climate. She then slept soundly on her bed, "hard as a rock" and draped with mosquito netting.

The next day the Houston party took a walk in the city. "O it is beautiful," Betsy wrote. "Began with a narrow Far East street and on to bridge with temples and brass statues en route. Walked out over the wide river (Bagmati), dock works on side, men wading (fishing?) and filling baskets with sand. Everyone cheerful and intrigued with us. Smiles." The American trio then took a taxi to the British embassy,[12] where they had cocktails with Sir George and Lady Falconer and met Major H. W. (Bill) Tilman, a well-known British mountaineer who had just come from a five-month trip in the Annapurna region of Nepal. It would turn out to be a most fortunate encounter.

The following day, after sightseeing the old section of Kathmandu known as Durbar Square, they returned to the British embassy, where Ambassador and Lady Falconer were "at home" to members of the diplomatic circle, the Maharajah-Prime Minister, and his brothers. It was a remarkable gathering:

> *[The Maharajah's brothers] assemble first, it is all very impressive, red tunic-ed servants, a great many soldiers along the route from town. Everyone dressed in his best (including us). At about 7 (we having been passed trays of drinks in the meantime) the first dignitaries arrive; Commander-in-chief of the Army, then various other generals and excellencies. These are all Rana brothers; then a young man or two (these are sons of the Maharajah). Finally His Highness, the Maharajah Mohan Shamsher Jung Bahadur Rana. He is taken around the circle of guests by Sir George and introduced. I say, "Good evening your Highness" and we shake hands. He is small, elderly, sweet-faced and*

Figure 7.1 "Tears in a Katmandu Street," 1950. Photo by Betsy Cowles. (Courtesy American Heritage Center, University of Wyoming. Copyright restricted.)

quiet voiced, moves slowly and thoughtfully around the room, then is ushered into an adjoining one.

I talk to Tilman, Colonel Lowndes, Mrs. Lall (who is there with her husband), various of the Indian embassy, then am passed down the line of generals and from one excellency to another by Lady Falconer. They are lovely, very quiet and gentle-seeming, several stutter. Many have been to the USA, all want to go. His Excellency the First Nepalese Ambassador to England—must be about the next in succession to the present Maharajah—tells me about tiger hunting; the circle of elephants that closes in on the prey. He has shot sixty himself!

At about 8:15 the Maharajah reappears, goes gravely around the circle of guests again, shaking hands and leaves.

Although certain parts of the city and valley were off-limits to foreigners, Betsy and the Houstons were able to do many of the same things that today's

Figure 7.2   Nell Houston attracted an audience in Kathmandu in 1950. Westerners were a novelty at that time. Photo, originally a 35mm slide, by Betsy Cowles. (Courtesy American Heritage Center, University of Wyoming. Copyright restricted.)

tourists in Kathmandu do: They visited Buddhist temples and Hindu shrines, took photographs, and shopped. They were entertained lavishly; in 1950 only nine Europeans resided in Kathmandu and new faces were welcome.

In late afternoon, Betsy often sat on the guest house porch; she came to "love" watching flocks of snowy egrets—"paddy birds"—as they flew overhead. Kathmandu reminded her of Colorado, especially at sunset when the shadows were long on the skyline of high hills that ring the city.

The Maharajah put a driver and car at his guests' disposal plus a guide who spoke almost no English. The Houstons and Betsy struggled to communicate with him:

> *We are anxious not to do anything improper or out of keeping with the tradition of the place so we are constantly asking Mr. Ditha Ram [the guide] if we may go here or there, photograph this or that. The nature of the Nepalese reply—an affirmative-negative inclination of the head and ambiguous shrug of the shoulders—leaves us completely mystified.*

*"May I climb up onto the platform?" I ask. (Mr. Ram seems to say "yes"—
or is it "no"?) I try again. "Would it be all right for me to take a picture of
the bell-ringer?" (Now he looks as if he were saying "no"—or is it "yes"?)
In desperation I decide to move towards the objective in question. Mr. R.
smiles happily, so I conclude that he meant "yes" all along!*

Betsy and Oscar worked out a system for taking pictures of the curious
townspeople who pressed close to get a better look. She took Oscar's crowd
and he took hers.

On October 12, at 10:30 in the morning, the first commercial airplane
ever to fly into Kathmandu landed on a dirt airstrip equipped with a wind
sock. The Indian ambassador to Nepal emerged and was covered with gar-
lands. Recognizing Oscar, Nell, and Betsy, whom he had met in Delhi, he
greeted them cordially. Betsy made sure that Round-Robin Letter #3 rode the
first commercial flight *out* of Kathmandu.

Betsy and the Houstons met the Maharajah-Prime Minister several times
and began to have "friendly" feelings toward him, which they thought he
reciprocated. They also met the King.

*He is…in uniform with shiny boots (and shiny diamonds) but his eyes
don't shine any and one gets the impression that the life of a figurehead sovereign isn't much fun. Now we go up, one by one, and get presented to him by the Maharajah who definitely is having a good time.
When I come up he says to the King: "She is the one who wants to go
up the south side of Mount Everest" (a slight exaggeration, your Highness, I think to myself) but the King only fastens a glum eye on me and
says nothing. (He can't speak in public.) We all curtsy and say "Good
afternoon, your Majesty"—doesn't it sound like a musical comedy? It
really was. I kept thinking I'd never had a chance to say "your Majesty"
to anyone before and never would again—so spoke up good and loud
and tried not to fall down while curtsying (and didn't.)*

Betsy obtained permission to photograph the King and the Maharajah-
Prime Minister sitting under the historic Jang Bahadur's tree, named for the
Rana who had been the first member of his family to rule Nepal.[13] Betsy
feared that the photo might be too dark, but consoled herself that her subjects' diamonds shone so brightly that perhaps it would turn out after all.

Betsy noted that Nepalese time was eight minutes earlier than Indian and
world time "just to be independent." (Charles Houston says that for many

Figure 7.3   Betsy took this shot of the Maharajah's palace as seen across the *maidan* (parade ground) in Kathmandu in 1950. Photo, originally a 35 mm slide, by Betsy Cowles. (Courtesy American Heritage Center, University of Wyoming. Copyright restricted.)

years Nepalese time has been *thirty minutes* different from India's.) She found the Nepalese anthem to be

> *an odd piece, made to sound odder by the fact that one band is two bars or so behind the other. This is on purpose which is oddest of all...half the tune is slow and sombre, then suddenly it sounds like a morris dance!...Then with a roar like the last judgment, the soldiers all fire their rifles and every blessed gun in the valley goes off. (This is called a "feu de Joie" and the Nepalese love it).*

Cannons also announced the beginning of curfew at 10 P.M. and its end at 5 A.M.

The Houstons and Betsy had a private audience with the Maharajah-Prime Minister at his white-columned, European-style palace known as the

Singha Durbar. They were shown inside and led up stairs, then down a long succession of rooms, one with a mural of a tiger shoot on all four walls, another a great stateroom with a throne at one end and a fountain in the middle. When Betsy passed a grandfather clock made of cut glass so that it resembled "a huge perfume bottle," she tried to imagine it being carried on the back of a porter over several high passes.

Finally, the Houstons and she were ushered into a sitting room where the ruling potentate and his second son, who was the foreign minister, awaited them. The Maharajah wore a black, long-coated outfit and a military hat, which he kept on, decorated with an insignia bejeweled with a diamond in its center "big as the Cullinan" and crossed diamond *kukris* (Nepalese curved daggers).

Betsy regarded the Maharajah as a "very fine and...very able man," although she found him difficult to understand because he mumbled into his very large, gray mustache. She thought that he was genuinely interested in the group's trip; he asked his son to give Oscar and Betsy every assistance he could. The Houstons and Betsy expressed gratitude for this offer and for his hospitality. They said they had been having a marvelous time in Nepal; when Betsy told him it reminded her of Colorado, which was one reason she felt at home, the Maharajah "smiled sweetly."

He talked about Nepal, its old isolation, and the effects and dangers of opening it up. He said that danger to Nepal lay to the south from India, not from the north where the great mountains served as a barrier. "I sometimes wonder how many of the people have the faintest idea what a parliament is," he said, commenting on Nepal's new one. Although he was interested in the United States, he was one of few members of his family who had never been there.

The audience lasted for about half an hour. At its conclusion, the Houston party presented His Highness with a Polaroid Land Camera and a snapshot they had taken of their guest house. "He seemed pleased," Betsy wrote, "and so did his son...[I] had the distinct feeling the son was going to try his darndest to take it over." Betsy wondered why the Maharajah had not given *them* any presents.

As they were leaving, he called their attention to a nearby anteroom, which was lined with Coney Island-style mirrors brought to Kathmandu from London in 1908; he said they always made a hit with people. To demonstrate, the ruler of Nepal stood in front of one; indeed, the effect was "marvelous." Everyone shook hands and Nell, Oscar, and Betsy retraced their steps out, past all the long rooms, "feeling very warm in the heart towards Nepal and the man who runs it." Almost no one—certainly not the Houstons, Betsy, or the

Maharajah—had the least idea that a political hurricane would strike Kathmandu on November 6, while the Houston party was approaching the town of Phedi.

Although the Houstons and Betsy went to Kathmandu mainly for the purpose of sightseeing, they accomplished a great deal more. Soon after their chance meeting with H. W. Tilman, Oscar began plotting to persuade him to join their expedition. Tilman and Oscar's son, Charles, had become friends on the Nanda Devi expedition of 1936, when Tilman and Noel E. Odell had made the first ascent of Nanda Devi, at the time the highest mountain ever climbed. Charles Houston might well have shared in that first ascent had he not come down with food poisoning at the highest camp.

Tilman knew the Himalayas as few people did. The Sherpas called him *Baloo Walla,* the Bear Man.[14] Since 1930 he had poked around the range's devilishly inaccessible valleys and glaciers for the sheer fun of exploring, sometimes making first ascents of unnamed peaks in the process. His good friend Eric Shipton was a frequent companion. Tilman had made two attempts on Everest from the Tibetan side, leading one of them in 1938. He had written five books about his mountain adventures in Africa and Asia, which had sold well. The man himself was somewhat enigmatic, even to his friends. Although known to be taciturn, when he did choose to talk he was also known for his dry wit and ability to "fence with quotations."[15] Eric Shipton and he were outspoken advocates of the small, fast Himalayan mountaineering party, a concept directly counter to the then-current fashion of hiring hundreds of porters to carry supplies into a base camp and of using oxygen.

In 1950 Tilman was fifty-two years old. He had never married, and in fact had the reputation of being a misogynist. But Oscar knew that this tough, competent man, whatever his idiosyncrasies, would add an expertise that the party lacked. And so he invited Tilman to lunch with him, Nell, and Betsy. Initially H. W. declined to join the trek but later reversed himself.[16] Betsy wrote:

> *I expect that Charley's coming is what did the trick. [[17]] But it might have been Oscar's salesmanship; he was superb, couldn't have been better had he been arguing an important case before the Supreme Court. Anyway: we are delighted. Tilman will make a very strong addition to the party and we feel beyond words lucky.*

Betsy and the Houstons spent their last two days in Kathmandu as guests of the Falconers in the British embassy. The night before their departure one of the Maharajah's servants arrived, laden with fifteen presents for the American

Figure 7.4 Today Kathmandu's bustling, modern airport contrasts sharply with the wind sock and dirt airstrip of 1950. Betsy and the Oscar Houstons were passengers on the second-ever commercial flight from Kathmandu to India. Photo, originally a 35mm slide, by Betsy Cowles. (Courtesy American Heritage Center, University of Wyoming. Copyright restricted.)

guests. "The loot included kukris, a lovely ivory and sandalwood box, some fine brass figures, Nepalese jewelry for Nell and me and two evening bags."

On October 19, the Houstons and Betsy flew out on the second commercial flight ever to leave Kathmandu. The pilot made "great spirals to gain altitude," giving his passengers a fine look at the distant high peaks. "They are all terrific," Betsy wrote. "One feels like the country boy accustomed to buildings on the scale of a Rexall store in a country village when he first lays eyes on Rockefeller Center."

In Calcutta, which Betsy described as "hot, wet, filthy," Tilman joined them for dinner. As they discussed final plans, Betsy found the mood of the party "confused" and Tilman "subdued." She gave him her two cameras, which had "acted up" in Kathmandu, so he could arrange to have them repaired in a local Eastman Kodak store. On the following day, Betsy, Nell, and Oscar flew to Delhi. They went through mail waiting for them at Cook's and wired Andy Bakewell and Bill Tilman that they would leave Delhi by train on the 27th.

The next few days were frenzied, for they had to make final purchases for the trek, mail exposed film back to the States, and sort all their food and equipment into logical loads for the porters. John Hotz, secretary of the Himalayan Club in Delhi and a nephew of the Swiss woman who ran the Hotel Cecil, gave them advice. So did Frank Thomas, a Himalayan explorer. He had just blown in from a long trip in Tibet—or so he said. Charles Houston states: "The whole story about Frank A. C. Thomas has never been told; it involved all of us and Betsy was a participant. Thomas undoubtedly was a spy, perhaps a double agent! He was determined to go with us but my father, smelling something wrong, refused."[18]

Betsy's diary said only that Frank Thomas had heard about the Houstons' upcoming trek and so had looked them up, accompanied by Gyaljen, a Sherpa he "thought the world of." Thomas suggested that Gyaljen join the Houston party, because he was eager to visit his home in Namche Bazar, a trading center right on the party's route. Furthermore, Thomas suggested that Gyaljen act as Betsy's Sherpa.

Betsy took an immediate liking to Gyaljen, "small, wiry, alert with eyes like bright little buttons set in an olive Mongolian face." (Tilman had a quite different impression of Gyaljen, who, he said, "was obviously too superior to be asked to carry a load but he made an admirable lady's maid."[19]) Betsy dubbed her man "Gyaljen Junior" or "Little Gyaljen," to differentiate him from "Gyaljen Senior," also known as "Big Gyaljen," who was their cook. Both Hotz and Thomas helped Betsy make out a vocabulary list of Urdu so she could communicate with Little Gyaljen by something more than smiles and nods.

On the 26th, Charles Houston arrived by plane, "cute and full of life." The next day he, Oscar, and Betsy boarded the train to Jogbani, where they were to meet the other two members of the party. Betsy shared a four-bed "cell" with Oscar, Charley, and Gyalgen Junior. She wrote that Oscar, Charley, and she thought of all the women that would have envied her but asked, parenthetically, if any men envied them? The three talked about a "mahseer" fish, about the geology of Everest, about how full the days were going to be. And they discussed Tilman. Betsy made a cryptic entry in her diary that indicated when she ordered potatoes in a restaurant, Tilman had come around and said, "What are you going to eat those things for? Just pure starch. I'd just as leave eat a boiled shirt." Charley assured her that Tilman's bark was worse than his bite.

An hour before midnight on October 29th, they arrived at Jogbani and connected with Andy Bakewell and Bill Tilman, who had just met each other the previous day. Unofficially, Andy would be the expedition scientist. Although his degree from Saint Louis University had emphasized mathematics, geophysics, and astronomy, he was also a naturalist. Andy had been on expeditions that collected amphibians, poisonous reptiles, birds, mammals, and plants in North and South America for such institutions as the St. Louis Zoo, Harvard's Arnold Arboretum, and the American Museum of Natural History. He had explored and climbed in the Yukon as well as in the Santa Martas and was an avid and excellent hunter.

Andy and Oscar and Nell Houston were fast friends, having met in the early 1940s in New York City, when Andy was a staff member of the American Geographical Society of New York working in the Department of Exploration and Field Research and in the Department of Mathematical Geography.[20] Charley was living in New York City also, a medical student at Columbia College.

Several years later, Andy moved to St. Mary's College in Kurseong, India, just south of Darjeeling, where he studied to become a Jesuit priest. So, after Oscar received permission to trek in Nepal and to explore an approach to Mount Everest, he invited Andy to join the party and asked him to work out a route. Immediately Andy called on Dr. John B. Auden (brother of the famous poet W. H.) of the Geological Survey of India.

Although Nepal was considered a sensitive area at the time, John Auden managed to procure the appropriate maps for the Houston party. He also loaned Andy his aneroid barometer because it read to 25,000 feet, higher than any Andy had. Because the Houston party was to be allowed only thirty-six days for their trek, it was necessary to use vehicles to the fullest possible extent.

Andy called in the famous Sherpa Ang Tharkay and his wife, Ang Yang Tsen, who were living in Darjeeling. Ang Tharkay had been the head Sherpa (sirdar) on a number of British Everest expeditions and was a member of the elite Tigers designated by the Himalayan Club. Tilman once said that Ang Tharkay "is probably the best Sherpa porter ever known."[21] Ang Tharkay, Andy, and a Canadian Jesuit priest who was also at St. Mary's College examined a map of eastern Nepal. Largely due to Ang Tharkay's knowledge, a route was worked out that would eventually follow the regular Sherpa trade route between the Solu-Khumbu and Darjeeling. From the railroad's terminus at Jogbani, the Houston party would bounce in a Land Rover to the road's end at Barakshetra, where the Sun, Arun, and Tamur Rivers meet. Then they would start walking.

Both before and after the Houstons' historic trek in Nepal, Andy deliberately maintained a low profile regarding his part in the journey. He did not want his presence to be misinterpreted., because, at the time, delicate negotiations were taking place between a Jesuit priest, Father Marshall Moran, and the government of Nepal regarding the establishment of a Catholic school in Kathmandu. (The talks proved to be successful. Shortly after the Houston party trek, St. Xavier's school came into being.[22])

Betsy met Andy for the first time at Jogbani. Then, after transferring to a bus, the party drove to a jute mill guest house prearranged by the mill owner, whom they had met in Kathmandu. There were no passport checks or guards of any kind, even along the border between India and Nepal. Betsy and her companions found the lack of formalities "fascinating."[23]

The next day a fifty-mile "wild bumpy ride" took them to Dharan. Along the way they drove through a forest of sal trees, whose entangled roots Betsy found quite beautiful, and they glimpsed a jackal. Today a fine highway roller-coasters north from Dharan to the ridgetop town of Hille, reducing to a half-day bus ride what took the Houston party three days to walk. But in 1950 Dharan was the end of the road. So it was there that the Houston entourage heaved all the food and duffels out of the truck, amid a mob of fascinated spectators. Bill Tilman took charge, "ordering and overseeing." He hired sixteen porters who then loaded up and set out.[24]

Notes

1. Glad Morath, "Woman of the Week," copy of article from an unknown Colorado Springs newspaper, courtesy of Ben Hammett, Ph.D.
2. Dorothy Teague Swartz, interview with the author, January 14, 1993.
3. Elizabeth S. Cowles, "The Tetons to Me [Part II]," *Trail and Timberline* no. 354 (June, 1948): 79.
4. "Lecturer Betsy Cowles Has Climbed the Highest Mountains But Doesn't Subscribe to Anything Man Can Do Woman Can Do Better," article from Colorado Springs newspaper, April 19, 1951, Archives, American Heritage Center.
5. William Ryder, M.D., letter to the author, August 8, 1994.
6. Elizabeth S. Cowles, text for talk, "Men Against Women," n.d. Archives, American Heritage Center.
7. Unless otherwise noted, all information about the Houston Expedition to Nepal in 1950 comes from a transcription of Elizabeth S. Cowles's diary, made by her second husband, General Earle E. Partridge, or from one of the seven Round Robin letters she wrote, or from the written text of a speech she wrote, "North to

Everest." All are housed in the Archives of the American Heritage Center in Laramie, Wyoming.

8. J. R. L. Anderson, *High Mountains & Cold Seas: A Biography of H. W. Tilman* (Seattle: The Mountaineers, 1980), 245.

9. Charles S. Houston, M.D., comments on the manuscript, December 1995.

> *I don't remember Walter Wood being invited. My father called me in the spring and asked me to go; I could not. Then in July Lowell Thomas persuaded me to go to Lhasa but that fell through. My father called me as they were leaving the U.S. and said, "If you could go to Lhasa, why not come with us instead?" After my partners agreed, I cabled him in Delhi and went.*

10. Karl Samson, *Frommer's Comprehensive Travel Guide: Nepal*, 2d ed. (New York: Prentice Hall Travel, 1992–1993), 166.

11. Jana Everett, Ph.D., letter to the author, September 19, 1995.

12. Rishikesh Shaha, *Modern Nepal: A Political History 1769–1955*, 2 vols. (Riverdale, Md.: Riverdale, 1990), 1: 144, and 2: 178, 181. Under the terms of the Treaty of Sugauli, ratified in 1816, a British representative resided in Kathmandu, although he did not have any power or responsibility for Nepal's internal affairs. In 1947, Nepal and Britain agreed to raise the status of their legations in London and in Kathmandu to those of embassies. Nepal also agreed to establish diplomatic relations with the United States. For several years, the American ambassador to India served as the ambassador to Nepal as well.

13. *Ibid.*, 1: 246–48. In 1856 Jang Bahadur "persuaded" the reigning monarch to sign a document that gave complete powers to the Rana family and its male descendants.

14. Anderson Bakewell, S.J., letter to the author, September 12, 1994.

15. Jim Perrin, introduction to H.W. Tilman, *Nepal Himalaya,* from *The Seven Mountain-Travel Books* (London: Diadem Books Ltd./Seattle: The Mountaineers, 1983), 9. This anthology is paginated as though the books constitute one large volume.

16. Tilman, *Seven Mountain-Travel Books*, 868. Tilman attributes part of his decision to join the Houston party to the fact that Major J. O. M. (Jimmy) Roberts, M.C. of the Gurkhas, whom he met on the way down to Raxaul, called him a "fool" for not going. As Tilman rationalized,

> *the journey would be of supreme interest; apart from viewing the south side of Everest there was the fun to be expected from seeing Sherpas, as it were, in their natural state. [Eric] Shipton and I had often discussed such an unlikely happening and here it was offered to me on a plate. In 1949 the Himalayan Committee had asked the Nepal Durbar for permission to send a party to reconnoitre the south side of Everest, but this had been refused and the Langtang Himal offered in its place.*

17. Houston, comments. "Tilman and I had been good friends and there's no doubt that he accepted because of me. The party was so weak that he would not have joined otherwise."

18. *Ibid.*

19. Tilman, *Seven Mountain-Travel Books*, 870.

20. Houston, comments. "Bakewell was a close friend of my family, and actually courted my sister for a time. He was a socialite at the time, going to all the parties, captivating women. We all loved him."

21. Tilman, *Seven Mountain-Travel Books*, 767.

22. Information about the role of Anderson Bakewell, S.J., in the trek, as well as his background and his observations on the trek, comes from five sources: (1) a copy of Anderson Bakewell's photo album containing his black-and-white photographs of the 1950 trek and other information, including a copy of a letter from Anderson Bakewell to John B. Janssens, S.J., written in 1951; (2) the curriculum vita (1936–1993) of Anderson Bakewell, dated November 1993; (3) an interview with Anderson Bakewell by the author, August 13, 1994; (4) a letter from Michael Tyrrell, S.J. (Executive Assistant to the Provincial, Oregon Province of the Society of Jesus) to the author, August 20, 1994; (5) a letter from Anderson Bakewell to the author, September 1994.

23. Houston, comments.

24. Charles S. Houston, M.D., "Towards Everest, 1950," *Himalayan Journal* 17 (1951): 10.

CHAPTER EIGHT
To Tengboche

The rest of the party "started off bang in the roaring heat of noon by going up 3000 feet." It included several Sherpas who had accompanied Andy Bakewell from Darjeeling: Gyalgen Senior, who served as both sirdar and cook; Da Namgyal; the Sherpani Dicky, and her man, Sarki. The first two had been with Tilman in the Annapurnas. Earlier that year, Sarki had carried to the highest camp on Annapurna when the French made the first ascent of that mountain. Dicky was to serve as the party's chief guide to Namche Bazar because she had been there very recently.[1] (Tilman made disparaging remarks about her and especially objected to her "cackle."[2])

The first night on the trail, the party camped a thousand feet below a pass with a view of the world's third-highest mountain, Kanchenjunga, "at sunset, by moonlight and tinged with the early morning colors when the sun rose." They could not see Everest, Betsy commented in her diary, obviously not realizing that on this route Everest would not be visible until they reached a hill above Namche Bazar.

The Houston party was relying on maps that were, as Charles Houston put it, "rather good topographically [but] weak on trails." Even today maps of the area are not to be completely trusted. Spellings vary from map to map; many are different from those on the maps used by the Houston party. Betsy and her companions were by no means sure they would reach their destination. But they *were* on their way, finally. "I feel happy and content, (and lucky)," Betsy wrote in her diary after the first day out. Camp was cheerful and full of fun. Bill joked that the "greatest danger on Everest is bed-sores."[3]

Figure 8.1   Betsy labeled this 1950 photo, "Our Sherpas." *Back row, left to right:* Dicky, Sarki, Gyaljen Senior, Pa Narbu, Sonam Tensing. *Front row, left to right:* Da Namgyol, Gyaljen Junior, Dawa Nurbu. (Courtesy American Heritage Center, University of Wyoming. Copyright restricted.)

The next day they continued their descent to the valley floor. Because the route coincided with one of the main north–south trade routes between Tibet and Nepal, they passed many people (Charley estimated 1,200). Betsy walked, mostly, but occasionally rode a pony.

The traffic is terrific and everyone who passes us stops to look. When we sit down, crowds assemble—it is impossible (practically) to get privacy enough for some of life's small necessities! We are dropping down to the Tamur R.—(beautiful greenery)—I saw the biggest spider web, about 30 ft., and a huge spider entrenched. [⁴] Tried a picture of it. Then down to the river's edge and along; the suspension bridge in sight. The river is rush and fine. On the bridge the pony I am on and me, we meet a gang of water buffalo in the middle. The W B win; I get off and walk past gingerly.

Betsy was quite taken with the people on the trail, especially the children, and ensured their good will by offering Life Savers. Although unwittingly Betsy was planting the seed that trekkers mean handouts, and tooth-decaying ones at that, her good intentions were above reproach; candy broke the ice and conveyed her friendliness to people whose language she did not speak. But Life Savers were only the first step. Betsy taught a few words of English to anyone willing to learn, and they would practice "thank you," "please," and "hello" as they walked beside her. One old soldier spoke to Betsy and concluded with, "Good evening, Mem Sahib." Another man said, with obvious pride, "Bon jour."

> *I wish you could see the traffic jam on the path if we sit down to eat lunch or so much as pause to draw a breath. The way to Dhankuta lies along one of the great north-south trade routes and it is filled with lines of coolies carrying salt, potatoes, oranges and cotton cloth. One coolie would catch sight of us and a low whistle would go down the line— then they'd all stop and look and soon they'd be four and five deep and no room to move. In the populated lowland areas one feels great public curiosity and not much else, but now that we're off the beaten track we find warmth, humor and interest and not a day passes without a human experience that is interesting and touching.*

The party camped on a small knoll that overlooked the town of Dhankuta, gaining at least some privacy from the onlookers they had picked up in the town's main street. A "press reporter of newspapers of Nepal," who was also headmaster of the local school, interviewed them in excellent English.[5] The governor of the province, Colonel Shumshere, a member of the Rana family whose full name was Brigadier Colonel Kham Shumshere Jung Bahadur Rana, rode a white horse up from Dhankuta to call on his visitors. His coat smelled of mothballs. That night Betsy wrote in her diary, "I am happy and feel useful and liked."

The next day she and her companions visited Dhankuta, which they found "lovely." Its streets were swept twice daily. Chinese lanterns suspended from bamboo poles lined the main street. Dhankuta was especially "scrubbed and shining" because a major festival was about to take place. (Probably it was Tihaar, which is celebrated throughout Nepal in mid-November.) The previous day all the houses had been replastered, as they were twice a year.

The party toured the school and were impressed at what the 400 pupils learned. Some of the blackboards showed math problems involving "tough

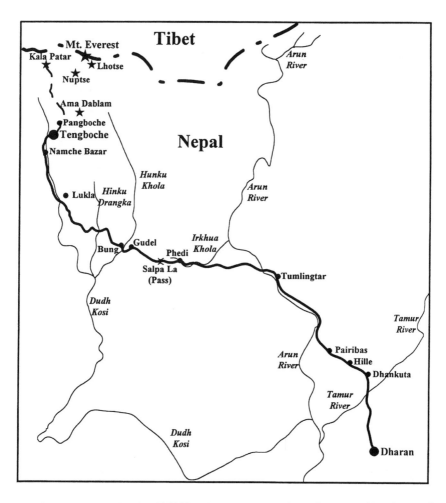

Map 2   Map illustrating the 1950 Houston party route through eastern Nepal toward Mount Everest. (Map made by David Robertson.)

compound fractions," which Betsy said she would be hard pressed to answer correctly. English was taught in all classes from the fifth grade on. On the blackboard were sentences written in English and diagrammed.[6] On an outside wall of one of the classrooms someone had chalked: "Gather courage. Don't be a chicken hearted fellow," a phrase that the Houston expedition adopted as its motto. The town's lending library even had a few books in English, including *A Life of Theodore Roosevelt, David Copperfield,* and *Now*

Figure 8.2 The main street of Dhankuta in 1950. Photo by Betsy Cowles. (Courtesy American Heritage Center, University of Wyoming. Copyright restricted.)

We Are Six. (After they returned to the United States, Betsy, Charley, and Oscar presented the Dhankuta library with new books, pasting into each one a bookplate printed with their names as donors.[7])

Colonel Shumshere gave the Houston party fresh ponies, as well as an escort to ease their way through his province until the party entered the province of the next governor; the escort consisted of a *jemadar* (officer) and his four men. As it turned out, the Houston party never did encounter the governor of the next province, and so the five men from Dhankuta accompanied them during the entire journey, not daring to leave the Houston group without an escort. (Besides, Betsy explained, they were having a very good time.) The next day they walked to a field below Pairibas Pass, where camp was set up.

The Houston party was traveling through country that almost no Westerners had ever seen. The first European to see the area had been the English botanist-doctor Sir Joseph Hooker; in 1848, he crossed the Tamur River, not traveling quite as far north as Dhankuta.[8] In 1934, at the invitation of Nepal's Maharajah-Prime Minister, the same John B. Auden who later procured maps for the Houston party, visited Dhankuta, inspecting damage caused by a catastrophic earthquake that had occurred on January 15. He then made his way northeast back to Darjeeling.[9] The first known Americans to visit the area had done so just three years before the Houston party. In 1947, Dr. S. Dillon Ripley of Yale University headed a party that made an ornithological survey, traveling to Dhankuta and then north, always on the east side of the Arun River, before returning to Dharan.[10]

While camped on the Pairibas Pass, the Houston party marveled at a splendid view of the 8,000-meter peak Makalu, and of Chamlang, set off by yellow-green rice fields in the foreground. Betsy wrote:

Item; above Pairibas all 3 sahibs bathe in a pool—big audience. I meet a sweet woman there with 2 daughters; she offers me her necklace, brings flowers and then offers me a rupee (?) all so touching. When she leaves, she touches her eyes to say there are tears in them. She counts out on her bare toes and fingers 20—to show her daughter's age. All our human contacts are warm and bright.

Betsy took a photograph of the immersed sahibs and said she wished she had brought her bathing suit. Apparently she had no understanding that it was highly offensive for a woman to show her legs in Hindu country. In fact, because she never commented on the matter, one may assume that Betsy simply did not understand that her long pants—and, even worse, the shorts she sometimes wore—were shocking to the people she encountered. Likely her attire attracted even bigger crowds than did the novelty of five tall, pale

Westerners and their retinue of porters. Yet, without fail, the people Betsy met were warm and friendly.

Because trail signs were almost nonexistent (and are still uncommon today), it was easy to get lost. On the third day out the party became separated. Bill Tilman, apparently assuming that camp would be close to the Arun River, went ahead. Accompanying him were some of the porters and Gyaljen Senior, who was carrying the day's food sack and most of the pots and pans. Those left behind ate a "very odd and limited meal served by a sub-cook in the pitch dark to some tired and rather dispirited expeditionaries."[11]

On November 2, Charley mistook the laughing and singing of the porters as a sign that it was time to get up and so, thinking it was 5:30, roused everyone at what turned out to be 4 A.M. They got up anyway and ate oatmeal, eggs, and little tart tomatoes, much the same breakfast that trekkers eat today. Then Betsy, Charley, and Oscar hit the trail and continued a long, steep descent to the Arun River, only a thousand feet above sea level. Betsy reveled in being able to wash and stepped into the river, undeterred by quicksand and a swift current. A man approached the group and threatened that an Indian sergeant would kill them all if they didn't go back to Dhankuta. The man appeared to be drunk, so they ignored him.

The Arun River is the main watershed of eastern Nepal. For three days the Houston party walked beside its broad waters, through lush green fields of rice, across two waist-deep tributaries, and up and down steep red hills. It was torrid, but by leaving early in the morning, they could enjoy four hours hiking in the coolth.

On November 3, the party confronted a landslide that turned the high path into little more than footholds on a cliff above the river. The ponies were forced to turn back, which relieved Betsy. "You know me and horses!" she wrote her friends. "[A]s the going gets rougher it's really less harrowing to walk, I find, and I have been." North of Tumlingtar the party crossed the Arun River on the local state-supported ferry.

[It was] more darn fun—long tree hollowed out and you sit in the bottom (bilge swishes over your rear), 3 oars-men—2 fore, 1 aft, they strike out from shore then hit the current & paddle like mad to reach opposite shore—boat lists and rolls and tips, being round, tree form, you wonder what keeps it from spinning around?) We land about 1/4 mile further down the shore than where we started—get out. Then boat goes back (6 loads.)

Oscar took movies of the crossing. The party "stunned the ferryman with a tip—the first paying passengers in the history of the ferry."[12]

Somewhere near the town of Dingla, within sight of the Irkhua Khola's waters, the party stopped at a farmhouse and purchased six dozen oranges at a cost equivalent to two cents a dozen. Then they stopped at a house whose owner, an old and dignified man, took Betsy by the hand and led her in. Seating her in a chair, he made a speech which Bill translated to mean that he was putting himself, his house, and its contents at her disposal. Betsy and her companions thanked him, gave him Life Savers, took his picture, and left. He pursued them with a present of yet more oranges. They found such hospitality extraordinary. Charley speculated about what would happen if a group of Nepalese people were to wander through his home town in Exeter, New Hampshire: Would the Americans greet visitors with a similar welcome?

By the time they were a week out, the party had settled into a routine. Because the days were short, breakfast was simple—oatmeal and/or eggs and occasionally small tomatoes. Bill Tilman made loaves of yeast-leavened bread which his companions came to call "foot bread," so named because some flour usually fell on Bill's feet as he kneaded the dough.[13] Sometimes Bill made a cake by adding sugar and dates and nuts cut up by Betsy.

After breakfast Oscar and Betsy were usually the first to start out, leaving by 5:30 or 6 A.M. Close to 11 o'clock they would stop for a lunch of Tilman bread, cheese, butter, jam, sardines, and perhaps an orange. Then they would hike again until 2:30 or so. This gave everyone time to wash body and clothes. Sometimes Betsy's Sherpa, Gyaljen Junior, would dry Betsy's pink nightgown by the fire.

Before the trip began, Betsy had decided that she would be Head Housekeeper of the party. "I want to be of real service to the expedition," she explained to her friends in Round-Robin Letter #5. "Hope very much to earn my keep and fix it so they eat better, live better and have a nicer, cheerful and more comfortable time than if it had just been men." In Kathmandu, Nell and she had discussed what Betsy's role ought to be and had concluded that it should include darning socks for herself *and* for the sahibs, as well as planning menus. In a Round Robin letter, Betsy wrote, "If it doesn't work out, I shall be really sad and apologetic and promise to stop bothering people to take me places."

Betsy considered Oscar Houston's welfare and comfort to be mainly her responsibility. At sixty-eight, he was the oldest member of the party; Charley and Andy were in their late thirties, Betsy was forty-eight, and Bill fifty-two.

Figure 8.3   Bill Tilman making "footbread", 1950. Photo, originally a 35 mm slide, by Betsy Cowles. (Courtesy American Heritage Center, University of Wyoming. Copyright restricted.)

Frequently Betsy and Charley discussed Oscar: "how to save him, keep him having fun and still get on with things." For the first few days of the trek they encouraged him to conserve his strength by riding rather than by walking, although he disliked doing so.

Betsy took great satisfaction in watching Oscar and in seeing that he had "things to suit him." Despite the hardships, Oscar retained his sense of humor and enjoyed "being in a land the hand of a white man never set foot in." With obvious approval, Bill Tilman later wrote that "Mr. Houston" thought raw milk was "more inimical to health than raw brandy and much less pleasant to take."[14]

Betsy and Andy got on quite well. She found him to be "agreeable and cheerful, less forceful than the others perhaps but very sweet." Andy regarded her as "a perfect lady" who was "always on the lookout for what needed to be done and unobtrusively doing it." Sometimes the two discussed poetry.

Charley Houston's medical background made him an invaluable member of the party, of course, as did his knowledge of big mountains gained from the Nanda Devi expedition of 1936 and the K2 expedition two years later. But Betsy delighted in the man himself, finding his jokes and comments to be high points in the days of tough walking. Charley, she wrote, was a "wonderful" person and a "joy from sunrise to sunset."[15]

The only member of the party whom Betsy could not enjoy without reservation was H. W. Tilman. Even in her diary, Betsy did not mention how things started off between them, but Charley made no bones about it in his: for the first three days, Bill Tilman walked a mile ahead of the party, alone, "but within a few days Betsy and Tilman had become close and walked side by side. It was amazing."[16] Still, Betsy found Bill to be moody.

Certainly she *wanted* to like the man. On November 2, she wrote: "T[ilman] warms up at times (gave me a piece of orange, peeled a while ago), smiles cutely when making one of his dry jokes. Like 'trouble with America is you are all package minded.' I think he is quite a man and will be happy if we end by being friends." Betsy recognized that he was essential to the expedition, for on November 4 she wrote,

> *C[harley] & I have a talk about the expedition—I saying that it is amazing to me that we'd have considered doing it without him or T[ilman]. This is wild country; one could get into an awful pickle, really dangerous. C[harley] agrees we were not being very sensible—imagine O & me with only Andy or some of these strangers we might have taken on who know Nothing. Feel, myself that C[harley] & T[ilman] are rocks of Gibraltar.*

By November 7, Betsy thought she was making progress with Tilman, noting that he was "warming up" and that he "sang a little song at tea!" But the next day she confided in her diary that "I irk HWT sometimes, but must try not to be too pervasive." And on the day after that, "HWT's abysmal pessimism is a real load for everyone to carry." At least by November 10 Betsy had learned to not take his dour moods so personally. "HWT in a bad temper but I feel better about it now he is mad at everyone and not just me."

Each day was physically demanding. Even the trail beside the Arun River was not a gentle grade, but rather an up-and-down grind made all the more grueling by the heat. After leaving the Arun River, the route climbed into the coolness of higher elevations, but it also crossed the grain of the land so that each day the party gained and lost several thousand feet.

Sometimes the trail was a mile-long stone staircase devoid of switch-backs. The local people learned how to go up and down the paths—fast—when they were toddlers. By the time they were adults carrying loads of 50 or 100 kilos *or more*, they could trot downhill unerringly from stone to stone or could skitter down smooth, dry mud, often barefoot, with an agility that amazed Betsy and her companions.[17]

Originally, the Houston party had planned to supplement the food supplies carried by porters with local fruits, vegetables, meat, and rice. But this proved difficult: Betsy and her companions were traveling through country that produced almost no surplus food except for oranges and bananas in the lowlands. They had first encountered the local sweet oranges at Dhankuta and had gorged on them all through the lowlands, thinking what a good export crop they would be. Rice was scarce at this time of year because people had little left from the previous year's harvest and had not yet reaped that of the present one. During the first week out, the party did manage to buy a few eggs, a "brace of very tough chickens," a goat (also tough, but delicious when curried), and *saag*, a local spinach.

Finding porters to carry their loads also proved to be a problem. The Houston party had modified its original route slightly so that they would not have to gain unnecessary elevation by going through the town of Dingla. Later they realized that this decision had probably been a mistake, for they had trouble picking up porters in the sparsely populated countryside. Because porters often quit suddenly or committed to carrying for only a few days, finding replacements was a constant job.

By the time the party reached the major settlement of Phedi, the rice crop was ripe. This meant that every able-bodied person was helping with the harvest and had no interest whatever in portering. Suddenly the Houston party was faced with the complete breakdown of the trip. Unexpectedly, the military escort from Dhankuta came to the rescue. Although these five men were definitely not porters, they simply heaved the loads onto their own backs and began the arduous climb from Phedi up toward the Salpa La (Pass). Their touching act enabled the expedition to continue.

The jemadar from Dhankuta became a favorite of the Houston party. He knew almost no English other than the names of the bones of the body, the organs of the different body cavities, and the sections of the heart. After each category he would stop and ask Charley, "*Teak Hi*, Sahib?" (Okay?) "Big intestine, small intestine, pancreas, spleen," he would say, sending Betsy and her companions into such laughter that they forgot about the rigors of the trek. The jemadar also knew "right," "left," "very good," and "red cap."

An hour below the Salpa La, the party set up a camp in the fog.

Nov. 7 (Day 9) Now it is Tuesday and we are at this moment camped at 9700 feet and will cross the Salpa-La tomorrow. It is beautiful up here. There are big trees and a grassy meadow where our tents are arranged cozily. Two wooden boxes (they hold biscuits) make a dining room table. We sit around it on the medicine chest, Andy's instrument case and assorted rocks. Our gasoline lantern goes on the table when it gets dark (which is soon) and we have a fine camp fire at our elbow. Five o'clock is dinner time and before 6 it is pitch dark. By 7 everyone begins to think of bed. The last few nights I've been reading the Kon-tiki Expedition aloud. We love it because it's such a change from this. When we have coolie worries or food troubles or wonder about the distance ahead, it's a great tonic to think of that little raft sailing across the Pacific. It's been a long hard pull today; 4000 steep feet up from our rather too centrally located camp at Phedi. The main path to the town ran right under one of my tent ropes (level places were scarce). Rather awkward for the citizenry but no casualties, not even after dark when a line of men and women carrying the rice harvest on their backs and with lighted brands in their hands wound their way up to the village…. My long red underwear is marvelous!

Next day, the party made the final push to the pass. They exclaimed less at the snowy peak of Numbur than they did upon seeing their first *chorten* (Buddhist shrine), bedecked with prayer flags. The Salpa La is on the eastern border of the Solu area of Nepal, which, coupled with the Khumbu area, is home to the largest number of Sherpas in the country. After the pass, the route began skirting ancient *mani* walls (made of stone tablets on which Buddhist prayers are carved), often covered with lichens that obscured the characters. Betsy learned to walk on the left of the walls, as all good Buddhists do. Andy noticed that after they entered the Solu-Khumbu, "Dicky's steps quickened and her chatter became more vociferous." Gyaljen began to reminisce; this was his first visit to the Khumbu since he left it at the age of seven.

Figure 8.4 "The Three Musketeers," Sherpas whom the Houston party encountered near Phedi in 1950. Thanks to these men, the expedition was able to continue toward Mount Everest. Photo by Betsy Cowles. (Courtesy American Heritage Center, University of Wyoming. Copyright restricted.)

While ascending the Salpa La, the Houston party encountered a trio of Sherpa men bound for Phedi, their carrying baskets heavily laden with salt, probably collected in the dried-up lakes of Tibet. The party persuaded the men to drop their salt in Phedi, turn around, and join them as porters. The men, whom they later dubbed "The Three Musketeers," proved to be as delightful as they were strong. A few days later more porters hired on, ending the crisis.

The rigors of the route west of the Arun River were demoralizing because the Houston party was behind its hoped-for schedule. Humping up and down several thousand feet, day after day, was taking longer than they had estimated it would and was eating into their allotted thirty-six days. Charley and Bill would have to scramble to get a look at the approach to Everest from this side.

Figure 8.5   Photo of Charley Houston negotiating one of the tamer bamboo bridges that the party crossed on the 1950 trek. Photo, originally a 35 mm slide, by Betsy Cowles. (Courtesy American Heritage Center, University of Wyoming. Copyright restricted.)

After the party arrived at their campsite, located in the town of Gudel, they despaired. From Gudel they could look across what they now realized was a steep, deep valley to the town of Bung. In reading their imperfect and very large-scale maps, they had optimistically assumed that the route from Gudel to Bung would be "straight-forward," although Betsy remarked that in retrospect they should have known that "in Nepal, no descent exists of that sort." Now they could see there was no avoiding a knee-wrenching plunge to the gorge of the Hongu (Hunku) Khola (Stream), which was so far down they could catch no glimpse of it. That evening Betsy had her only experience of claustrophobia on the trip. She felt "enclosed in the vast spaces like walls." Bill Tilman summed up the group's feeling by writing a little poem:

In frightfulness naught can excel
The prospect of Bung from Gudel
And words die away on the tongue
When we look back to Gudel from Bung.[18]

The descent from Gudel to the Hongu Khola was as unrelenting as the group had feared it would be. Worse, the bamboo bridge that spanned the Hongu Khola was disconcertingly high and very wobbly. The expedition had begun encountering bamboo bridges soon after they crossed the Arun River. Betsy found them unnerving despite her good balance.

Those bridges! They are usually made of bamboo logs lashed loosely together. They bobble around as you walk across, holding on to two banister logs (that also bobble). The whole business sags and swings, especially when you're in the middle, with the torrent roaring below. Quite sensational! No wonder that the Sherpas, who are good Buddhists, always go through a little incantation before they start over.

On November 10, Charley wandered off by himself to take pictures and in so doing made a wrong turn, which was dubbed "Lost Doctor Pass. The following day, November 11, the Houston party crossed the Innukhu (Hinku) Khola "on another of those nifty bamboo bridges," climbed thousands of feet up to a ridge, and dropped down into the valley of the Dudh Kosi (the Milk River). At long last the Houston party was in the drainage of the silt-laden river whose tributaries are born on the glaciers of Mount Everest. Almost certainly they were now in country never before seen by Westerners.[19] Betsy was ebullient, writing:

We all feel marvelous. Beautiful snow peaks on every hand and a crystal clear sparkling blue day. Namche Bazar is just three days up the valley and somewhere—not far away now but still hidden behind the intervening ridges is Mt. Everest. Or is it purely mythical? We're really beginning to wonder.

Their trail paralleled the Dudh Kosi on its west bank, unlike the present-day trail, which follows the river on its east side, serving as a pedestrian highway for those who begin their journey at the town of Jiri and for those who fly into the town of Lukla.[20] Today guest houses and tea houses line the way, advertising their advantages and menus on signs written in Nepali-style English. In 1950 very few tea houses existed and certainly there were no signs written in English.[21] Travelers commonly relied on the good will of local residents, borrowing pots in which to cook the rice they carried and sleeping on rugs in a home. And, of course, there was no airstrip in Lukla; the present one was built in 1964.[22]

Figure 8.6   Betsy photographed this *mani* stone in Nepal, 1950. Today some are painted in bright colors. Photo, originally a 35 mm slide, by Betsy Cowles. (Courtesy American Heritage Center, University of Wyoming. Copyright restricted.)

As the Houston party made its way upriver, the air grew colder. They began meeting people who were warmly dressed, many of them Tibetans whose peaked hats were edged with fur. Sherpas passed them, often wearing necklaces consisting of a long, flat bead, usually mottled and gray in the center, flanked by two round ones, usually pink. They encountered a monk from Lhasa who was making a pilgrimage to raise money. Betsy felt that the people on the trail exuded "good will and cordiality," although she observed that the women were sometimes "hesitant and afraid." Betsy found the children enchanting.

> *The bandobust had paused at a farm to see if we could get some rice and maybe a sheep. While the negotiations were going on, I sat on a knoll writing in my diary. I looked up to find a row of little children around me, watching intently. I got out Life Savers and we had some conversation about how good they are to eat, please try one, and who was whose sister or brother, and what pretty bracelets, beads and nose rings everyone had on. Two boys were perfectly darling with bright eyes, sweet expressions and rosy cheeks under their brown color. A pair of little girls had their small brothers on their backs. All wear woolens here (it's cold) and every foot has on the woolen legged, leather soled Tibetan boots, trimmed in bright colors. Wonderful to find one can tell by gestures and inflections and arrive at complete friendliness and understand.... When I rose and said goodbye, all my little people said goodbye back, in the sweetest little imitative voices. I just loved it.*

Word of the party, which by then consisted of twenty-seven people, raced ahead. After the trail left the river, Betsy and her companions began "toiling up a steep zigzag trail on the big 3000 foot pull" to Namche Bazar, the Sherpa trade center of the Khumbu. The climb was hard on everyone, especially Oscar. And then, just where the trail leveled out, Betsy and her companions heard cheerful bells coming down. Soon four little horses with bright saddle blankets appeared, accompanied by two head men from Namche and the local police officer. Everyone shook hands and made polite speeches, and four members of the Houston party mounted the little horses. As they rode into Namche, curious onlookers jammed the narrow streets and packed the windows of the buildings. Betsy wrote:

> *It is a town like nothing I've ever seen; houses of stone, in rows, dark woodwork—looks a bit like Southwest cliff dwellings, fits right into the amphitheater it's built against. We smile at everyone and say "salaam."*

Figure 8.7   The Sherpa trade center of the Khumbu, Namche Bazar, in 1950 when
the buildings were in the muted tones of wood and stone. Today there are many
brightly painted shutters and the buildings have more stories. Betsy and members of
the Houston party took the first photos of the town and its surroundings. Photo by
Betsy Cowles. (Courtesy American Heritage Center, University of Wyoming.
Copyright restricted.)

> *Everyone greets us enthusiastically. We dismount and are led up some*
> *dark steps into an upper room where we have some lunch. The room*
> *is crowded with people watching and children who are periodically*
> *chased out. Tents are set up outside on a dirt terrace—the whole vil-*
> *lage watching our every move from above and below.*

Three or four Sherpa veterans of past expeditions to Kanchenjunga and
Everest welcomed the Westerners; one had walked from Thami, a settlement
several miles to the north. Betsy described them as "fine looking men" who,

with great pride, showed off their porter's books and chits signed by famous mountaineers such as Eric Shipton and Hugh Ruttledge. Sonam Tensing presented the party with a gift of yak butter. He had been with Bill Tilman on the 1938 Everest expedition, dressing so nattily that his nickname became "Foreign Sportsman."

Charley recalls that for him one of the highlights in Namche was being served buttered tea in the home of one of the local head men. The smoke inside was "choking." Posters from Communist Russia decorated the walls.[23]

Betsy climbed up one side of the valley that enclosed Namche Bazar, in order to take a picture, leaving behind most of the crowd that had been following her. Clouds hid Everest. After returning to camp, she, Charley, and Bill set to work dividing their food into two parts. One part was for Betsy, Andy, and Oscar, who would stay at Tengboche (which Betsy spelled "Thyangboche"), a Buddhist monastery, or, more accurately, a *gompa*. The other part was for Bill and Charley, who would continue north to reconnoiter Mount Everest. For six days, possibly seven, the two parties would be separated.

Although Betsy found Namche Bazar to be picturesque and the children "so bright and rough and cute," she was unnerved by living in a "goldfish bowl." It was as though all business had been suspended so the locals could watch Andy, Bill, Charley, Oscar, and Betsy. Families even brought food and threw bedding beside the expedition's tents, spending the night so they would not miss anything. Betsy was relieved to quit Namche and to head north where they would finally see Mount Everest for the first time.

Or so they hoped. A thick cloud bank moved in and, during the night, it began snowing. Betsy called it a "blizzard," but Charles Houston thinks that the term is too strong; although the storm was briefly intense, it dropped only an inch or so. Still, one question was on everyone's mind: had winter arrived, or was the storm only a brief interlude?

Bill and Charley left Namche first, accompanied by Sarki, Da Namgyol (one of the "Three Musketeers"), and a young Namche boy, Donu, to carry. A few hours later, Oscar, Andy, and Betsy set out into the "whirling snowy mist." "It was a mean day," Betsy wrote, "and our feelings weren't helped by the sight of our faithful coolies trotting ahead in their paper-thin clothes." Betsy's favorite, Amrit, had carried a heavy load all the way up from Dharan, often giving Betsy a pang when she saw the look of "patient weariness on his face at the end of a hard day." Going up the final steep hill to the gompa, Betsy passed Amrit and "his quick cheerful smile shone out on that dark day like a spear of the brightest sunlight."

At noon they arrived at Tengboche.

Notes

1. Anderson Bakewell, S.J., "Southern Approach to Mount Everest," manuscript for article in *Der Bergsteiger* (ca. 1951), Archives, American Heritage Center.
2. Anderson Bakewell, S.J., phone conversation with the author, September 8, 1994.
3. Jim Perrin, introduction to H.W. Tilman, *The Seven Mountain-Travel Books* (London: Diadem Books Ltd./Seattle: The Mountaineers, 1983), 433. Tilman mentions that Shipton had spoken about the danger of bedsores on mountaineering expeditions.
4. Identification was made by the late Edwin L. Licht, Museum Curator Adjoint, University of Colorado Museum, Boulder, from a verbal description during a phone conversation on September 2, 1994. The genus is *Nephila*; the species is either *maculata* or *robusta*.
5. Lakshman Raj Joshi, B.A., letter to Elizabeth S. Cowles, February 2, 1951, Archives, American Heritage Center.
6. Charles S. Houston, M.D., comments on the manuscript, December 1994.
7. Elizabeth S. Cowles, Archives, American Heritage Center. In his comments on the manuscript, Charles Houston said that the books took a year to arrive but that someone had told him that they were indeed in the Dhankuta library.
8. F. F. Ferguson, "Sir Joseph Hooker, K.C.S.I., M.D., D.C.L., F.R.S., Early Travels in Nepal and Sikkim," *Himalayan Journal* 16 (1950): 86.
9. J. B. Auden, "Traverses in Nepal," *Himalayan Journal* 7 (1935): 76.
10. The expedition was funded by Yale University, the Smithsonian Institution, and the National Geographic Society. Dillon Ripley wrote a book about the journey titled *Search for the Spiny Babbler: An Adventure in Nepal* (Boston: Houghton Mifflin, 1952).
11. Elizabeth S. Cowles, text for a slide talk, "North to Everest," given in Colorado Springs, Denver, Chicago, New York, Boston, Philadelphia, Pittsburgh, London, and other places in the 1950s. Archives, American Heritage Center.
12. Tilman, *Seven Mountain-Travel Books*, 872. Today the ferry is still operating, although a wooden boat made of boards has replaced the hollowed-out log; there is also a well-built suspension bridge several miles to the north.
13. *Ibid.*, 875.
14. *Ibid.*, 878.
15. Elizabeth S. Cowles, letter to Emilie S. Smith, 1950, Archives, American Heritage Center.
16. Houston, comments.
17. Kanak Mani Dixit, "The Porter's Burden," citing studies by Nancy Malville, Ph.D., *Himal: South Asia* [formerly *Himal: Himalayan Magazine*] 8 (6) (November/December 1995): 35, 37.
18. Tilman, *Seven Mountain-Travel Books*, 874. On the way back, Bill Tilman wrote that the village of Bung, "a name which appeals to a music-hall mind...provoked another outburst...because its abundant well of good rakshi [rice wine] on which we were relying, had dried up." He dashed off another limerick, instructing the "hypercritical" that the "a" in "chang" was properly pronounced with a short "u."

> *Hope thirstily rested on Bung*
> *So richly redolent of rum;*
> *But when we got there*
> *The cupboard was bare*
> *Sapristi. No raksi. No chang.*

19. In 1949 a man named St. George and a companion made a journey from Kathmandu to the Solu Khumbu. This would have put them south of the Houston party's route, but exactly how much farther south is unknown, because there is no published account of the trip. Charles S. Houston, M.D., "Towards Everest, 1950," *Himalayan Journal* 17 (1951): 10.

20. Dawa Sherpa of the Himalaya Hotel in Lukla, conversation with the author, November 1993.

21. Houston, comments.

22. Sir Edmund Hillary, *Nothing Venture, Nothing Win* (New York: Coward, McCann & Googhegan, 1975), 258, 259. In 1964 a 1,000-foot airstrip at Lukla was constructed on 6 acres of land for a cost of $2,000. Although the airstrip has since been lengthened and refined, it still offers passengers exceptionally thrilling landings and takeoffs.

23. Houston, comments.

CHAPTER NINE

"Sceneries All Round"

When Charley and Bill arrived at the Tengboche gompa, they were "wet, cold and discouraged." Although Betsy later wrote that word of their coming had not preceded them, and that the lamas (or monks) were astonished to see their first white men, Charles Houston says this was not the case. The lamas had heard they were coming and "rushed out" to meet them. Although some were "surprised," others had been outside Nepal and seen white men before.[1] Thick Tibetan rugs for sitting on were offered, as were charcoal braziers.[2]

Several hours later, Andy, Oscar, and Betsy arrived, escorted by the head man from Namche, who made arrangements with one of the lamas for the three Westerners to stay on the second floor of an unused and somewhat dilapidated stone house, the first floor of which was a stable. One end of their quarters contained a kitchen with a cooking hearth where the Sherpas would sleep; the Houston party's quarters were in the larger room at the other end, which contained a fireplace. A hole in the ceiling served as a chimney. Benches, rugs, and braziers were brought in.

In this new home, Charley and Bill had lunch with the rest of their party. Then the two men left on their trip up the valley of the Khumbu, leaving the "stay-at-homes" somewhat depressed.[3] The snow continued. In the late afternoon the "faithful Gyaljen" made tea and the Sherpas laid out mattresses and sleeping bags. Hot toddies in front of a roaring fire cheered everyone. After a huge dinner, Betsy read a little *Kon-tiki*. It was still snowing when they went to sleep. "But the next morning," wrote Betsy, "something miraculous, unbelievable, absolutely astounding had happened."

Figure 9.1   The stone house on the grounds of the Tengboche gompa where members of the Houston party stayed in 1950. The building no longer exists. Photo, originally a 35 mm slide, by Betsy Cowles. (Courtesy American Heritage Center, University of Wyoming. Copyright restricted.)

We opened the shutters and looked out at the most beautiful scene in all the world. There are no words for it. There were the buildings of the lamasery [gompa], snow on the ground, black accents against it made by a myriad of yaks lying around. The sky was a heavenly deep blue. On every hand were mountains of the like I had never seen before or dreamed of. Incredibly lofty—so high up it made your neck hurt to look. Delicate, tapering, shining and with the fluted sides that one sees nowhere else but in the Himalayas. We gasped, saw stars, pinched ourselves, said to each other—when we could speak—Isn't it Terrific, incredible? The photographers went absolutely stark staring mad. I got, positively, cramp in the shutter finger. Nobody thought of breakfast and had to be reminded about lunch.

The lamas began calling on the Westerners. There were twenty-five at the gompa, half of them boys, a few only eight years old. Betsy discovered that a

Figure 9.2   The Tengboche gompa as Betsy photographed it in 1950. Note Mount Everest in the center background, peeking over its neighbors. Snow blows off the Nuptse-Lhotse Ridge to the right. The Royal Geographical Society selected this photo as its official 1951 Christmas card. (Courtesy American Heritage Center, University of Wyoming. Copyright restricted.)

lama was "a most lovely, happy, warm and intelligent human being." Thronging around their guests, the lamas brought rugs for them to sit on and presents of yak butter, yak cheese, yak milk, and oranges. A little girl whose family lived in the area adopted Betsy, bringing her frequent gifts of freshly cooked potatoes. Everyone in the vicinity of Tengboche was fascinated with the visitors. One day, in fact, callers arrived before Betsy, Oscar, or Andy had arisen.

The local residents liked to watch Betsy write in her diary, probably because they were fascinated by the "flowing quality of English writing." It was so different from Tibetan writing, "chopped into separate syllables," which Betsy thought resembled shorthand.

Figure 9.3   Oscar Houston entertains the young Tengboche lamas while enjoying quiet days at the gompa in November 1950. Photo, originally a 35mm slide, by Betsy Cowles. (Courtesy American Heritage Center, University of Wyoming. Copyright restricted.)

There are 12 people (ages vary from 8 to 50 years) within distances of from 20 feet to one foot of me, this very minute. Mostly they are young lamas but we also have one old lama with a sweet peaceful face. All are delightful and delighted. In between these sentences I am writing, I teach them ONE-TWO-THREE-FOUR (etc). Then point to my nose and say NOSE (and they all say "nose"). This has gone on for hours. We progress to SHOE, SOCK, TEETH, HAIR—they only need to hear once and they have it. If my train of thought seems jumpy, Dears, it's because I have just finished demonstrating to my audience how zippers work. Wish you could have heard the amazed chorus that went up when I un-zipped the little pocket at the back of my mountain coat and pulled the hood out! (Now they are trying on my glasses). A tiny creature has just brought us 4 small (hot) potatoes as a present. Delicious.

Andy chatted with the lamas and was amazed to discover that they had traveled to places like Lhasa, Darjeeling, Kalimpong, Calcutta, Kathmandu, and Delhi. Some had gone over 20,000-foot passes "carrying only what they wore on their backs."[4] One young lama told Betsy the names of all the mountains visible from Tengboche, which she wrote in her notebook and which he then transcribed in Tibetan. Charles Houston confirms that it was Andy Bakewell who worked out the precise direction of the peaks, assigning them degrees and elevations, which Betsy also copied into her diary.

The lamas were enthralled by the group's field glasses, and by Oscar's small pocket telescope. Sometimes the young ones were so taken with the novelty of their guests that they apparently forgot to perform a duty or were late for a service. When this happened an older lama would come to enforce discipline, always with "understanding and sweetness." Then the little boys would run off, their red robes swinging. "This is a very happy place," Betsy wrote. "The little Lamas are just like any young fry: they roughhouse, chase each other and go off into roars of giggles. In the services (we've been to several) there are two, especially, who carry on to beat all."

Shortly after Andy, Oscar, and Betsy arrived at Tengboche, they were invited to a religious service (*pujah*), held in the main room of the gompa. Gyaljen Senior instructed them on how to behave. Altogether they attended three or four pujahs, and, as Betsy later commented, they did not remind her in any way of Sunday morning at Grace Church. She and her companions sat on benches at the side of the large main room.

The ceremonial room is elaborately painted and carved—banners hang from ceiling & what look like lamp shades with silk flounces. 4 red columns in center of room, painted in primary colors; gives an elementary, rather naive effect until you come close and see the detail & the design which is lovely.

Lining two sides of the room were Tibetan books, each consisting of loose sheets of handmade paper printed from hand-cut wood blocks. The sixteen-year-old religious leader of Tengboche, correctly called the *Rimpoche* although Betsy never used this term, sat on a "bench-like throne" at one end of the room. Betsy noted that he looked "as if he'd like to give a friendly grin if only it were proper." (Although she referred to him as the "head lama" or "abbot," she should have reserved that term for the gompa's administrative head; this rotating position was held in 1950 by the first cousin of the Houston party's cook and sirdar, Gyaljen Senior.)

The old lamas sat on benches around the sides of the room, while the young ones sat on benches that formed two lines down the center. All wore

Figure 9.4   The sixteen-year-old Rimpoche at the Tengboche gompa in 1950. Photo by Betsy Cowles. (Courtesy American Heritage Center, University of Wyoming. Copyright restricted.)

dark red homespun robes with "notes of sulphur yellow," dull blue, and maroon, a combination of colors almost "too beautiful." As a lama later explained, a heavy fur-lined woolen layer was worn under the colorful outer robe. Occasionally during the pujah, Tibetan tea was served, "thick and buttery and…stewed for hours." A large pot was passed around the room to keep cups full. Betsy learned to take only small sips so she would not be "drowned."

    "Music plays an important part in the ceremonies," Betsy wrote. "The lamas chant, led by one of the patriarchs with a deep rich bass. Then, at intervals, like a kind of chorus, everyone picks up some kind of instrument and absolute bedlam bursts forth—the music is not melodic but rather rhythmical—and it is very loud." The musical instruments consisted of two great long horns, large seashells that Betsy erroneously called "conchs"; small horns;

cymbals; bells; a castanet-like sound-maker; and three large drums.[5] One lama let Betsy beat his drum.

After the chanting was over, Gyaljen motioned Betsy and Oscar to come forward. (Probably Andy was out exploring.) They did, bearing hastily assembled gifts that consisted of thirty rupees, a ballpoint pen, and Betsy's tan Swiss silk scarf decorated with chalets. Gyaljen led them up to the Rimpoche, whom Betsy thought was "a dear boy." Serving as translator, Gyaljen then expressed the visitors' thanks and appreciation. After presenting their gifts, Oscar and Betsy bowed and left the room.

Following the pujah, several lamas gave their visitors a tour of the gompa's upper floor. Betsy and Oscar viewed a collection of "wonderful painted masks," which were housed in cabinets; statues of Buddha made of brass, gold, silver, jade, or crystal; silver prayer wheels; vases used in ceremonies; incense burners, and painted silk scrolls (*tankas*).

The lamas also showed off their library, which was, as Charley later observed, "an unusually fine one," upon which a "staggering" amount of labor and time had been lavished. Each book was perhaps four inches by eighteen, "enclosed in painted boards…wrapped in rose-colored silk and labelled with colored silken tabs" that hung over the end. Every volume was slipped into its own cubicle in the wall. Consisting of 600 or so books, the library was "handsome" and had an atmosphere of "tender loving care." It was a rare and valuable collection.

A photo session was held in the afternoon. Preparations took half an hour due to "lots of decorating and primping."

Peacock fans, flower vases (with false flowers), banners, silver prayer boxes, tea cups, rugs laid on ground and banners hung up behind. I took lots of closeups of the old lamas and of Gyaljen's cousin…. Lots of laughter as I drag the lamas over and say "don't look like this" (making a solemn expression). Little groups on balcony duck when I point my camera up but finally I do succeed in snapping them. Then Head Lama [Rimpoche] arrives, gets a red peaked cap put on him and then we let loose; pictures from all directions, and distances. It is an incredible sight—little dog keeps appearing in the forefront (and before that, in church) but nobody seems to mind…we bow low, express our appreciation and depart. Completely bushed!

After lunch, Betsy and Oscar sat in the sun. Soon a crowd gathered and Betsy resumed teaching an anatomy lesson she had begun earlier. Her pupils progressed to "elbow" and "armpit." Oscar dozed. When afternoon clouds moved in, obscuring the sun, school ended. The Rimpoche's mother and another young woman brought a pot of Tibetan tea along with rice, milk, and potatoes. Betsy dabbed a little perfume behind the women's ears; they giggled and liked it, but refused to look at themselves in a mirror.

Neither Betsy nor Oscar stayed healthy at Tengboche. Soon after her arrival, Betsy felt a cold coming on and began taking penicillin. She "dosed" Oscar for diarrhea, an ailment that became especially miserable at night when he had to descend a ladder in the cold dark.[6] The 12,000-foot elevation made them both very sleepy. And the temperatures were low, going down to 18 degrees, in contrast to the 118 degrees F. they had experienced in the Arun River Valley.[7] By midafternoon, when the clouds began drifting up from the valley, Oscar and Betsy would retreat to their stone house. After closing the shutters and lighting a fire, they would sip hot drinks and chat quietly. Or they would fall asleep, sometimes to the roar of distant avalanches or to "bursts of weird music" emanating from the gompa.

Without fail, at 4:30 A.M., drums announced the beginning of the day at Tengboche, a custom Betsy objected to. "I must say," she said in a speech she gave many months later, "I came to feel that there must be something, really something, in Buddhism. Everyone seems so happy and at peace and fond of each other. But at 4:30 in the morning, it really seems as if, after all, the conventional U.S.A. time table [is] a lot better."[8]

Andy Bakewell was the only one of the three who remained completely healthy and energetic. Therefore, while Betsy and Oscar took it easy, he climbed the lower reaches of nearby peaks to take photographs of Everest's surroundings. The day after arriving in Tengboche, Andy and the Sherpa Pa Nerbu explored the ridge east and a little south of the gompa, which steepens into the summit of 22,000-foot Kantega. The early morning sun lit up several chortens along the route, infusing them with a "brilliant white light" that rested like a halo...resulting in an unearthly appearance." Andy later discovered that the effect was caused by hoar frost clinging to the branches that supported the small prayer flags on top.[9]

Soon Pa Nurbu and he were forced onto a steep rock slope made slippery with snow. They roped up, but could not stick their ice axes deeply enough into the ground for an effective belay. Moving very carefully, they finally achieved a small promontory that they estimated to be at 15,000 feet. While Pa Nerbu built a large cairn, Andy photographed the Himalaya in all directions; unfortunately, the great ridge of Nuptse and Lhotse continued to hide the bulk of Everest as effectively as it had lower down. They returned to Tengboche in time for late tea.

The next morning the same pair left in darkness, this time going north-west in the direction of Everest but avoiding the village of Pangboche, which was under quarantine because of an epidemic. Their goal was to climb as high as possible on the southern slope of Taweche. By noon they reached 17,000 feet or so. Everest, which we now know was some eight miles away, still remained mostly hidden by the Nuptse–Lhotse ridge. Once again Andy pho-tographed while Pa built a cairn, albeit a more modest one than the previous day's. At dusk they returned to Tengboche.

During one of their rest days, Gyaljen guided Oscar and Betsy down the steep north side of the Tengboche site to the Buddhist convent at Duboche, located in a wooded grove. Each of the seventeen nuns lived in her own small house, complete with a stone wall and stack of firewood. Betsy met three of them and found them to be "cheerful though shy." One rushed off to change into her best clothes. Another put her hand against Betsy's and giggled. The main court contained a big room with a large prayer wheel connected to a bell that rang after each revolution.

Seven years later, the anthropologist Kristoph Fürer von Heimendorf stated in his book, *The Sherpas of Nepal,* that there would have been more lamas at Tengboche if the Duboche nunnery (a source of wives) had not been so close. One of the conditions of being a lama there was—and is—celibacy. However, Charles Houston had a different slant on the subject, saying that he and his companions were told, "confidentially of course and with leers," that it was because of the nunnery's proximity that there were so many young lamas at Tengboche.[10]

On November 18, the twentieth day of their trip, Betsy asked the lamas if she might witness a dance and was told, quite politely, that perhaps her male companions might watch but that women were strictly forbidden. "I wasn't a bit cross about this," Betsy wrote, "having...a great sense of privilege for so long it seemed high time I should be excluded from something." After Oscar and Andy left the stone house to go up to the gompa, Betsy settled down to do darning. Soon, however, a lama came "flying down," saying that Mem Sahib should come up. So Betsy *was* permitted to watch the dance after all, and to photograph it. Oscar took movies. Four lamas wearing colorful robes and headdresses swayed gracefully and "with dignity." Betsy's two favorite little lamas—the ones who always "cut up" so at the services—blew the long horns.

On November 19, Charley and Bill returned from their reconnaissance, exhausted but gratified by what they had accomplished. After leaving Tengb-oche on the 14th, they had set up camp in a shepherd's stone hut on the

Figure 9.5   The practice dances for the 1950 Mani-rimdu festival at the Tengboche which, eventually, Betsy was permitted to watch. Photo, originally a 35mm slide, by Betsy Cowles. (Courtesy American Heritage Center, University of Wyoming. Copyright restricted.)

outskirts of Pangboche. The next morning, a bitterly cold one, they continued up the valley, reaching the confluence of two tributaries of the main river by morning.[11] (This was just below Dingboche, where the Imja Khola merges with the Dudh Kosi.) At first they were uncertain whether to turn right or left. Finally they realized that they were not looking at the true south face of Everest but rather at the "tremendous rock and ice buttress" of Lhotse and Nuptse and that, in fact, they could not even see Everest. Thus, they decided to use what little time they had left to take a look at Everest's west side. Turning left, they crossed a large level plain which they were sure was an old lake bed; it abounded in "snipe-like birds" eating shrubs and plants. At noon Bill and Charley set up camp in an area containing a few stone walls and chest-high bushes and junipers in the vicinity of what is called Pheriche today.

After lunch the pair climbed high enough to gain splendid views of Chamlang, Makalu, and Ama Dablam, which they called "Amdanglungma." However, they were disappointed at their inability to climb high enough to examine the south face of Lhotse. That night they built a huge bonfire and Bill Tilman talked for hours.

The next day Charley and Bill resumed their reconnaissance and made a right-angle turn toward the north. Their original plan had been to camp as high as possible in the valley of the Khumbu Glacier in order to inspect its head and to take a look at the West Cwm (valley) directly beneath Everest's south face. But the going was too slow and they had to retreat "gloomily" in the dark to their windy, cold camp.

Starting out early the next morning, they found a good route across the glacier and climbed to well over 18,000 feet on what they thought was Pumori but which was, in fact, Kala Patar.[12] (Today it is a popular trekking destination because it offers such a fine view of Everest.) Charles Houston later wrote his and Bill Tilman's impressions:

Well below and almost due east the upper Khumbu glacier curved tortuously around the rocky "corner" we had tried to turn on the day before, falling in fantastic pinnacles to the lower glacier. This was the mouth of the West Cwm, a narrow ice-chocked corridor less than 1,000 yards wide, through which is crowded all of the snow and ice which falls from the Lhotse-Everest saddle (the South Col). From our vantage point we could see no obvious route up this ice-fall. Not only was the glacier badly broken and crevasse-ed, but it also appeared to be swept from side to side by falls of ice and rocks from above. We both believed that the ice-fall could be forced, but it did not appear to offer a very attractive route of access to the upper West Cwm, a view of which was still denied us by intervening ridges.

By then they could see the two "steps" on the northeast ridge in silhouette and the Yellow Band as well as the Great Couloir, both features named by the British on their Everest attempts from the Tibetan side. They were surprised at the lack of snow on the summit, a sign of terrible winds. Charles Houston and Bill Tilman were the first Westerners to set foot on the Khumbu Glacier. (The English mountaineers George Herbert Leigh Mallory and Guy Henry Bullock were the first Westerners to actually *see* this glacier, which they viewed from the Tibetan side of Everest in 1921.)

As Charles and Bill sat in the shelter of huge sun-warmed boulders, they speculated on the possibilities and impossibilities of climbing Everest from this side; Bill was more pessimistic about the route's feasibility than Charley was.[13] They knew that an attempt on Everest in November, as opposed to one in the spring months, would mean fewer hours of daylight and lower temperatures. However, Charles concluded that "all in all, the perfection of the weather and the freedom of the high rocks from snow should offset the cold and shorter days, and if the snow is adequately consolidated lower down, the post-monsoon season would appear to me to be the best season for an attempt on the mountain."

Reluctantly, the men left their spot and climbed down. They made their way along the Khumbu Glacier's western moraine, noting that it was full of large, flat meadows and streams that would make it suitable for a base camp from which to attempt Everest. The scarcity of firewood would be a problem, though. As had been pre-arranged, their Sherpas met them at camp and soon made a roaring fire. In the morning the Sherpas warmed up the handles of the sahibs' ice axes.

Bill shaved, such an unexpected gesture that Charley teased him about doing it because of Betsy. In response, Bill "growled."[14]

Dawn found Sarki very ill, probably due to a recurrence of malaria. He was given medicine and carried, but after a mile or two he recovered enough to walk on his own. In late afternoon the party arrived at Tengboche.[15] Andy, Oscar, and Betsy joyously welcomed them; after a "fine reunion dinner" the lamas dropped in, one by one, to pay their respects. The porters also appeared, wearing warm clothes although many were still barefoot.

The following morning, the Rimpoche received Betsy and her friends. "We were greatly impressed by the appearance and bearing of this young lama, though he spoke only a few words to us," Charles later wrote. The five Westerners were escorted to the front of the Rimpoche's dais. He gestured, whispered prayers, and hung a small charm box around the neck of each. Then he draped ceremonial scarves (*katas*) around their necks and handed each one a small packet of ceremonial food to ensure their safe return. They were later informed that each charm box contained the ashes of a dead lama. Though the reception was brief, Betsy and her friends found it impressive. Charles said it confirmed their respect for the religion of their host.

At Tengboche, Charley held sick call, just as he had almost daily on the trek. As he puts it, "I saw the lame, the halt and the blind every day on the way in and out."[16] Mostly he dispensed good will. However, once Charley handed out a pill to the jemadar who complained about "pouring rice" all night—his way of saying he had had a headache. It worked. The next day Gyaljen Junior requested medicine for his cold; Charley gave him pills. Dicky requested a cure for her sore knee; Charley gave her sunburn cream.

Figure 9.6 The Houston party of 1950 posing for a photograph in front of the Tengboche gompa, most wearing *katas* and lockets containing the ashes of a dead lama. *Left to right:* Anderson Bakewell, Oscar Houston, Betsy Cowles, H. W. Tilman, Charles Houston, M.D. (Courtesy American Heritage Center, University of Wyoming. Copyright restricted.)

The Houston party presented gifts to the lamas (everything they could spare) and candy to the children living in the village at the foot of the hill. Then, with sadness, they turned their backs on the gompa and began retracing their steps down the hill. For a while the little girl who had brought Betsy potatoes walked beside her down the hill, holding her hand. Betsy gave her a balloon—"My little child, whom I love." The day was warm. Betsy wrote in her diary that the walk from Tengboche was the "loveliest" of her life.

Lunching on a sunny rock, they gazed at Taweche and Tramsurku, which they called "Tamusurmu." Betsy thought that all the mountains surrounding Everest were "infinitely more beautiful and impressive" and that the only thing Everest had going for it was height. And then, perhaps realizing how ungracious this sounded, she added, "Not that it isn't a thrill to be so near the highest mountain in the world," and said she liked to watch it as the sun went down because the last rays of the day shone on Everest long after all the other towering peaks lay in darkness. Still, she regarded Everest as a "great hulking form," whereas she called Ama Dablam "a wedge-shaped beauty…a Matterhorn raised to the nth power." Her favorite mountain was Tamusurmu, "a Milan Cathedral in mountain form. Not one summit but four or five, and all connected by the most delicate and graceful, shining, airy and fluted snow ridges."

After lunch, Betsy mostly walked by herself. She picked gentians, probably the blue and white tubular ones, *Gentian prolata*, and kept looking back up, trying to see Tengboche.[17] Later she wrote that it was "the most beautiful place in all the world." Almost certainly Betsy realized that she would never see it again.

As they neared Namche, the Houston party heard the tinkle of bells, ponies sent to meet them. Betsy rode one for a bit, then got off to take pictures. After the group arrived in town, friendly mobs swarmed to get a look, but the fishbowl life did not seem to disturb Betsy as much as it had before. The party wrote messages for couriers to take out ahead. Charley gave his Dobbs hat, as Betsy called it, to the head man of Namche, who promptly put it on in place of his own fur-trimmed Tibetan hat. Betsy thought it transformed him so completely that if he had cut his hair and worn a new suit of clothes he could have walked down the main street of Colorado Springs without attracting any second glances.

That night the porters and Sherpas celebrated late in a last fling before the long walk out. The next morning, November 21, the party breakfasted on livers from a sheep the cook had purchased in Namche. "[The] carcass is coming along with us," Betsy wrote, "looking vast and bloody and simply wild." By now all the porters had rejoined the group, some so bundled up in warm clothes that they were hardly recognizable. Betsy's pony boy was still barefoot. The head man, wearing his new hat, came to say goodbye. He brought his family with him, the women showing off their finest jewelry. Then, taking Charley's hand and placing it on his own head, he said, "My house…your house." The head man brought Betsy a bottle of rakshi with flowers fixed in the cork.

Betsy and Oscar were first on the trail. "O what a beautiful day," Betsy wrote her diary. At lunch she took off her long red underwear, washed, and put on clean clothes. Feeling "marvelous," she walked with the Houstons. They

Figure 9.7   The head man of Namche Bazar. Photo by Betsy Cowles. (Courtesy American Heritage Center, University of Wyoming. Copyright restricted.)

made camp early and poured the head man's rakshi into their tea. "Feel warmed and cheered," Betsy wrote in her diary. "Think that they like me and that I've been useful." A girl tied Betsy up in her zipper hood, salaamed three times, and gave her an orange. Another girl held Betsy's hand, saw that it was cold, and put it inside her coat to warm it. Tibetan bowls, probably brass, were for sale. Oscar, an excellent bargainer, purchased seven. Bill Tilman bought one for Betsy.

Betsy decided that the local people on the trail seemed friendlier than they had on the way in. Certainly the members of the Houston party were more talkative, more relaxed on the trip out. Campfires were "mirthful" partly because Bill seemed to have loosened up.[18] One afternoon, as they walked through a "druid" forest of rhododendron trees hung with moss, Bill picked wild raspberries and gave some to Betsy. That night he described his fifteen years in Kenya and told stories about mountain climbing in Persia.

By now everyone was extremely fit. Betsy wrote: "Our muscles are terrific. Think I never before have had the power to walk so strongly." They could now go four or five hours without stopping "even when a long steep ascent" was involved, as it inevitably was. Still, Betsy thought that everyone was suffering from a sense of anticlimax. And "Tilman is grumpy so I leave him alone."

After they crossed the Salpa La and ate lunch, Betsy climbed back up, by herself, to say goodbye to the snowy Numbur and to the whole range of mountains. Now she and her companions were leaving the Sherpas' country and would soon be in the tropics.

Later Betsy wrote that it would be hard to imagine a "finer and more vigorous people" than the Sherpas. She found them to be "gay and endearing," fun-loving, thoughtful, and hard-working, and so "wonderfully imitative" that she was sure they could learn English in a week. They had a knack for doing what needed doing, cheerfully. Immediately after the party decided on a campsite, the Sherpas would "whip up the tents, blow up the air mattresses, lay out the sleeping bag and all your gear, give you hot water to wash in and announce tea." When there was no work to do, the Sherpas "cut up like kids after school." They wrestled, climbed trees, made up contests, and played jokes on each another. Charley improvised a modern nursery rhyme, "Hi Diddly Dee—A Sherpa's life for me!" Betsy made a resolve to be as "Sherpish as possible in the future."

Although the Houston party singled out the Sherpas as being delightful, in fact they commented on the warmth and charm of all the people they encountered. Each member of the expedition, Westerner and Nepalese alike, had taken at least one turn on the wooden Ferris-wheel swings "always placed for maximum view" by the trail. For most of the year, only the supports stood there. However, during the festival of Tihaar, wooden seats were added, simple, ingenious contraptions. (Today they are much less common because the Nepalese government strictly regulates the cutting of wood, and because the cost of lumber has soared.[19])

Figure 9.8   Sherpas delighted in taking a whirl on the Ferris-wheel-like swings installed for the annual festival of Tihaar, in 1950. Photo, originally a 35mm slide, by Betsy Cowles. (Courtesy American Heritage Center, University of Wyoming. Copyright restricted.)

Oscar commented that the Nepalese were the only people he had ever run into who appreciated a view, for they almost always put their villages and trail resting places in sites with a special vantage point. At the start of the trip, Bill Tilman received a letter that illustrated this. It was from the same Sherpa woman, Ang Yang Tsen, whose husband, Ang Tharkay, had greatly assisted Andy in selecting the Houston party's route. Bill described his friend Ang Tharkay as the "head of all the Sherpas in Darjeeling."

> *Dingbuzy [Dingboche] has nothing but sceneries and sceneries all round and it is told that the beauty and grandeur are simply marvelous and enchanting.... I wish I were a man and not a woman to accompany you to these darling places to see with my own eyes those hills where we often played a childish hide and seek game with much frolics and those snow-capped hills and yonder mountains where our eyes never got tired of looking at the majestic beauty.... When you reach those places, my dear Sir, do please remember us and think in your mind that your Ang Tharkay and his beloved wife are actually with you to show all that they possibly could do in their power to be as much helpful as they would be.[20]*

In 1950, as now, the Nepalese planted flowers in their yards. They made chains of marigolds and strung them along mani walls, bridges, windows, and doors, even haystacks. Porters put freshly picked blossoms on their carrying baskets. On the day of Tihaar that honors bovines, Nepalese entwined marigolds in the horns of yaks, cows, and zoes (a cross between a yak and a cow). Sometimes a Sherpa in the Houston party would pick two flowers, one for himself and one for Betsy.

On November 28, the party returned to the house of the old man who had been so welcoming to them on November 5. "All is ready for us," Betsy wrote, "little gray leaf plates hold sugar, dahl, rice (token gifts) and there are two big baskets of oranges of which we eat tons—they are peeled and split for us; everyone so sweet and attentive. Earnest eyes fixed on us. (O has a chair brought for him—mat and rugs for us). We give presents of a plastic flask, Mary Chess compact(!) balloon, etc." They went on to the village and were met with gifts of flowers, bananas, and more oranges.

The next day, November 29, after the Houston party had forded a side stream south of Tumlingtar, they noticed a cigarette wrapper with English printing on it, and Charley spied a box from a kind of film different from that which anyone in their group had been using. An Englishman had been through four days earlier, they were informed. Was it Thomas?

Figure 9.9   Betsy arranging flowers for the Houston party's Thanksgiving feast on the way out from their historic visit to the Khumbu in 1950. Photo by Anderson Bakewell. (Courtesy American Heritage Center, University of Wyoming. Copyright restricted.)

On the thirty-second day of their trek, November 30, the Houston party celebrated Thanksgiving. Although it was hot, they strode vigorously along the Arun River, finally setting up a grassy green camp by the Manga Khola (stream). Everyone was in high spirits. "Even HWT was nice," Betsy said. She and he had a conversation in which they agreed that Americans were too gullible and that he was too suspicious.

Thanksgiving dinner began with hot rakshi toddies served in little silver cups provided by Andy. Then the five celebrants toasted the king, President Harry S Truman, themselves, and so on. Decorations consisted of lacy white flowers picked by Oscar and a centerpiece of two ears of miniature corn swiped from a field by a Namche Bazar man accompanying the party. Betsy set out a cloth of mosquito netting, laying it on a wooden packing box raised up on rocks so that it really was like a table. Everyone sat on "high rock seats." Napkins were Kleenex tissues. Some Tibetan brass bowls held candles; others served as dishes for nuts and after-dinner mints. Andy said a blessing. Then the party devoured a feast of chicken, ham, rice, chocolate mint pudding, and some of Bill's "foot" cake.

On December 1, the expedition climbed up from the Arun River valley to the Pairibas Pass, taking four hours to gain approximately 5,000 feet. December 2 was their penultimate day, "to which HWT replied, 'Thank God.' (Our being late for breakfast aroused all this)," Betsy wrote in her diary. "He is often dour and cross and says biting things—but has been an essential on the trip I think."

During their trek, the Houston party had been relatively healthy and free from injuries. To be sure, Betsy had removed two wood ticks that she picked up somewhere north of Bung, and Bill discovered lice during a "flea and louse hunt," which the Sherpas had found very amusing.[21] (Betsy gleefully reported that she had had none.) But these incidents were merely annoying. Of greater medical significance were three trends that Charley said he had found surprising: that each member of the party had picked up a cough, had felt the altitude so much, and had slept badly above 8,500 feet.

The Houston party's route out was slightly different from the one they had taken in. On the advice of the jemedar, who had had word of political troubles in Nepal, they avoided Dhankuta, and instead turned straight south. They then crossed the Tamur River on a little car attached to an overhead cable, while the Sherpas crossed on a large boat that ran on a track in the river directly beneath the cable. Two policemen in red fezes met them, sent by the governor of Dhankuta after he realized that the Houston party would require official escorts out. During their trek a revolution had taken place in Nepal! (As the Houston party found out later, King Tribhuvan and his family had left Nepal and taken refuge in India, welcomed by Prime Minister Jawaharlal Nehru himself.[22])

Betsy and her companions walked on a path built into the side of the gorge until they came to the site of a proposed dam, not yet approved, which was to be 1,000 feet high. If built, the dam would back up the Arun, the Tamur, and the Sapt Rivers to provide power for India. The site was torn up with test tunnels and two dredges digging down into the river bed; huge compressors and gas drums lay by the path. At the dam headquarters in Barakshetra, the staff invited the Houston party to have tea in the guest house. They sipped tea while sitting in real chairs and munched "good things" under the glare of electric lights.

Then, while four members of the party walked through orchid forests, Charley Houston borrowed Betsy's air mattress and floated down the Sapt Kosi all the way to Chatra. From there Bill telephoned Jogbani to arrange for someone to pick them up and found that it would be Thomas. Betsy then went rafting with Charley, holding on to his feet.

On the final day, number 36, before anyone else arose, the Dhankuta boys left. At 6 the Three Musketeers took off. The rest of the day dragged on as the party waited for the vehicles to arrive. Donu, the Sherpa, climbed a tall dead tree "just like a monkey" and placed a large skull in its highest branch, for a target. He and his friend threw rocks at it. Charley and Bill shot rapids. It grew so late that the Houston party began to worry. Finally Thomas showed up with the truck. "He is so helpful," Betsy wrote in her diary, an opinion she no doubt later revised.[23]

After spending the night in Jogbani, they hopped the train to Lucknow and then another to Delhi, where they were besieged by reporters, including one from the *New York Times*. "We...find ourselves very famous," Betsy commented.

Notes

1. Charles S. Houston, M.D., comments on the manuscript, December 1995.
2. Charles S. Houston, M.D., "Towards Everest, 1950," *Himalayan Journal* 17 (1951): 12.
3. In his comments on the manuscript, Charles S. Houston recollects that he and Bill stayed the night in Tengboche, leaving the next morning. Betsy states that the pair left shortly after lunch on the day of their arrival. Bill Tilman corroborates this on page 879 of *The Seven Mountain-Travel Books* (London: Diadem Books Ltd./Seattle: The Mountaineers, 1983).
4. Anderson Bakewell, S.J., copy of letter to John B. Janssens, S.J., 1951, and photo album of 1950 trek in Nepal, collection of Anderson Bakewell, S.J.
5. From photographs taken in 1993, Dr. Shi-Kuei Wu, Professor of Natural History and Curator of Zoology at the University of Colorado Museum in Boulder, has identified the seashells as Australian trumpets. They belong to the family Melongenidae; their scientific name is *Syrinx aruanus* Linnaeus, formerly called *Fusus proboscidiferus* Lamarck. Their distribution is limited to Queensland, North Australia, and to islands in the Arafura Sea. Presumably, these are the same seashells, or at least the same species, that Betsy noted in 1950.
6. Although Betsy never specified what Oscar's ailment was, Charles S. Houston did in his comments on the manuscript, December 1995.
7. Elizabeth S. Cowles, "North to Everest," *Vassar Alumnae Magazine*, n.d., 7, Archives, American Heritage Center.
8. Elizabeth S. Cowles, text for a slide talk, "North to Everest," given in Colorado Springs, Denver, Chicago, New York, Boston, Philadelphia, Pittsburgh, London, and other places in the 1950s, Archives, American Heritage Center.
9. Anderson Bakewell, S.J., "Southern Approach to Mount Everest," manuscript for an article in *Der Bergsteiger* (ca. 1951), Archives, American Heritage Center.
10. Houston, comments.
11. Kosi means river, but Betsy Cowles, Charles Houston, H. W. Tilman, and others used it as though it were the name of a river, as in Kosi River.
12. Houston, comments.
13. *Ibid.*
14. Anderson Bakewell, S.J., letter to the author, September 12, 1994.
15. H. W. Tilman's account of the incident involving Sarki, in *Nepal Himalaya* as it appears in *The Seven Mountain-Travel Books* (London: Diadem Books Ltd./Seattle:

The Mountaineers, 1983), 884, differs somewhat from Charles Houston's account in his article, "Towards Everest, 1950."

16. Houston, comments.

17. Identification made from a captioned photograph in the Sherpa Museum at Namche Bazar.

18. Houston, comments. "Yes, the march out was more pleasant and we were indeed relaxed. Tilman had been in rare form for many days already."

19. Jangbu Sherpa, sirdar for Sagarmatha Trekking Company, conversation with the author, November 1993.

20. Elizabeth S. Cowles, Nepal diary, November 7, 1950, quoting a letter sent to H. W. Tilman dated October 20, 1950, from Darjeeling, Archives, American Heritage Center.

21. Tilman, *Seven Mountain-Travel Books*, 885. Bill said his lice were due to the fact that a porter, Donu, insisted on carrying some of his spare clothes in Bill's rucksack until Bill "broke him of the habit."

22. On November 6, while Betsy and her companions were walking up to the village of Phedi in the midst of a rice harvest, the king and his three sons, driving their own cars and accompanied by their wives and the five-year-old heir apparent, Prince Biendra, left the royal palace. As they came abreast of the entrance to the Indian embassy, they suddenly swung through the gates, "to the shock and bewilderment of the Rana government's guards posted outside." Protocol was muddy about what to do when a reigning monarch sought asylum in a foreign embassy in his own country. Initially the Rana government was inclined to force the Indian embassy to surrender the king and his family. However, recognizing that this would incur the wrath of India, it shut down the airport and attempted to persuade the king to release the eldest son of the Crown Prince. King Tribhuvan refused. Thus, at 2:45 P.M. on November 7, the Rana government enthroned the king's second-oldest grandson, four-year-old Prince Gyanendra, who along with four younger siblings, had been left behind at the royal palace. Finally, on November 11, the Rana government permitted King Tribhuvan and his family to fly from Kathmandu to India, where the Prime Minister himself, Jawaharlal Nehru, received them when they landed at the Palan airport. Prolonged discussions between Nepal and India then ensued, the latter "playing the role of midwife in delivering democracy to Nepal," while England and the United States threw in their opinions of what to do next. Finally, King Tribhuvan and his family returned to Kathmandu on February 15, 1951. From Rishikesh Shaha, *Modern Nepal: A Political History 1769–1955*, 2 vols. (Riverdale, Md.: Riverdale, 1990), 2: 208, 238.

23. Houston, comments. The Houston party later found out that Frank Thomas had followed them nearly to the Salpa La before he turned back. He rode the train back with them to Delhi, grilling them intensively. Finally Oscar said they would not answer any more questions. Thomas revealed nothing about himself. Houston:

> *Our embassy hinted many things about Thomas; I confronted him and saw his passport, finally. Years later he was jailed in India for crossing the Inner Line and I was asked to intervene. A complicated tale. Whether he or any one knew that part of my task, had I gone with Lowell Thomas, was to treat a clandestine radio operator in Tibet, is unknown.*

CHAPTER TEN

"America's Foremost Woman Mountaineer"

Time magazine reported on the Houston party's trip to Nepal: "Mrs. E. S. Cowles of Colorado Springs, the only woman along, was welcomed with the rest and even allowed to witness impressive Lamaistic rituals—a very unusual honor for a woman, but Mrs. Cowles is one of the world's leading alpinists. Perhaps the teen-aged Buddha was too much impressed with her to treat her as a female."[1]

Betsy sorted her Nepal slides; typed out a talk based on her diary and round-robin letters; sent her speech-making costume, a sari, to the cleaners; and began giving illustrated lectures around the country.[2] Tickets for "North to Everest," presented at the Colorado Springs Fine Arts Center, sold so fast that 200 people were put on a waiting list. Betsy gave a second show that also sold out. A thousand people attended her next "North to Everest" talk, at Phipps Auditorium in Denver. Sponsored by the Colorado Mountain Club and promoted by the western section of the American Alpine Club, it raised money to help publish the first edition of Bob Ormes's book, *Guide to the Colorado Mountains*, a book Betsy had strongly supported.

In November 1951, Betsy presented yet a third well-attended slide show in Colorado Springs, this one titled "Caravan to Katmandu." Then she went east. During the next two weeks, she spoke at the Philadelphia Cricket Club, the Shipley School for Girls in Bryn Mawr, the American Alpine Club's annual meeting in Boston, and the Anglers Club in London. In 1952 she lectured about Mount Everest at a meeting of the Chicago Mountaineering Club; in 1953, she would talk was at the Naturalists Club of the Carnegie Museum in Pittsburgh.

In her talks (and in her articles as well), Betsy often quoted from books and conversations that appealed to her. Often she drew from such notables as Shakespeare, Robert Frost, and Dorothy Parker. But she also quoted the authors of mountaineering books and her own friends, such as Bob Ormes.[3]

Audiences loved her, and they were hungry to hear about Nepal. "*The Dinner* was followed by a splendid program," one listener wrote. "Betsy Cowles was tops." A Philadelphia reporter called her "one of the foremost climbers of her sex" and wrote that "Mrs. Cowles doesn't have to answer the 'Why Climb' question. The answer is in her enthusiasm, her experiences and her photographs." A British angler wrote that "Mrs. Cowles…proved to be a fascinating speaker and a sparkling personality…. She practically hypnotized the audience." It was, he said, the "best and liveliest Ladies Night" in the club's history. Laura Gilpin, well-known photographer of the Southwest, described Betsy's slides as "superb," and a reporter for the *Santa Fe New Mexican* declared that Mrs. Cowles's illustrated lecture was as good as one given by Thor Heyerdahl two years earlier.[4]

Betsy and her trip to Nepal made good copy. Some reporters, completely ignorant of mountaineering, claimed that Betsy had "scaled the Himalayas," or that she had been a member of an expedition "up the south face of Everest," or that she had climbed most of the world's major mountains other than Everest. According to one newspaper, Betsy was "very feminine in spite of her exploits."[5] The Pittsburgh *Post-Gazette* called Betsy a "Grandmother Mountain Climber" and described her speech as "engaging" and "peppered with such feminine words as 'darling,' 'sweet,' and 'spic and span.'" Betsy was "pert, slender and almost saucy…. Youth is one thing she seems to exude. People spot her as 30 and she won't clear up the birth date beyond saying she graduated from Vassar in 1923 and has a year old granddaughter."[6]

Britain's Royal Geographical Society selected Betsy's black-and-white photograph of the Tengboche gompa to appear on its official 1951 Christmas card for members. Her black-and-white photographs of the 1950 trek were exhibited at the Colorado Springs Fine Arts Center. *Look* magazine used some of her photos for an article about Nepal written by Charles Houston.[7] *American Magazine* featured Betsy in an article about "America's Interesting People."[8]

In the fall of 1952, when Betsy had been away from Colorado Springs for more than four months (climbing in Switzerland for part of the time), she wrote to a friend from New York City:

I leave Friday for the West and shall have big feelings when again I see my mountains. They always look a little squat and unimpressive after the Alps but I love them dearly and have always felt it was mutual. There will be so many places in the hills to re-visit; I always feel they wonder about me when I'm away and are happy to have me back.

The house on Culebra Avenue had been sold, so Betsy first stayed with Uncle Phil and then moved into a little house, which she rented, at 12 Pourtales Place, near the Broadmoor Hotel. She began looking for a new residence and finally found one shortly before Thanksgiving of 1952. High above the bustle of town, 1317 Hermosa Way was "the right size," had a view of the mountains, a "nice" kitchen, and room for a piano. "It will be a home for me, which I have needed." Several months later Betsy wrote, "I love my house so. It has a profound effect on me; something very comforting and enfolding; I feel more peaceful and quiet in my spirit than for years."

She hemmed curtains, planted flowers and trees, weeded, and built a stone wall—"No Glue to stick it, just gravity and good-will!" Betsy hung her many photographs and paintings on walls so there would be "mountains everywhere you look, not only out of the windows."[9] She took up cooking and baking again, apparently after a long hiatus. "[M]y son Dick's birthday tomorrow; need to bake a cake, or what wd [would] you think of candles stuck in a nice homemade APPLE PIE??" She also delighted in "Grandbaby Day," which occurred weekly when little Steffie (Stephanie, Richard's daughter) came to visit. Betsy called her small granddaughter "a most beguiling little creature around whom the whole world revolves (she sees this plainly!) Small secret smiley look of complete pleasure and her place in it."

Betsy and Emilie became ever closer, frequently visiting each other in their respective homes and taking driving trips across the country to check up on their father in Santa Barbara.[10] "I think SISTERS ARE WONDERFUL," Betsy once wrote a friend. Often Betsy and the Macauley Smiths vacationed together, in Wyoming or the Southwest or Betsy's beloved Switzerland. Sometimes they were joined by the Strong sisters' first cousin Richard Sewall and his wife Lil. Although, as Betsy tactfully put it, "Emmy wasn't destined to be God's Gift to alpinism," Emilie did make an effort to enjoy trails and "rough walking" so she could accompany her mountain-climbing husband, Mac, and Betsy into such rugged areas as the Wind Rivers of Wyoming. Her sister became, in Betsy's words, "the best camp cook north of the Mason-Dixon line. Lucky the climbers that start upwards fortified by Emmy's marvelous menus!"[11]

Betsy was now Colorado's unofficial ambassador of mountaineering. When Maurice Herzog visited Denver in March 1953, to promote his book about the 1950 ascent of the first 8,000-meter peak ever climbed, Annapurna, Betsy invited him to visit at her home in Colorado Springs. An article and photograph of the pair appeared in the local newspaper. Mr. Herzog was quoted as saying, "I am glad to have had the opportunity to come here and call on Mrs. Cowles. She is an accomplished mountain climber and is widely known for what she has done."[12] Betsy reveled in the experience.

> We sat out on the terrace, he in a deck chair, and talked of mts., and of Nepal—then a fine lunch (good Rhine wine) and up to Denver.... Hundreds turned away from his lecture and no one there but was deeply moved at what he told and what he was. I introduced him (very short) and when he came out on the stage he said, "Restez ici" and then made the sweetest little response about our being "fellow Nepalese."[13]

In early 1954, the year after Mount Everest was first climbed, members of the successful expedition toured the United States. The "NY people running the Everest lecture" wired Betsy to sit on the stage at Carnegie Hall, attending the festivities of the first Everest show in America. Uncle Phil paid her way to New York, saying he had always wanted to get Betsy on the stage at Carnegie but it was so difficult to do because she couldn't play anything well.

In March, the Everest climbers stopped in Denver. Three of the group, George Lowe, Dr. Charles Evans, and James Morris, accepted an invitation from Betsy to visit her in Colorado Springs, relaxing and taking a little hike up Cheyenne Canyon. (Sir Edmund Hillary, one of those to make the first ascent, was tied up in Denver for the day.) An article and photograph of Betsy and the trio of expedition members appeared in the local paper.[14] Betsy wrote a friend that their visit was a "wonderful experience," and called them "marvelous men, intelligent, perceptive, un-egotistical;...and they LOVED Colorado."[15]

Betsy needed people. And yet sometimes she felt there was "too much going on and too many people here and too much to do. My life has accustomed me to time alone, and I have grown to need solitude. Head starts buzzing after a while and I begin to see stars." One January 1, she wrote, "I did

Figure 10.1   Betsy Cowles in her home on Hermosa Way in Colorado Springs, circa 1956. Note the wall of mountain photographs and paintings. Artist-mountaineer Belmore Browne painted the picture of Tengboche (middle picture, top row). (Courtesy Emilie S. Smith.)

not 'see the New Year in' gay fashion—just had a quiet evening here and went to bed early. Much better!"

Betsy often sought peace and quiet in the hills behind her house. Her personal letters abound in references to what she saw on these hikes—deer, an eagle dozing on a rock, and once a mountain lion who "high-tailed it" away from her. Many of Betsy's letters attest to the restorative powers of her walks: "I am TERRIBLY busy, running the drive for our symphony orchestra this fall. I snatch little walks early in the morning, only time I have. It helps so."[16]

In January 1955, Betsy was elected to a three-year term as president of the Colorado Springs Fine Arts Center Board of Trustees. (Bob Cowles had also served on the board and had long supported the institution with contributions.) Betsy, knowing she had taken on a lot, wrote a friend, "I think I shall feel I've done a little to pay the dear town and country and mts back for all they do for ME."[17] After taking office, Betsy commented that "in mountaineering one always refers to the 'team,'" and that she thought of the trustees and the staff as a team. In a newspaper interview, Betsy stated that her goals were to enlarge the center's scope and to get the building in order. The reporter wrote, "If her accomplishments in this field compare with those in others like mountaineering, lecturing, photography (and she can cook too!), she will achieve them."[18]

Betsy owned works by Boardman Robinson, Adolph Dehn, and Edgar Britton, all nationally established artists who were associated with the Broadmoor Art Academy, later to become the Colorado Springs Fine Arts Center. She had visited many of the world's great art museums because they were located in cities that were "pathways to mountains."

A staunch booster for Colorado College and a long-time member of the Woman's Educational Society, Betsy gave a speech to raise money for the college building fund and once addressed female students who were about to graduate. Although the latter speech rambled, it was one of Betsy's most personal and summed up her philosophy on life.[19] She started out by confessing that when she was in front of a "trapped" audience, she found it almost impossible to talk about anything but mountains. Then she drew parallels between high mountains and living, which had occurred to her over the years as she had "plodded up a steep snow slope or followed a splendid leader along a beautiful rock ridge." The "love of the hills and sense of their value and helpfulness" are what give meaning to the mountaineering experience. Of course, one could find "grim adventures," especially in the "big leagues of Himalayan exploration." Mountain climbing was more fun in the "bush leagues" where she played.

But no matter what the "bracket," getting up a mountain asked a lot of one. And it was "pretty marvelous" to make an all-out effort, to give all you had. "The 100%ism of mountaineering is a revelation of directness and simplicity," Betsy said, leaving one without any energy "to waste on useless qualms, on self-consciousness, personal vanity or the wandering attention that so often muddies the waters of our daily life. Nothing left over to jangle or feel restless, no unused residue, just that fine sense of having employed mind and muscles to the utmost." When it was possible to apply the "give it all you've got" quality of a hard climb to everyday life, the results could be "absolutely astonishing."

Betsy believed it was a mistake to think that people gave their best performances when they were absolutely sure of themselves. She felt that the best jobs, in both life and mountains, were done "by people with tremendous misgivings about themselves." Betsy spoke of the benefits of exercise, not just to "hold on to…muscles…and figures," but also for respite and revitalizing.

> *I should find it hard to put into words to you tonight what it has meant to me over the years to slip off on a mountain path for an hour when I needed to or how often I've worked out the tangles and problems of life as I plodded along through the quiet of a high pine forest.*

It was "fearfully important in life," she said, to have a pursuit in which you could completely lose yourself.

Although Betsy's days of hard climbing were now over, her persona increasingly seemed to be fused to her mountain adventures. Privately, at least, Betsy appeared to relish the public's description of her as "America's foremost woman mountaineer." According to one acquaintance, Betsy could be quite vindictive in guarding what she regarded as "her" turf, that is, mountain climbing.[20]

After Betsy and Bob Cowles were divorced in 1938, Betsy became involved with a succession of men, one of whom, at least, was less than half her age. As her sister put it, "One of Betsy's charms was that she was frequently, though never lightly, in love." Dorothy Swartz expressed it differently, saying that an attractive and vivacious woman like Betsy, "involved in a male-dominated sport where she was in contact with exciting and athletic men, day after day in isolated mountain areas, couldn't help but become very close to many of these men."[21] A lot of Betsy's men were mountain climbers.

She found the ending of one serious relationship especially devastating, because she felt that a major factor in its demise had been her inability to bear children. "You'd think he came from a family of whooping cranes," she commented to Emilie.[22]

An affectionate and prolific correspondence between Betsy and Miecio (Miezyslaw) Horszowski offers a portrait of her that would otherwise be lost. Miecio, a concert pianist and close friend of Pablo Casals, apparently saved every postcard and letter that Betsy wrote him. Altogether there are over 160 pieces, the first written in 1950 and the last in 1971.

Betsy met Miecio through Emilie, who came to know him when he performed in a chamber music series she and her friend Fanny Brandeis were managing. Later, Betsy and Miecio became better acquainted at the Casals Festival in Zermatt, "one of the great musical experiences" of Betsy's life. They climbed the Breithorn and the Kleine Matterhorn together.[23] Fanny, Miecio, and Betsy became so close that they referred to themselves as "Nous Trois."

Most of the communications were during 1952, 1953, and 1954. Betsy sent Miecio brownies, frequently cautioned him to take rests from his "strainful" life, invited him to join her party in Switzerland, and knit him a pair of socks "in plenty of time for the 1954 climbing season." He sent Betsy jars of jam, books about composers, and favorite records (sometimes of his performances). Betsy tried to learn more about music but often apologized for not doing her homework. In New York City, she tried to turn the pages for Miecio as he played the piano—but turned them at the wrong time! Apparently, Miecio chastised Betsy for calling a Mahler piece "very tiresome," and she responded by saying that "Ignorant Opinionateness is so dreadful…. Yes, thought there were some beautiful moments but still not My Style." In Colorado Springs, Miecio played "Happy Birthday" for Betsy on her own piano, making a "LOVELY piece out of it." (He performed at a Colorado College concert that Betsy had arranged for him.[24])

Knowing that Miecio liked mushrooms, Betsy sent him a postcard of Mushroom Rock in Death Valley. From St. Louis, she sent him a postcard of a St. Louis Zoo chimpanzee playing the piano. "Do you think he's as good as you?" she asked, following with a drawing of a happy face.

Betsy sent Miecio her sympathy when the conductor, Arturo Toscanini, died: "I know your deep and sad feelings about Mr. Toscanini, your dear old friend." Sometimes she apologized for writing about humdrum matters: "What a boring letter! oh dear." And, in the only political comments of Betsy's that survive, she wrote the following postcard to Miecio on October 3, 1952.

> *I am voting for e [Dwight Eisenhower, the Republican candidate]. Who are you voting for? Fanny [Brandeis] mad as mad at me; she is for s [Adlai Stevenson, the Democratic candidate]. I shall be glad when the whole thing is over, won't you?"*

Betsy usually began her missives with "Dearest M." and ended them with, "So much affection." At some point, perhaps during the summer of 1954, Miecio apparently made a declaration of love to her. Betsy's reply was masterful. The correspondence continued.

Miecio dear

I am sitting down in the hotel garden green and cool, pretty flowers, and the lake beyond. The Dents du Midi look wonderful.

My dear, I feel confused about things and not sure that I understand—but I want to write you a few things about myself which I want you to know in any event.

I love the man I was going to marry very much; now things do not seem to be going well. There are drawbacks to our marriage and now they seem to loom very large. I don't know how it will turn out.

I don't know what you have had in your mind, or really, what you feel about me—but if a loving and warm friendship will add happiness and warmth to your life, you have it from me. I have loved our days, and all the fun with nous trois, and the sense of our affection and like-mindedness. I know you did too. That they meant a great deal to Fanny.

I count on this going on and think that we can have great value for each other in this way. I don't want (I could not bear) to bring unhappiness to you, Miecio. Please let us hold on.

With Affection, Betsy

On November 7, 1956, Betsy met a good-looking four-star U.S. Air Force general, Earle Partridge, known as Pat. He had moved to Colorado Springs, in July 1955, to head the Continental Air Defense Command, which was later transformed into the North American Air Defense Command (NORAD) with the addition of Canada. Betsy and Pat met at a party given by mutual friends, followed by a Julliard String Quartet concert.[25] They began keeping company and, according to the local newspaper, were seen at all the Colorado College hockey games.[26]

Articles in *Newsweek* said that Pat Partridge had been noted for his "Apollo-like physique" at West Point. Colleagues described him as a "tall, lean, perfectly poised" man with "quiet eyes and easy smile," who, when he shook hands, "in a couple of seconds...seem[ed] to zip you open, take full stock of your contents, file for future reference and zip you up again." The general played a "dazzling tennis game."[27]

Born in 1900 in Winchendon, Massachusetts, Pat grew up in nearby Ashby. He enlisted in the army at the end of World War I. Following graduation from West Point and Air Flight School, Pat rose steadily through the military hierarchy. He commanded the Fifth Air Force in Korea and the Far East Air Forces in Tokyo, receiving many decorations and medals for his service. Soon after Pat moved to Colorado Springs, he and his wife of thirty years separated; eventually they divorced. They had two grown daughters, Patricia and Kay.

Eleanor Davis Ehrman, a well-known mountain climber and friend, remembered that when Betsy told her about Pat, she said, "Oh Eleanor, I'm marrying a wonderful man. And he likes mountains, too, and that's just the frosting on the cake!"[28] Ten days before the marriage, Betsy wrote Miecio "the happy news" that she was to be married soon to a

> *wonderful man...good, fine, able.... Many things are new to him = music and the mountains among them. It has been wonderful to see his heart open to them, loving to hear the Prades records and yours, wanting to know and hear, loving all I could tell him of Mr. Casals and you, dear Miecio.... Dear, he will be your friend and I believe you will love him. And I know, as my dear dear friend, that you will be happy for me.*[29]

On February, 24, 1958, Betsy and Pat were married in a ceremony performed by her father, then ninety-one years old, at his home in Santa Barbara. Betsy was nearly fifty-six years old and Pat fifty-eight. The only guests were members of the family and Mrs. Jessica Swift of Colorado Springs and Vermont, who was Uncle Phil's sister.

Several months after her marriage, Betsy joined the local Aero Club and began taking flying lessons. "A crazy idea...for an ageing lady who isn't a bit bright about mechanical matters?" she later wrote. "Yes, perhaps. But that's one of the reasons for this article; that I have always been so sure that if I could learn to fly, anyone can." She soloed in September. "I made enough mistakes so that overconfidence was never a problem, like mislaying the Lamar airport because I kept looking for it in Rocky Ford." Always she blessed Pikes Peak for showing her the direction home. Once she endlessly circled the airport at Trinidad, Colorado, searching for a wind sock so she could figure out which runway to land on. Later Betsy discovered that Pat, highly amused, had been observing her from above in a B-57.[30]

She "managed" to pass the written exam in January and by the middle of March "got through...somehow" the final flying test. Pat and she logged hundreds of miles together, first in a Cessna 172, then a 182, and finally in a

Figure 10.2 Betsy Cowles Partridge and her husband General Earle (Pat) Partridge, USAF, at a reception, circa 1958. (Courtesy United States Air Force Academy Library.)

Beechcraft Bonanza. Betsy never had any illusions about who was the "real airman" of the family, but she routinely spelled Pat on long flights. She once said that for her, flying, like climbing, offered a "lifting of heart."[31] After Pat's retirement from the Air Force in 1959, he became a consultant for Lockheed Aircraft; he and Betsy then traveled for business as well as for fun. On trips in the United States they usually piloted their own plane.

The summer after they were married, Betsy took Pat to the Tetons for his first climb. He did "wonderfully," so Betsy took Pat closer to home on the very long, but not technically demanding, Pikes Peak.[32] Thereafter she said that her husband was "her favorite convert."[33]

In 1967 Betsy and Pat went to Africa, first on safari and then to hike. They did not take a camera, "with the idea of giving the experience every bit of our concentrated attention both of eye and ear."[34] After climbing to 16,300 feet on Mount Kenya, Betsy commented, "Pretty good for two elderlies." Encouraged, she and Pat then tackled Mount Kilimanjaro, an extinct volcano that is Africa's highest mountain.[35]

It began well. They left their hotel, the Marangu, at 10:15 in the morning and arrived at the Bismarck Hut (the names of many of the huts have since been changed) at 3:20, gaining 10 miles and 4,500 feet in a little less than four and a half hours. The next day, January 16, they climbed to the Peters Hut and, the day after that, still feeling good, to the Kibo Hut. On January 18, they started for the summit at 1:30 A.M. and reached the lowest point on the rim of the crater, Gilman's Point, 18,640 feet. Toward the end they had been very slow.

Most hikers regard the point as summit enough to have climbed the mountain and Betsy was quite willing to do so. (This was, after all, before the common use of drugs that mitigate the unpleasant and sometimes dangerous effects of high altitude.) But no, Pat insisted that they plod on to the highest point of the crater, Uhuru, which is 19,340 feet—and, in the end, Betsy was glad that he had. Two hours later, when they reached the top, their guides sang a song, did a dance, and congratulated them with "real pleasure." After Betsy and Pat returned to the Marangu Hotel, their guide begged to ask the ages of the "Bwana and Memsahib." When told that Betsy was sixty-five and Pat sixty-seven, he requested a picture of "the oldest and most illustrious" clients he had ever guided.

In February and March of 1969, the Partridges took an extensive trip to the Caribbean. Pat piloted their plane in a great circle from West Palm Beach southeast through the Bahamas to the island of Saint Lucia, then west to Curaçao and the coast of Colombia, and finally north-northwest via Panama, Guatemala, Mexico, and Texas. Although Betsy stated that she was "NOT a tropical personality," she survived the heat and the humidity. Usually they flew in the morning. Then, after arranging for a room, preferably in a small, intimate inn, Pat and Betsy would explore their surroundings on foot. "Cannot get over how fine I think it is to be a WALKER," Betsy wrote in her diary, because it "always gives you something to *do*, keeps you healthy, doesn't cost a cent (an afternoon deep-sea fishing...costs 50 bucks) and you end up by knowing the lay of each land you visit. We have walked almost four hours (3½ mile hike) each day and thoroughly enjoyed it."[36]

Betsy loved looking down on the water, especially during their flight over the Great Exuma chain. "Never have we seen such water—opal colors of all the blues, greens, pale creams in swirls, arcs and circles and looking, at times, as if they had solid thickness like deeply carved shapes." They flew over Venezuela and Colombia. It gave Betsy a "vast thrill" to look down on the Santa Marta Range, especially on La Reina and Ojeda and The Guardian, which she had not seen since her 1940 trip. North of Mexico City they flew over the high volcanoes, Orizaba, Ixtaccihuatl, and Popocatapetl. Betsy recalled that she had planned a trip to climb them in late 1941 but that the bombing of Pearl Harbor had intervened. She and Pat decided to "do" them some day...they never did.

In 1970, Betsy returned to Nepal, this time to the Annapurna region. She and Pat flew to Kathmandu by way of Pat's old Asian stomping grounds. They attempted to climb Mount Fuji in Japan but were turned back by the weather. In Korea they visited some of Pat's long-time friends and did some sightseeing. After Pat could see that Betsy was obviously enjoying herself, he confessed that he had hesitated to take her there, that he had been afraid that she would be bored. She replied, "You don't seem to know me very well yet." By then they had been married twelve years.

In Kathmandu, they met their friends Bill and Laney House, who were to be their trekking companions. Betsy found that she could not get her bearings. "The king's palace seemed so much bigger and not where expected... many shops, cars (!), *people*. And the sacred cows acting as if they owned the place."[37]

A few days later they flew to their starting point, Pokhara, where they were met by (Colonel) Jimmy Roberts, a former member of the Ghurkas, who was working for the adventure travel company that handled their trek. On October 15, the foursome and their entourage started west and slightly north, eventually dropping down to the magnificent gorge of the Kali Gandaki at Tatopani. From there they trekked as far north as Jomsom, making a side trip to the Tilicho Pass before retracing their steps. Although the large numbers of trekkers bothered Betsy, she still found Nepal enchanting.

Betsy, who by this time had "lost her interest in photography," did not take a camera.[38] She and Pat, now sixty-eight and seventy years old, found it hard going at first. The grade was "much more extensive and constant" than anyone of the party had walked on in years, "but you do have the feeling of progress," Betsy wrote, "and I bet we come out of this strong as horses." They did, and to Betsy, at least, it felt good to acquire "MUSCLES."

Immediately Betsy started learning the names of the Sherpas on their trek, and soon found out their backgrounds. By the end of the trip, she was worrying how to help them improve their English, to the point of asking Jimmy Roberts how she could go about accomplishing this. Betsy taught English to children she met and handed out presents to them. Two incidents marred her gift-giving, the only "acts of unkindness" she saw in Nepal. A young mother took a Life Saver out of her baby's hand when she thought Betsy wasn't watching, and a boy stole a tablet of paper from a younger one, who then complained to Betsy.

But mostly the trip was full of delights. One night a "big Indian-British mob…though they seem very agreeable" camped nearby told the Houses and Partridges about a fine "exhibit" of fireflies beyond the lights of the camp. "We went to see—Fourth of July—marvelous." Another night, when no one was looking, Betsy sat in the seat of one of the many Nepalese Ferris-wheel swings that were set up along the trail, and took a few turns. "Great," she wrote in her diary.

Laney House recalls the pleasure of hiking with Betsy, who, having forgotten her pack, insisted on carrying Laney's every day. When they came to a narrow part of the trail with a dropoff on one side, Betsy would put her hand behind her so Laney could take it. "It was very reassuring," Laney said later. "I would always get a little nervous. [Betsy was]…very thoughtful."

Betsy conscientiously described the wildlife and vegetation along the way but, as always, reserved her highest compliments for the mountains. From their camp below 14,000-foot Tilicho Pass, the party had a fine view of the great 8,000-meter Dhaulagiri. Betsy wrote, "The evening scene with light on the peaks and rosy glow with the sky most wonderful. Wind was blowing on Dhaulagiri's summit and a border of icy mist rose from the last night. Worth coming a million miles (on foot) to see."

After a day of rest, Bill led Betsy and Pat up a nearby "handsome summit." "Wonderfully thoughtful," he frequently stopped for Betsy; Ang Nima, the head Sherpa (*sirdar*) and a porter "sprinted" along. Pat climbed twenty-five paces, then rested, reminding Betsy of her father counting steps in Switzerland and saying, "Since I could go X paces, I can go X more." Finally they were near the top, which they estimated to be 16,000 feet.

We then contoured over to a grassy col with our peak ahead and there had lunch. And here came the great moment ahead of us. North and far below was Tibet, bare, hilly, vast. To one side (our right) Muktinath…. A whitish band ahead (or rising rocky ground) marked the end of Nepal—next, Tibet, looking blackish, dark grayish as to soil. A saw-tooth distant line of peaks above all this with one black summit much higher, with a dab of snow on top. We could see the broad track leading above the Kali Gandaki into Tibet, now closed, and Mustang, the last Tibetan town, was behind a tan mound beside it. All the other dazzling peaks were in plain view in a great circle around us, or were, when we reached our small rocky mountain top 20 minutes or so after leaving the col. Fun to have a little bit of rock work to land us on it and there to find ourselves perched up above everything. No wind—not

hot—not cold—an absolutely perfection of a day, and we, three people
from the other side of the world having this tremendous experience.
 Can't vouch for the others, but for me unequaled in my mountain
life. Even when seeing Everest that morning at Thyangboche twenty
years ago—perhaps because of being older and valuing things
more? Dunno.

By all reports, Betsy's marriage to Pat Partridge was a happy one. According to a close friend, Betsy "fell for [Pat] like a ton of bricks" while he became "absolutely glued" onto her.[39] Although their personalities were very different, they seemed to complement each other rather than to clash. In their bathroom hung two certificates, one commemorating Betsy's first solo flight and the other commemorating Pat's climb of a peak. Kay Partridge has said that she "always felt that those two achievements epitomized their mutual devotion, each wanting to participate fully in a profound passion of the other."[40]

Several women have remarked that although Pat was civil enough to them socially, they did not think he regarded them as worth bothering with. He was a "one-woman man" and Betsy was the woman. Her natural warmth and vivacity drew him out. Once he remarked, "Who can be down around Betsy?"[41] Sometimes Pat and Betsy would waken in the middle of the night and he would talk to her for hours about things that had happened to him in war. He always neatly folded his clothes on the floor, probably a habit developed for a quick getaway during combat.

In Colorado Springs Betsy and Pat slept in a bed that was three-quarters the width of a standard double bed, so narrow that it "made anyone laugh who saw it."[42] On their African safari and climbs of 1967–1968, their tent was furnished with twin cots; in a trip critique Betsy wrote, she said that Pat and she had agreed that their "wonderful trip" would have been improved if "1) there was a double bed 2) more exercise and 3) always a nearby stream of clear water."[43]

Betsy admired Pat's patience and his skills as a pilot, and he knew things that she did not.[44] When they were flying over foreign countries, such as Iran, he could draw a map to orient her. In Africa, when she told Pat that she had caught sight of the Southern Cross, he replied, "Fine—only you are looking northwest." (When she wrote this in her diary, she drew a picture of a happy face.[45]) He filled her in about revolutions in Guatemala, about soldiers training to protect the Dalai Lama, and about the political history of Korea.[46]

Pat and Betsy traveled well together, falling easily into a common rhythm, whether it was talking, visiting a museum, taking a stroll, trekking, or simply agreeing that they were tired and wanted to nap. Betsy often mentioned in her diaries that she regarded books as an extremely important piece of "equipment" while traveling. Pat and she would each carefully select one, read it and then, once finished, swap. They had lively discussions about what they read. On their Caribbean jaunt, Betsy read *Nicholas and Alexandra* while Pat worked on *The Territorial Imperative.* In Africa, Pat read a novel by Ernest Hemingway, while Betsy enjoyed *Living Free.* In addition, Betsy read books about the history of the country she was to visit and noted in her diary that she was not sure whether it was better to read such books before or after the trip. She concluded that it was best to do both.

Throughout her life Betsy remained slim, and deplored overweight women in general and those who wore revealing clothes, such as miniskirts, in particular. (She also damned women on cruise ships whose main interest seemed to be "SHOPPING," although, in fact, Betsy certainly loved to shop.[47]) She was always well groomed, even on the trail. Although she felt that a mountain "beauty standard" should be lower than an urban one, Betsy stated, "I've never been one to feel that the rough life became more and more delightful the worse you look." She thought that lipstick was an "important essential" that did not weigh too much to bring along.[48] However, in the damp heat of the tropics she remarked that although she did not think she looked her best, it was not important.[49] For hiking and climbing Betsy wore baggy twill pants with a belt, purchased in Europe, color-coordinated with her jacket and sweater.

In her younger years, Betsy had "very pretty" brown hair, which remained tidy even when jammed under a wool hat.[50] As she grew older, her hair changed color, which seemed to bother her not at all. When Betsy was nearly sixty-five, she wrote Emilie when she returned to her hotel after climbing Kilimanjaro, "Wish you could see my brown face. Think I have quite a lot of more grey hair, too—kinda like it."[51] After her 1970 trek to Nepal, Betsy went to a beauty salon in the Hotel Oberon in New Delhi, where she had her hair done in a fashionable bouffant style. She wrote in her diary, "and Pat likes it [drawing of a happy face]. So maybe from now on: a new ME."

The Partridges maintained a busy social life in Colorado Springs. They belonged to the Cheyenne Mountain Country Club, the Broadmoor Golf Club, and the Kissing Camels Club. Betsy even played golf to keep Pat company. As always, she hiked, often with Pat but frequently by herself, and continued her memberships in the American Alpine Club, the Colorado Mountain Club, the Ladies' Alpine Club of England, and the Club Suisse de Femmes Alpinistes.[52]

Many weekends found Betsy and Pat relaxing at their cabin in the foot-hills near the Carrol Lakes northwest of Colorado Springs.[53] Visiting friends and relatives all over the country continued to be part of Betsy's routine, now usually accompanied by Pat. Em Smith recalls that once she and Macauley and Pat and Betsy took a trip to the Grand Canyon, switching off riding in a car and flying in the Partridge airplane.

As had been her habit for many years, Betsy corresponded with dozens of people, usually by postcard. Her handwriting was so tiny that she could cram an amazing amount of news into a small space. Sometimes she acknowledged a good time by sending a gift, often a book, accompanied by one of her personal calling cards with a message scribbled on it such as "Fun this weekend, Betsy C."[54] During the Christmas season, Betsy mailed post-cards, never conventional holiday greetings.

In December 1972, Betsy wrote a cheery postcard to Laney and Bill House, with a reproduction of a Degas painting on the front. She and Pat were returning from their annual medical checkups at a private clinic in New Mex-ico, a "grueling" multiday experience that they both "abhorred."[55] "Checkups were SUPERB," Betsy wrote, followed by a picture of a happy face, "and we go home today with lovely words, 'Whatever you've been doing, go right on' ring-ing in our ears."[56]

A year later she was diagnosed with cancer. No one, least of all Betsy, could believe that it was terminal.[57] Her friends were especially shocked, because she had always kept in such good shape.[58] When she was dying, Charles Houston, at her request, flew out to see her. "Charley," she said, "I've done everything the doctors asked me to do; I've done my duty. Now can't I just go?" A week later, on June 12, 1974, she died at home, surrounded by family.[59]

Pat and Betsy had firmly agreed that there would be no publicity about her death. But the lack of a newspaper notice created such consternation and practical difficulties for those who mourned her that finally one of her closest friends arranged for an obituary to appear.[60]

Pat's daughter Kay never forgets August 1, "tipping my hat to Switzerland and to Betsy. She really did make a band of joy around her."[61] Swiss Day was Betsy's special day and Switzerland her special country. Indeed, Betsy Cowles Partridge often said that after she died, her fondest wish would be to return as a cow in Switzerland grazing in an alpine meadow, with a great bell hung around her neck.[62]

Notes

1. *Time* (December 18, 1950), 75.

2. Marka Webb Stewart, interview with the author, March 25, 1994. Marka recalls that Betsy wore a sari when she gave her speech in Colorado Springs.

3. Emilie S. Smith compiled quotations kept by her sister, Elizabeth S. Cowles, and her brother, William Strong, into a "Book of Gems."

4. Calla Hay, "Audience of 600 Thrills to Adventure of Betsy Cowles through Nepal to Everest," *Santa Fe New Mexican*, April 25, 1951, Archives, American Heritage Center.

5. "Himalayas Scaled by Woman Here to Lecture April 25," *Santa Fe New Mexican*, "The Women" section, n.d., Archives, American Heritage Center.

6. Ray Waterkoth, "Everest from Distaff Side," *Pittsburgh Post Gazette*, n.d., Archives, American Heritage Center.

7. In addition to Elizabeth S. [Cowles] Partridge's own articles and talks about her 1950 trek, the American Heritage Center contains numerous articles about the trek written by others, such as one authored by Charles S. Houston, M.D., "Venture into Forbidden Nepal," *Look Magazine*, (January 1951).

8. "America's Interesting People," *American Magazine*, n.d., Archives, American Heritage Center.

9. Elizabeth S. Cowles, postcards and letters to Miecio Horszowski (1952, 1953), collection of Emilie S. Smith.

10. John H. Strong's first wife, Eliza, died in 1946. After marrying again, he and his second wife moved to California.

11. Elizabeth S. Cowles, 'Have You a Mountain Widow in Your Home?" *Sierra Club Bulletin* no. 6 (June 1949), 21.

12. "Famed Mountaineer Witnesses Troops' Rock-Climbing Exhibit," *Gazette Telegraph* [Colorado Springs], March 24, 1953, Archives, American Heritage Center.

13. Elizabeth S. Cowles, letter to Miecio Horszowski, [March] 1953, collection of Emilie S. Smith.

14. Ed Zakusky, "Everest Conquerors Take Jaunt Up Cheyenne Cañon," *Gazette Telegraph* [Colorado Springs], March 2, 1954, Archives, American Heritage Center.

15. Elizabeth S. Cowles, letters to Miecio Horszowski, January 10, 1954, and March 4, 1954, collection of Emilie S. Smith.

16. Elizabeth S. Cowles, letters to Miecio Horszowski, January 1, 1953, and September 28, 1954, collection of Emilie S. Smith.

17. Elizabeth S. Cowles, letter to Miecio Horszowski, January 27, 1955, collection of Emilie S. Smith.

18. "Fine Arts Center Profiles," *Denver Post*, n.d. [ca. February 1955], Archives, American Heritage Center.

19. Elizabeth S. Cowles, text for talk to the Women's Educational Committee of Colorado College, n.d., Archives, American Heritage Center.

20. "B.," letter to the author, January 23, 1992. The following incident was recounted by a woman, not a mountain climber, who requested anonymity. "B."'s husband, a member of the American Alpine Club, was one of Betsy's long-time friends and admirers.

When Maurice Herzog came to Denver after his climb of Annapurna, a dinner for American Alpine Club members and their guests was held in his honor. After the receiving line had broken up, one of our guests, a blond beauty in her late twenties, and I observed the guest of honor standing alone in the center of the huge panelled room at the University Club. Everybody else was standing around the perimeter like a bunch of wallflowers, chatting away and totally ignoring the guest of honor. Mr. Herzog spoke no English. I knew that Betsy spoke a little French and assumed that perhaps she had decided to give others a crack at Herzog as we understood that she had been his escort for the previous two days in Denver. Aware of this, and that seemingly there were no takers, my guest and I, with my husband's copy of Annapurna *in hand, advanced on Mr. Herzog with a request for his autograph and to practice our French.*

The three of us had an absolutely wonderful time and one of the dinner's organizers, noticing the fun we were having (because of our ability to communicate in French) seated us at the head table flanking Mr. Herzog. Some time after Herzog's visit, Sir John Hunt (the organizer of the first successful ascent of Everest by the British in 1953) came to Denver. Betsy insisted that I not be invited to any festivities given in his honor. This highhanded approach especially annoyed Jerry Hart, the prominent Denver attorney who later became president of the AAC and who was hosting one of the private parties for Sir John Hunt; Jerry and his wife disliked being told by Betsy whom they could and could not invite.

The matter was "happily resolved" when "B." suggested to Jerry that he reject the normal rules of etiquette and send an invitation to her husband, omitting her name, so that only "B." would be boycotted. "B." says of the incident:

It was always my impression that [Betsy] protected her mountain climbing turf from others of her sex. She did not tolerate competition and could be rather vindictive....I think it was very silly of Betsy. I had no interest in participating in her sport, and therefore could not possibly have been perceived as a threat.

Later "B." gave a dinner for a member of one of the early Everest expeditions and invited Betsy. Thereafter, as "B." put it, she was "the object of [Betsy's] gratitude for having delivered her a famous British Everester. The evening was a great success as Sir Jack and Betsy charmed one another."

21. Dorothy Teague Swartz, comments on the manuscript, October 10, 1994.
22. Emilie S. Smith, interview with the author, March 24, 1992.
23. Elizabeth S. Cowles scrapbook of letters, Archives, American Heritage Center. This includes information from #29 in the list of letters at the beginning of the scrapbook, as well as a postcard from Miecio Horszowski to Betsy. In comments that Emilie S. Smith wrote to the author (March 1996), she said that Fanny Brandeis was a niece of the United States Supreme Court Justice Louis Brandeis. Miecio, born in Poland, studied under the same Leshetizky who had taught Betsy's aunt in Vienna. After 1940, he lived in New York City.

24. Unless noted otherwise, all information and quotations come from letters that Elizabeth S. Cowles [Partridge] wrote to Miecio Horszowski, collection of Emilie S. Smith.

25. Elizabeth S. [Cowles] Partridge, Nepal diary 1970, Archives, American Heritage Center.

26. Leo Zuckerman, "Air Defense Chief, Springs Woman Wed," *Rocky Mountain News*, February 24, 1958, Archives, American Heritage Center.

27. "Earle E. Partridge Changes in Command," *Newsweek* 36 (21) (June 4, 1951): 19; "Air Force Trio," *Newsweek* 36 (4) (July 24, 1950): 16–17.

28. Eleanor Davis Ehrman, interview with the author, May 14, 1985.

29. Elizabeth S. Cowles to Miecio Horszowski, two letters; one undated, ca. 1955, and the other February 14, 1958. Both letters are from the collection of Emilie S. Smith. On April 15, 1963, Miecio performed a concert, part of the Colorado College series, dedicated to the memory of John Henry Strong, who had become a good friend of Miecio's. The two shared a love of music and God.

30. Elizabeth S. (Cowles) Partridge, "Only for Those with Husbands Crazy about Flying," *Entries* (September 1967), 18, Archives, American Heritage Center. In Emilie S. Smith's comments on the manuscript (March 1996), she quotes from a letter Betsy wrote her: "My passengers piloting my first long flight were Pat and Jimmy Doolittle [Pat's closest friend]. They would say, 'Betsy, let's go over there for a look.' [To which she would reply,] '*NO*, I'm staying right on course!'"

31. "Aloha, Mrs. Partridge," *Entries* (July 1959), 6, Archives, American Heritage Center.

32. Jane Hoelscher, "First Lady of Mountaineering," *Entries* (October 1958), 5, Archives, American Heritage Center.

33. "Aloha, Mrs. Partridge," 5.

34. Elizabeth S. [Cowles] Partridge, text for talk, n.d., Archives, American Heritage Center.

35. Elizabeth S. [Cowles] Partridge, Africa diary 1967–1968, Archives, American Heritage Center.

36. Elizabeth S. [Cowles] Partridge, Caribbean Circle diary 1969, Archives, American Heritage Center.

37. Unless otherwise noted, all information about the 1970 trek in Nepal comes from Elizabeth S. [Cowles] Partridge, Nepal diary 1970, Archives, American Heritage Center.

38. Bill and Laney House, interview with the author, October 15, 1992.

39. Laney House, interview.

40. Kay Partridge, letter to the author, April 6, 1993.

41. Laney House, interview.

42. Emilie S. Smith, interview with the author, March 24, 1992; Emilie S. Smith, comments on the manuscript, March 1996.

43. Elizabeth S. [Cowles] Partridge, Africa diary 1967–1968.

44. Elizabeth S. [Cowles] Partridge, Caribbean Circle diary 1969.

45. Elizabeth S. [Cowles] Partridge, Africa diary.

46. Elizabeth S. [Cowles] Partridge, Caribbean Circle diary.

47. *Ibid.*

48. Elizabeth S. Cowles, "Round-Robin Letter #6," Archives, American Heritage Center.

49. Elizabeth S. [Cowles] Partridge, Caribbean Circle diary.

50. Laney House, interview; Dorothy Teague Swartz, interview with the author, January 14, 1993.

51. Elizabeth S. [Cowles] Partridge, letter to Emilie Strong Smith, January 14, 1969, Archives, American Heritage Center.

52. Elizabeth S. [Cowles] Partridge, biographical information sheet (October 31, 1968), Colorado Room of the Penrose Public Library, Colorado Springs.

53. In 1964, according to data copied from the homeowners' book by Stuart Dodge, General Earle Partridge purchased Cabin Y from Beryl Ritchy.

54. Dorothy Teague Swartz, interview with the author, January 14, 1993.

55. Kay Partridge, letter to the author, September 23, 1994.

56. Elizabeth S. [Cowles] Partridge, postcard to Laney House, Christmas 1972, collection of Laney House.

57. Robert M. Ormes, "End of the Trail: Betsy Partridge," *Trail and Timberline* no. 669 (September 1974), 219.

58. Stuart Dodge, interview with the author, October 29, 1994.

59. Charles S. Houston, M.D., "In Memoriam: Elizabeth Cowles Partridge," *American Alpine Journal* 20 (49) (1975): 250, 251.

60. Obituary of Elizabeth S. [Cowles] Partridge, *Colorado Springs Sun*, June 18, 1974. In a letter to the author (December 14, 1994), Kay Partridge says that her father was not pleased that the notice had been published.

61. Kay Partridge, letter.

62. Viola Ryder Nicholson, interview with the author, July 17, 1995.

Epilogue

During her lifetime Betsy was known for her quiet generosity. For example, she gave Bob Ormes money to hire a guide for a Matterhorn ascent, knowing that Bob's income would not permit him such a splurge.[1] To her friend, Vi Ryder, she permanently "loaned" several fine antiques and outright gave several paintings by Taos artists. Betsy gave Vi's daughter a trip to Europe as a college graduation present. Stu Dodge is almost certain that Betsy provided scholarships for students at Fountain Valley School.

After Betsy's death, friends and family set up a memorial fund at the Fine Arts Center, which was used to purchase an oil painting by the American artist Henry Arthur Elkins, titled "In the Colorado Rockies." Much earlier, Betsy had given her Edgar Britton sculpture, "Torso of a Woman," to the Center, stipulating that it remain in her home until she died. Other of Betsy's tangible bequests to the Center included several Adolf Dehn lithographs, an Edgar Britton oil painting, a couple of Boardman Robinson pen-and-ink drawings, some antiques, and other objets d'art.

Although Betsy remembered close relatives in her will, she stipulated that the bulk of her estate, effective after Pat Partridge's death, would go to Colorado College, to the Colorado Springs Fine Arts Center, and to the City of Colorado Springs Parks Department. Lesser, though very generous, amounts went to the American Alpine Club, Vassar College, and the Colorado Mountain Club. The music department of Colorado College inherited Betsy's Steinway parlor grand piano. Emilie added a plaque to it which reads, in part, "She made round her a halo of delight." Today, more than twenty years after Betsy's death, Emilie says simply, "I still miss her."

As Betsy recognized in 1950, her trek to Nepal was indeed the "trip of a lifetime." In addition to being the first Westerners to view the wonders of the Khumbu area, the Houston party visited Nepal when it was on the brink of historic changes.

After his exile to India, King Tribhuvan and his family did not return to Kathmandu until February 15, 1951. During the next few years he succeeded in establishing a constitutional democracy, thus ending the Ranas' reign of 104 years. Mohan's official residence, the Singha Durbar of a thousand rooms where Betsy, Nell, and Oscar had peered at the Coney Island mirrors, was converted into government offices.

In April 1951, Betsy wrote to the deposed Maharaj-Prime Minister Mohan, expressing gratitude for his hospitality and enclosing photographs she had taken and newspaper clippings (which he referred to as "cuttings") about Nepal. He replied, thanking her for the photographs and saying he was glad her stay in Kathmandu had been enjoyable. "It is gratifying," he wrote, "to note that you are impressed by the simple characteristics of the people of Nepal, their self respect, independence, hospitality and dignity."

Three years later, Betsy again wrote to Mohan, apparently to offer condolences on the death of his son, Bijaya, with whom Betsy and the Houstons had had especially friendly contacts in 1950. His reply to her, written from Bangalore in southern India, was much less formal than the first one. Mohan said he was "so so" and that the "sad death of dear Bijaya in tragic circumstances" had given him the "rudest shock" of his life. "The palace of eternity has been opened for him," Mohan continued, while those left "have yet to endure life as best we can." He said that times had changed a great deal in Nepal. "It would not be too much to say that one who re-visits the country is not unlikely to experience like Rip Van Winkle.' "[2]

King Tribhuvan ruled until 1955. Several weeks before his death, he turned over all royal powers to his son, the Crown Prince Mahendra Bikram Shah Dev. In 1972, Mahendra's son, Birendra Bikram Shah Dev, became king and remains so as of this writing. Nepal's struggle to become democratic has continued.

The 1950 Houston-Tilman reconnaissance of Mount Everest paved the way for a second, more thorough look at the Khumbu. The following year, a British party headed by Bill Tilman's good friend Eric Shipton essentially retraced the route of the Houston party. However, they started their trip in early September, nearly two months earlier than the Houston party had, and so overlapped the monsoon season. Rains swelled the rivers, washed out bridges, and made the trails "slimy with mud"; leeches infested the under-growth. On but a single twig, "a score of the creatures could be seen, stiff and erect, like a cluster of little black sticks, ready to attach themselves to our legs and arms and clothing as we brushed past."[3] The Houston party had reached Namche Bazar in two weeks; the Shipton party took nearly four.

Some time before reaching Namche, two young New Zealanders who had been climbing in the Garhwal Himalaya of India finally managed to catch up with the party as had been prearranged. As the expedition went higher, the weather became clear, at least in the morning. And so, setting up camp at about 18,000 feet, the climbers began exploring the approach up the Khumbu Glacier. They made the "exciting" discovery that there was a practical route from the West Cwm to the South Col, although a "mass of hanging glaciers" threatened the route with ice avalanches. The glacier itself was inhospitable enough; huge ice towers (*seracs*) toppled without warning while restless cre-vasses convulsed open or shut overnight. As Charles Houston and Bill Tilman had surmised, it was an exceedingly nasty route. But it was the only one. In the years to come, some would call the Khumbu Icefall the "Mouth of Death."[4]

In the spring of 1952, a Swiss team forced its way up the Khumbu Icefall to the South Col and finally onto the southeast ridge within 800 feet of Ever-est's summit. But brutal winds and cold thwarted them from pushing on. The Swiss returned in the fall but again weather conditions stopped them from exceeding their earlier high point.

A year later, in 1953, the British were granted a permit to climb Everest. They used a different approach from that of the Houston and Shipton parties, starting at Kathmandu and walking east to the Dudh Kosi, where their route then coincided with that of their Western predecessors. On May 29, two men reached the summit: Tenzing Norgay, a Tibetan who had lived in the Thami area of Nepal since childhood and who had been a member of the Swiss team that had come so close to the top a year earlier; and Edmund Hillary, one of the two New Zealand climbers who had joined the Shipton party on the 1951 reconnaissance.

Andy Bakewell and Betsy kept in touch after their Nepal trip. A letter sur-vives that Andy wrote in 1954 from the Singbhum District, Bihar, India, "deep in the jungle." He recalled a letter Betsy had written him and said that he had frequently thought of their wonderful trip together. He said he wished he could type the letter he was writing her, but that it was 3 A.M., and he would have to be up in an hour to take a girl with a "terribly infected hand" out to a hospital. She would have to be carried "like Herzog—for miles—then across the Kali River before we hit any sort of wheeled vehicles. [This referred to Maurice Herzog, who, after making the first ascent of Annapurna in June 1950, was so badly frostbitten that he had to be carried out to safety by porters.] We may save the finger but it will be close." Almost incidentally, Andy then mentioned that a bear had mauled him nearly four weeks earlier, but that he had killed it and was healed again.[5]

In 1951, Andy was ordained into the priesthood. He has since served in India, Maryland, Washington, D.C., and, for eleven years, in northern Alaska. Headquartered in Delta Junction, he was the only Catholic priest in permanent residence for a 35,000-square-mile area. As of 1978, he has lived in Santa Fe, New Mexico, first serving as chaplain for St. Vincent Hospital and then as chaplain for the Discalced Carmelite Monastery near St. John's College. Andy never returned to Nepal after his trek with the Houston party.

Oscar Houston died in 1969. The movies he took in 1950 of the Arun River crossing and of the Tengboche lamas' practice dances for what we now know was the Mani-rimdu festival are in the possession of his son, Charles. Their color has not faded in the least.

In 1953, **Charles Houston** and Bob Bates organized an expedition to K2 on which one member, Art Gilkey, died. Charley calls it a "major passage" of his life and has not climbed since.

Four years later, Charley and his wife, Dorcas, moved to Aspen, Colorado, to work in an "imaginative health program," and later in a small clinic. On New Year's Day of 1959, he participated in the rescue of a young man who had come down with debilitating symptoms after crossing a 12,000-foot pass near Snowmass Lake. Charley then treated the young man after he was evacuated to the Aspen hospital, where he quickly recovered. In 1960, at the urging of Dr. Paul Dudley White, Charley wrote an article for the *New England Journal of Medicine* titled "Acute Pulmonary Edema of High Altitude," in which he described the New Year's Day incident, as well as others, and their medical implications.[6] Because the article was the first on the subject to be both widely disseminated *and* written in English, it "stirred correspondence from literally all over the world."[7]

Since Charley was "catapulted" into high-altitude medicine, it has been a major focus of his life.[8] Sometimes referred to as "the father of high-altitude physiology," he has lectured throughout the world and written three books, in addition to numerous articles, on the subject.

In 1962, Charley left Aspen to direct the Peace Corps in India for three years. After a year and a half in Washington, D.C., working for the Peace Corps, he accepted a professorship at the University of Vermont in Burlington. He and Dorcas, have lived there ever since.

In 1981, Charley repeated the 1950 trek his father had organized, this time with his own son, who is also a medical doctor and a mountaineer. Although it was a "sentimental journey," Charley comments that "sadly, much had changed."[9]

Bill Tilman's diary of the 1950 trek to the Khumbu contains mostly lists of distances, and descriptions of mountains, the route, and food. In between these dry notations are a few personal comments: he is "fed up with Nepal"; the coolies "lied"; "the Yanks wouldn't touch breakfast"; "even Yanks now satisfied that no route exists on Everest."[10]

In 1952, Tilman's book *Nepal Himalaya* was published. It included a short section about the 1950 trek with the Houston party, in which he described his companions thus:

> *Besides the Houstons there were two old friends of theirs, Mrs. E. S. Cowles, an American climber of note and Anderson Bakewell who was then studying at the Jesuit College of St. Mary's at Kurseong near Darjeeling. Hitherto I had not regarded a woman as an indispensable part of the equipage of a Himalayan journey but one lives and learns. Anyhow, with a doctor to heal us, a woman to feed us and a priest to pray for us, I felt we could face the future with some confidence.*

Twenty pages later, Bill wrote, "Mrs. Cowles, of course, stole the show, and soon had them all, urchins and lamas alike, eating out of her hand."[11] One has to read all seven of Bill Tilman's mountain-travel books to understand the significance of the quoted passage; although the man occasionally praises women for their hard work and loyalty and mentions when they are pretty or buxom, nowhere else does he describe a female as charming. Indeed, he rarely makes comments about such personal characteristics as charm about any Western friend, male or female, although he sometimes mentions when they are strong, selfless, or competent.

Betsy's diary records the cross words Bill spoke to her and details cynical remarks he made. But it does not tell us that in the end, despite the setbacks, she and he became good friends. In her typically reticent fashion, Betsy's diary most certainly gives no hint that Betsy discussed marrying Bill with Charley and Dorcas Houston, eventually deciding that he would be much too set in his ways.[12] As Andy Bakewell commented many years later, "To see Betsy quietly bring [Bill] around was a source of wonder to us all."[13]

After his 1950 trek to the Khumbu, Bill Tilman never returned to the Himalaya. He had told Betsy that his two expeditions to the Langtang Himal and to the Annapurna Himal had made it clear that his ceiling was 20,000 feet, that he was simply "too feeble" to go higher.[14] For a year and a half, Bill tried the life of a diplomat, serving as the British consul in Upper Burma. (His biographer, Tim Madge, speculates that Bill might have been trying out a new career suitable for a wife—Betsy Cowles.[15]) However, the diplomatic service did not suit Bill and he took up serious sailing. Voyages to Patagonia, West Greenland, Baffin Bay, the South Shetlands, South Georgia, and the circumnavigations of South America and Africa provided material for eight books.

He and Betsy corresponded occasionally. Betsy visited Bill's home in Bodowen, Wales, in September 1953, and was received by his sister because Bill was away. In 1956, Betsy invited Bill to visit her. He replied cordially that "being an unsociable chap with very little to say for himself it is nice to think I should be a welcome guest in Colorado." (However, he never did accept the invitation.) Then, in typical Tilman-ese, he mentioned that he had the possibility of doing an highly lucrative article for *National Geographic Magazine* but that he doubted his pictures would be acceptable "as they are mostly of mountains without any females in red shorts in the foreground."[16]

Sometimes Betsy and Bill ran into each other at the American Alpine Club's annual banquets held in Eastern cities. At such a banquet in 1963, which took place a few months after the first successful American ascent of Mount Everest, one AAC member was "enchanted" to watch how Betsy took Bill Tilman in hand: "She straight-armed his anti-female digs and jollied him into submission. A curmudgeon turned into a pussycat before my eyes."[17]

Apparently Betsy gave Bill a letter which he hand-delivered to his sister when he reached home in Wales. He then wrote Betsy a letter: "Adeline… was delighted to have your letter. It was fun seeing you again. 'Age cannot wither, nor custom stale her infinite variety.' No doubt next time you come here it will be by your own plane. There is an air field quite handy. Yours ever, Bill."[18] (By that time Betsy had married Pat Partridge.) In 1970, Betsy and Pat Partridge were Bill's houseguests at Bodowen. Bill made "foot bread," which Betsy carried back to the United States with the intention of air-mailing some to Andy Bakewell and Charley Houston.[19]

Bill Tilman's niece has described her uncle as "terribly shy," but a "perfect gentleman of the old school and always a charming host." She feels that he was not a misogynist and that his reticence around women is explained by his hardly ever being exposed to any besides his mother, sister, or nieces; from the age of seventeen on he was either fighting in a world war, living on

Figure 11.1   In 1993, the fifty-nine-year-old Rimpoche of Tengboche looked at color copies of slides Betsy took of him when he was sixteen, in 1950. (Photo by David Robertson.)

an isolated Kenyan coffee plantation, mountain climbing, or sailing. He "couldn't stand...the women who fluttered their eyelashes at him.... Betsy was a woman who could be admired for doing something in his field and who had no designs on him."[20]

Still, Bill Tilman's books are sprinkled with anti-female and anti-marriage comments. According to a friend, Bill once told him that he had had his "peccadilloes...but the trouble with women is that they get in the damn way."[21] Although there is a story that H. W. Tilman resigned from the Alpine Club in 1974 after it voted to terminate its 117-year-old policy of not admitting women, in fact this is probably not the case. According to Tim Madge, after the Alpine Club rescinded its sexist policy, the board voted to make Bill Tilman an honorary member, thus forestalling any possibility of his resignation.[22]

Sometime after November 1, 1977, the boat on which Bill was sailing disappeared between Rio de Janiero and the Falkland Islands. He had hoped to spend his eightieth birthday on Smith Island in the Antarctic.

Shortly after the Houston party visited **Tengboche**, the young Rimpoche left to study in Tibet, returning to his gompa in 1956.[23] Since then he has divided his time between Tengboche and Kathmandu, occasionally traveling to other parts of Asia as well and, in 1995, to the United States. Known as the reincarnate Lama of the Tengboche Monastery, Nawang Tensing Jangpo has become an important spiritual leader of the Sherpas. He has reached out to the many trekkers and climbers, Western and Eastern, who visit Tengboche, permitting them to camp beside the gompa and to witness the Mani-rimdu practice dances *and* the actual festival.

On January 19, 1989, Tengboche burned to the ground. Most of the masks, costumes, relics, and books that Betsy and her companions had admired in 1950 burned, as did the decorated dais on which the young Rimpoche had sat.[24] The destroyed gompa was the second to occupy the site, the first having toppled during the earthquake of 1934. Tengboche has since been rebuilt with funds contributed by people from all over the world.

The stone building that Betsy, Oscar, and Andy occupied has disappeared. Because Sherpas often build stone structures without mortar, buildings and walls are erected and dismantled relatively easily.

However, the view from the gompa has changed very little. Many of the thousands of people who have visited Tengboche on a clear day would agree with Betsy's assessment that it is "the most beautiful place in all the world."

Notes

1. Robert M. Ormes, interview with the author, May 13, 1985.
2. Mohun [Mohan] (Shamsher), letters to Elizabeth S. Cowles, May 27, 1951, and March 4, 1954, Archives, American Heritage Center.
3. Eric Shipton, *The Mount Everest Reconnaissance Expedition* (New York: E.P. Dutton, 1952), 31.
4. Stacy Allison with Peter Carlin, *Beyond the Limits: A Woman's Triumph of Everest* (Boston: Little, Brown, 1993), 206.
5. Anderson Bakewell, S.J., letter to Elizabeth S. Cowles, June 29, 1954, Archives, American Heritage Center.
6. Charles S. Houston, M.D., *New England Journal of Medicine* 263 (September 8, 1960): 478.
7. Charles S. Houston, M.D., letter to the author, December 20, 1977.
8. Charles S. Houston, M.D., letter to the author, July 7, 1994.
9. Charles S. Houston, M.D., comments on the manuscript, December 1995.
10. H. W. Tilman, diary of Nepal 1950 trek with Houston party, Archives, American Heritage Center.
11. Jim Perrin, introduction to H. W. Tilman, *Nepal Himalaya,* from *The Seven Mountain-Travel Books* (London: Diadem Books, Ltd./Seattle: The Mountaineers, 1983), 868, 879.

12. Tim Madge, *The Last Hero Bill Tilman: A Biography of the Explorer* (London: Hodder & Stoughton, 1995), 124.

13. Anderson Bakewell, S.J., letter to the author, September 12, 1994.

14. Despite the fact that Betsy's diary says 24,000 feet (not 20,000 feet), it seems likely this is a mistake. In J. R. L. Anderson's *High Mountains & Cold Seas: A Biography of H. W. Tilman* (Seattle: The Mountaineers, 1980), the author quotes Tilman as saying that although a man in his fifties might perform well up to 20,000 feet, above that elevation "he is declining into decrepitude."

15. Madge, *Last Hero*, 171.

16. H. W. Tilman, letter to Elizabeth S. Cowles, February 26, 1956, Archives, American Heritage Center.

17. Andrews Black, letter to the author, January 22, 1992. (Note: This scene would have taken place after Betsy was married.)

18. H. W. Tilman, letter to Elizabeth S. [Cowles] Partridge, December 15, 1963, Archives, American Heritage Center.

19. Elizabeth S. [Cowles] Partridge, Nepal diary 1970, Archives, American Heritage Center.

20. Pamela R. Davies, letter to the author, July 14, 1992.

21. Jim Perrin, introduction to Tilman's *Seven Mountain-Travel Books*, 8.

22. Charles S. Houston, M.D., "In Memoriam: Harold William Tilman 1898–1978," *American Alpine Journal* 29 (54) (1979): 683. In a telephone conversation with the author in December 1994, Tim Madge, author of *The Last Hero Bill Tilman*, said he thought that the letter of resignation supposedly written by Tilman never existed and offered the explanation printed here.

23. Kristoph Fürer von Heimendorf, *The Sherpas of Nepal: Buddhist Highlanders* (Calcutta and New Delhi: Oxford Book, 1964), 133.

24. His Holiness Nawang Tensing Jangpo, Reincarnate Lama of the Tengboche gompa, conversation with the author through a translator, November 1993.

Mountain Trips of Betsy Strong Cowles Partridge, 1933–1970

1933–on

>**Colorado:** 54 of the high Colorado peaks of 14,000 feet and over. Second climbs of Lindsay, Sneffles, Evans, Humboldt, Castle, Sherman, Grays, Wilson Peak, Grizzly, Belford, Lincoln, Quandry. Numerous repeats of Pikes Peak and Democrat and of lower peaks and passes of Colorado.

1933

>**Switzerland:** Dent du Midi (Haute Cime), Petite Dent de Veisivi (traverse), Pigne d'Arolla (traverse), to Zermatt from Arolla over the Col d'Hérens with ascent of the Tête Blanche, Rifflehorn (Matterhorn couloir), Untergabelhorn (traverse), Zinal Rothorn, Matterhorn.

1934

>**Tetons:** Grand Teton.

1935

>**Tetons:** Grand Teton (traverse via east ridge) [first female traverse of the mountain].

>**Canadian Rockies:** Whyte, Niblock, Pope's Peak (traverse), Mitre, Edith (traverse with new route on ascent).

1936

Switzerland: Drei Schwestern (traverse), Piz Morteratsch (traverse), Piz Languard, tour of the Piz Bernina via Sella Pass and Bellavista Sattel, Piz Roseg (traverse via north ridge), Piz Palu (traverse), Rimfischhorn, Dent Blanche, Weisshorn, Weissmies (traverse by north ridge).

1937

Switzerland: Wetterhorn, Nassihorn, Grosse Fiescherhorn (traverse), Finsteraarhorn, Monch, Jungfrau, Wellenkuppe-Obergabelhorn (traverse with descent via Arbengrat), Matterhorn (traverse by Zmutt and Italian Ridges), Mont Blanc.

1940

Tetons: Middle Teton (traverse via north ridge, new route), Minga Spire (first ascent), Symmetry Spire (via north couloir), Buck Mountain (traverse with first ascent of the north face), Wister (traverse), Veiled Peak (traverse), Owen, Grand Teton (traverse by Exum ridge), Teewinot (partial traverse by south ridge), Moran (north ridge), Nez Perce (east ridge), Grand Teton (traverse via north ridge).

New England: White Horse and Cathedral Ledges.

1941

Sierra Nevada de Santa Marta (Colombia): first ascents of La Reina (18,170 ft.), Pico Ujueta (18,070 ft.), The Guardian (17,200 ft.).

Tetons: Grand Teton (traverse with first ascent of Petzoldt Ridge), Grand Teton (via Exum Ridge), South Teton (traverse), Moran (CMC route).

1947

Colorado: Chair Mountain.

1950

Switzerland: Petite Dent de Veisivi (traverse), Roussette, from Arolla to Zermatt via the Bertol Hut and Col d'Hérens with ascent of the Aiguille de la Za, Trifthorn, Zinal Rothorn (traverse via Rothorngrat), Matterhorn (traverse via Italian and Swiss Ridges), Crasta Spinez (traverse), Piz Morteratsch (traverse via Speranza Ridge), Piz Bernina (traverse via Biancograt).

Himalayas: Member of the Houston Expedition with first approach to Mount Everest from the south through eastern Nepal.

1952

Switzerland: Mont Blanc de Seilon (traverse), Arête de Bertol (traverse), Dent Blanche, Aiguilles Rouges d'Arolla (traverse), from Arolla to Moiry Hut via Col Couronne, with traverse of Grand Cornier to Mountet Hut, and traverse of the Zinal Rothorn (by north ridge) to Zermatt; Rimpfischhorn (traverse with descent via north ridge), Südlenzspitze-Nadelhorn-Stecknadelhorn traverse, Breithorn, Kleine Matterhorn, Monte Rosa (traverse via Dufourspitze, Grenzgipfel, Zumsteinspitze, and Signalkuppe to Margerita Refugio) and descent to Zermatt with traverse of Lyskamm.

1953

Switzerland: Ebnefluh, Mittaghorn, Bieschhorn (traverse via north ridge), Alphubel (traverse via Rotgrat), Obergabelhorn-Wellenkuppe traverse (with descent by Arbengrat), Täschhorn (traverse via Mischabel Ridge), Riffelhorn (by Matterhorn Couloir), from Kandersteg to Reid via Löetchen Pass, by Ferden Pass to Leukerbad, to Kandersteg by Gemmi Pass.

1954

Wind River Range (Wyoming): East Sentinel, Gannett, Koven, Sphinx, Rampart.

1955

Switzerland: Piz Languard, Piz Corvatsch, Piz Morteratsch (traverse by southwest ridge), Jägihorn, Jägigrat (traverse), from Saas Fe to Zermatt via Adler Pass and to Arolla via Col d'Hérens and Bertol Hut with ascent of Aiguille de la Za.
Wales: Tryfan (traverse).

1956

Tetons: South Teton, Grand Teton (Exum Ridge), Symmetry Spire, Mount St. John (traverse).

1957

Italian Tyrol: Marmolada.
Switzerland: Jazzihorn.
Wales: Snowdon.
Scotland: Ben Nevis.

1958

Tetons: Grand Teton (Exum Ridge), Storm Point.

1959

Bavarian Alps: Kramerspitze, Alpspitze (traverse), Hoher Gaif, Zugspitze.
Switzerland: Riffelhorn, Rimpfischhorn, Matterhorn.

1960

California: Mount Whitney.

1962

Bavarian Alps: Kramerspitze.
Italian Tyrol: Marmolada, Torre di Sella (One and Two).
Switzerland: Trifthorn, Wellenkuppe.
Wales: Cader Idris, Snowdon.

1967

Colorado: Mount Evans, Mount Sherman, Mount Lincoln.

1968

East Africa: Mount Kenya to Point Lenana (16,300 ft.); Kilimanjaro: Point Uhuru (highest point, 19,350 ft.).

1970

Nepal: Twenty-five-day trek in western Nepal via Kali Gandaki River to Jomson.

Bibliography

Allison, Stacy, with Peter Carlin. *Beyond the Limits: A Woman's Triumph of Everest*. Boston: Little, Brown, 1993.

Anderson, J. R. L. *High Mountains & Cold Seas: A Biography of H. W. Tilman*. Seattle: The Mountaineers, 1980.

Brower, Dave, ed. *Going Light with Backpack or Burro: How to Get Along on Wilderness Trails (Chiefly in the West)*. San Francisco: Sierra Club, 1951.

Clapesattle, Helen. *Dr. Webb of Colorado Springs*. Boulder: Colorado Associated University Press, 1984.

Collier, Peter, and Horowitz, David. *The Rockefellers: An American Dynasty*. New York: Holt, Rinehart & Winston, 1976.

Cowles, Elizabeth S. *Alpine Beginner*. N.p.: Privately printed, ca. 1934.

Cronin, Edward W., Jr. *The Arun: A Natural History of the World's Deepest Valley*. Boston: Houghton, Mifflin, 1979.

Dyar, Ralph E. *News for an Empire: The Story of the* Spokesman-Review *of Spokane, Washington, and of the Field It Serves*. Caldwell, Idaho: Caxton Printers, Ltd., 1952.

Haimendorf, Kristoph von Fürer. *The Sherpas of Nepal: Buddhist Highlanders*. Calcutta and New Delhi, India: Oxford Book, 1964.

Hillary, Sir Edmund. *Nothing Venture, Nothing Win*. New York: Coward, McCann & Googhegan, 1975.

Hodgins, Eric. *Mr. Blandings Builds His Dream House*. New York: Simon & Schuster, 1946.

Madge, Tim. *The Last Hero Bill Tilman: A Biography of the Explorer*. London: Hodder & Stoughton, 1995.

McKay, Douglas R. *Asylum of the Gilded Pill: The Story of Cragmor Sanatorium*. Denver, Colo.: State Historical Society of Colorado, 1983.

Ormes, Robert, with the Colorado Mountain Club. *Guide to the Colorado Mountains*, 6th rev. ed. Chicago: Sage Books, 1973.

Petzoldt, Patricia. *On Top of the World: My Adventures with My Mountain-Climbing Husband.* New York: Thomas W. Crowell, 1953.

Petzoldt, Paul K. *Teton Tales and Other Petzoldt Anecdotes.* Merrillville, Ind.: ICS Books, 1995.

Samson, Karl. *Frommer's Comprehensive Travel Guide: Nepal,* 2d ed. New York: Prentice Hall Travel, 1992–1993.

Shaha, Rishikesh. *Modern Nepal: A Political History 1769–1955,* 2 vols. Riverdale, Md.: Riverdale, 1990.

Shipton, Eric. *The Mount Everest Reconnaissance Expedition.* New York: E. P. Dutton, 1952.

Smith, Cyndi. *Off the Beaten Track: Women Adventurers and Mountaineers in Western Canada.* Jasper, Canada: Coyote Books, 1989.

Sprague, Marshall. *Newport in the Rockies: The Life and Good Times of Colorado Springs,* 3d rev. ed. Athens, Ohio: Sage Books, 1985.

Strong, William M. *How to Travel Without Being Rich.* Garden City, N.Y.: Doubleday, Doran, 1937.

———. *Photography for Fun.* New York: Leisure League of America, 1934.

Tilman, H. W. *The Seven Mountain-Travel Books.* Introduction by Jim Perrin. London: Diadem Books Ltd./Seattle: The Mountaineers, 1983.

Index

Ang Tharkay 118, 160
Alpine Beginner 41
Alpine Club, The 69, 93, 193
Ama Dablam (Amdanglungma) 152, 156
American Alpine Club (AAC) 21, 69, 72,
    89, 90, 94, 93, 97, 101, 103, 165,
    181, 187, 192
American Geographical Society 81, 103,
    117
Amlekhgaoi (Nepal) 106
Ang Yang Tsen 118, 160
Annapurna (Nepal) 108, 121, 168, 177,
    190, 192
Arahuaco Indians (Colombia) 75, 76,
    84–86
Artists
    Britton, Edgar 170, 187
    Dehn, Adolph 170
    Elkins, Henry Arthur 187
    Robinson, Boardman 170, 187
Arun River (Nepal) 1, 118, 126, 127, 131,
    133, 135, 150, 160, 161, 162, 190
Auden, Dr. John B. 117, 126
Auden, W. H. 117
Ayres, Fred 42
"Aunt Fannie." *See* Stewart, Sarah
    Cowles.

Bakewell, S. J., Anderson 72, 82, 103, 115,
    117, 118, 120n20, 121, 128, 130,
    132, 139, 143, 145–147, 149–
    151, 154, 160, 161, 189–192, 194
Bamboo bridges in Nepal 135
Barranquilla (Colombia) 74, 77, 78, 81, 85
Bates, Robert 62, 63, 65, 74, 76, 89, 93,
    190
Bell, Mr. 28, 30–33
Bergschule (Switzerland) 22, 53, 54
Biener, Marie 36
Boucher, Stanley W. 95, 96
Braden, Spruille 86
Brandeis, Fanny 172, 173, 183n23
Broadmoor Art Acadamy 170. *See*
        Colorado Springs Fine Arts
        Center.
Broadmoor Hotel 16, 21, 96, 167, 180
Brower, David 2, 97
Buck Mountain (Wyoming) 58, 59, 60, 198
Bullock, Fannie Bullock 69
Bullock, Guy Henry 153
Bung (Nepal) 134, 140, 141n18, 162

Cabot, Thomas 72, 74
Cabot Party 72, 77, 85, 86
Canadian Rockies 42, 72, 197

Capitol Peak 96
Caribbean Trip 1969 176,180
Carrol Lakes (Colorado) 51,181
Case,John 90,91
Chamlang (Nepal) 126,152
Chandragari Pass (Nepal) 2,107
Cheney,Laura 11
Cheney Brothers Silk Mills 12
Cheyenne Canyon (Colorado) 168
Cheyenne Mountain Country Club 16,180
Club Suisse de Femmes Alpinistes 181
Colorado Mountain Club (CMC) 42,51,
      95–97,165,181,187,198: CMC
      Juniors 95,96
Colorado College (CC) 11,16–19,95,
      170,172,173,187
Colorado Springs 15–20,22,50,51,54,
      93–95,97,102,103,156,165,
      167,168,172–174,179–181,187
Colorado Springs Fine Arts Center 4,165,
      166,170,187
Colorado Springs Symphony 4,95
Cook,Frances 93
Cook's 115
Cowles I,Alfred 12
Cowles II,Alfred12,15,18,20
Cowles III,Alfred 12,15,16,18,20–22,
      38n17,54,57,68n5,170,171
Cowles,Ann 17,54,93
Cowles,Elizabeth Cheney 15
Cowles,Elizabeth Livingston Strong.*See*
      Partridge,Elizabeth (Betsy).
Cowles,Richard Livingston 16,167
Cowles,Sarah.*See* Stewart,Sarah
      Cowles.
Cowles,Stephanie 167
Cragmor Sanitorium 16,37,38n2
Cromwell,Georgia Englehard 69,71
Culebra Avenue (Colorado Springs) 18,
      94,167

Da Namgyol 121,139
Darjeeling (India) 103,117,118,121,
      126,146,160,191
Davis,Eleanor.*See* Ehrman,Eleanor Davis
de Brette Peak (Colombia) 80,81,84

Dent de Satarma (Switzerland) 32
Dents du Midi (Switzerland) 22–25,173,
      197
Dhankuta (Nepal) 123,125–127,131,
      162
Dharan (Nepal) 118,126,139
Dhaulagiri (Nepal) 178
Dicky 121,132,154
Dingboche (Nepal) 152,160
Dingla (Nepal) 128,131
Dodge,Stuart 98,100n20,187
Donu 139,162
Duboche Convent 151
Dudh Kosi (Nepal) 135,152,189
Duke of Abruzzi 50

Eastman Kodak Company 39n26,51,115
Eberli,Max 74–81
EhEhrman,Eleanor Davis 69,174
Englehard,Georgia.*See* Cromwell,
      Georgia Englehard.
Eureka Climbing Club 41
Evans,Dr.Charles 168
Exum,Glenn 2,41,43,44,46,47,57,62,
      63,65,90,198,199

Falconer,Ambassador George and Lady
      108,109,115
Female mountaineers,attitudes of and
      toward 57,60,69,71,76,78,93,
      94,96,97,101–103,193
Ferris-wheel swings (Nepal) 158,178
Fletcher,Horace 8,9
Fountain Valley School 20,187
Froelicher,Elizabeth 20
Froelicher,Francis 20,22,41
Fryxell,Fritiof 42
Fuller,Edwina Fay 69
Fundacion (Colombia) 74,85

Geological Survey of India 117
Georges,Antoine 27,28,30–37,41
Georges,Josef 28,30,31
Gloomy Gulch (Colombia) 77,79,80,84
Grand Teton (Wyoming) 1,41,42–47,57,
      58,63,67,91,92,197–199

Grass, Kaspar 53
Guardian, The (Colombia) 80, 176, 198
Gudel (Nepal) 134, 135
Guide to the Colorado Mountains 165
Gyaljen Junior 115, 116, 128, 132, 154
Gyaljen Senion 116, 127, 143, 147, 149, 151

Hall, Henry 72, 78
Hammett, Ph.D., Ben 21, 38, 39n17
head man from Namche Bazar 143, 156, 157
Henderson, Kenneth 42
Hermosa Way (Colorado Springs) 95, 167
Herzog, Maurice 168, 182, 183n20, 190
Heyerdahl, Thor 166
High altitude, effects of 21, 77, 162, 176, 190
Hillary, Sir Edmund 2, 141n22, 168, 189
Himilayan Club 115, 118
Hodgins, Eric 11
Hongu (Hunku) Khola (Nepal) 134, 135
Hooker, Sir Joseph 126
Horszowski, Miezyslaw (Miecio) 171–174, 183n23, 184n29
Hotel Cecil (New Delhi) 104, 115
Hotz, John 115, 116
House, Laney 177, 178, 181
House, William (Bill) 62, 63, 65, 74, 76, 89, 93, 177, 178, 181
Houston, M.D., Charles (Charley) 77, 89, 90, 91, 103, 104, 107, 112, 114, 115, 117, 119n9, 120n20, 121, 122, 125, 127–130, 132, 133, 135, 139, 143, 147, 149, 151–154, 156, 162, 166, 181, 188–192
Houston, Dorcas 89, 90, 191
Houston, Nell 1, 93, 103, 106, 108, 111, 114, 115, 117, 128, 188
Houston, Oscar 1, 93, 98, 103, 104, 106, 108, 110, 111, 113–115, 117, 125, 127, 128, 129, 137, 139, 143, 145, 147, 149–151, 154, 156–158, 161, 188, 190, 191

Ice Mountain (Colorado) 51
Imja Khola (Nepal) 152
Innukhu (Hinku) Khola (Nepal) 135
Irkhua Khola (Nepal) 128

jemadar from Dhankuta 126, 131, 132, 154
Jogbani (India) 117, 118, 162, 163
Jomson (Nepal) 200
Jungfrau/Jungfrau Group (Switzerland) 25, 54, 198

K2 (Pakistan/China) 73, 89, 98, 130, 190
Kala Patar (Nepal) 153
Kali Gandaki (Nepal) 177, 178, 200
Kanchenjunga (Nepal/Sikkim) 121, 138
Kantega (Nepal) 150
Karachi (Pakistan) 103, 104
Kathmandu (Nepal) 1, 2, 104–115, 118, 128, 146, 177, 188, 189, 194
Khumbu (Solu-Khumbu—Nepal) 1, 118, 132, 137, 143, 153, 154, 188, 189, 191, 192
Khumbu Glacier 1, 153, 154, 189
Khumbu Icefall 189
Kilimanjaro (Tanzania) 175, 180, 200
Knowlton, Elizabeth 69, 71, 72, 74–80, 94

Ladies Alpine Club 181
La Chapelle, Dolores 101
La Reina (Colombia) 79–84, 176, 198
Langtang Himal (Nepal) 192
Leschetizky, Thedor 6, 183n23
Lhotse (Nepal) 150–153
Lochmatter, Franz 34
Longs Peak (Colorado) 22
Lowe, George 168
Lukla (Nepal) 135, 141n19

Maharajah Mohan Shamsher Jung Bahadur Rana 108–111, 113–115, 126
Makalu (Nepal) 126, 152
Mallory, George Leigh 33, 153

Mani-rimdu festival 190,194
Madge,Tim 192,193
Mathay,Fabian 23
Matterhorn (Switzerland) 9,25,34–37,54, 71,90,103,156,172,187,197–200
McCreery,Eliza Livingston. *See* Strong, Eliza L. McCreery
McCreery,William 6
Merrick,Mary 93
Merrick,Polly 90,91
Miller,Maynard 97
Molenaar,Dee 98
Mexican volcanoes 176
Monte Grande Pass (Colombia) 74
Moran,Father Marshall 118
Morris,James 168
Motilone Indians (Colombia) 85
Mount Bross (Colorado) 22
Mount Confederation 72
Mount Eolus (Colorado) 96
Mount Everest (Nepal/Tibet) 1,27,37, 73,102,106,111,114,117,118, 121,133,135,138,139,150– 156,165,166,168,179,188, 189,191,192,198
Mount Foraker (Alaska) 103
Mount Fuji (Japan) 177
Mount Lincoln (Colorado) 22,96,197,200
Mount Marcy (New York) 18
Mount Moran (Wyoming) 58,62,63,90, 102,198
Mount Oxford (Colorado) 41
Mount Sherman (Colorado) 22,197,200
Mount Wister (Wyoming) 58,198
Mr. Blanding Builds His Dream House, 11
Mummery,A. F. 42

Namche Bazar (Nepal) 1,115,121,135, 137–139,156,161,189
Nanda Devi (India) 114,130
Nanga Parbat (Pakistan) 71
Nawang Tensing Jangpo,reincarnate Lama of the Tengboche Gompa. *See* Rimpoche.
Nehru,Prime Minister Jawaharlal 162, 164n22,188

NORAD (North American Air Defense command) 173
Numbur (Nepal) 132,158
Nuptse (Nepal) 150–152
Nuptse-Lhotse Ridge (Nepal) 151

Oberon,Merle 79
Odell,Noel E. 114
Orcutt,Christine Reid 69,94
Ormes,Robert M. (Bob) 3,21,51,98, 165,166,187

Pa Nurbu 150,151
Pangboche (Nepal) 151,152
Partridge,General Earle E. (Pat) 173– 180,180,192
Partridge,Elizabeth Strong (Betsy)
   Appearance 2,16,180
   Attitude toward mountains 9,18,27, 36,42,57,72,81,144,155,167, 170,171,174,178
   Background/Childhood 5–12,21
   Bequests 187
   Death 181,185n60
   Flying 174–176,184n30
   Marriage to Alfred (Bob) Cowles III 12, 15–22,54,57
   Marriage to General Earle (Pat) E. Partridge 174–181
   Men 171,173,174
   Music 37,59,72,148,150,167,187, 172,174
   Organizations belonged to 4,20,95, 170,180,181
   Photography 48–51,52n8,60,73,86, 149,175,177
   Politics 172
   Role as Colorado's official mountain ambassador 168,171,182, 183n20
   Talks 78,165,166,170
   Trips:
      Africa 1967–1968 175,176
      Caribbean Circle 1969 176
      Colombia 1941 5,69,71–86
      Colorado 1942 93

Trips (*Continued*)
Nepal 1970 177–179
Nepal via Pakistan and India 1950 103–163
Switzerland 1933 22–37
Switzerland 1936 53, 54
Switzerland 1950 101
Tetons 1934, 1935 57–67
Tetons 1940 57–67
Tetons 1941 89–92
Tetons 1959 175
Partridge, Kay 174, 179, 181
Peary, Josephine Diebitsch 69
Perren, Elias 36
Petite Dent de Veisivi (Switzerland) 25, 27, 28, 32, 197, 198
Petzoldt, Patricia (Bernice) 72, 73, 92
Petzoldt, Paul 1, 5, 41–44, 46, 47, 57–63, 65–67, 72–80, 84–86, 89–93, 198
Phedi (Nepal) 114, 131–133
Pheriche (Nepal) 152
Pico Ujueta (Colombia) 80–83, 85, 198
Pikes Peak (Colorado) 18, 22, 174, 175, 197
Pittsburgh (Pennsylvania) 6, 166
Porters of Asia 50, 106, 107, 114, 115, 118, 127, 131, 133, 154, 156, 160, 190
Prentice, Alta Rockefeller 7
Prentice, Madelaine 8
Pueblo Bello (Colombia) 74–76

Rana Family of Nepal 107, 108, 111, 123, 164n22, 188. *See also* Colonel Shumshere, Colonel, and Maharajah Mohan.
Reid, Christine. *See* Orcutt, Christine Reid.
Rimpoche of Tengboche 147, 149, 150, 154, 165, 193, 194
Ripley, Dr. S. Dillon 126
Roberts, M. C., Major/Colonel J.O.M. (Jimmy) 119n16, 177
Rockefeller, Bessie. *See* Strong, Bessie Rockefeller.
Rockefeller, John D. 6, 10
Rockefeller, Nelson 85, 86
Royal Geographical Society 166

Runnette, Evelyn 97
Ruttledge, Hugh 139
Ryder, Dr. Charles 19, 20
Ryder, VI 19, 187

Salpa La (Pass) (Nepal) 131, 132, 158
San Sebastian (Colombia) 75, 76, 85
Sancocho feast 75, 77, 84
Santa Marta Range (Colombia) 1, 3, 5, 63, 69, 71, 72, 74–86, 92, 103, 117, 176, 198
Sapt Kosi (River) 162
Sarki 121, 139, 154
Sella, Vittoria 50, 198, 200
Sewall, Lil 167
Sewall, Richard 10, 167
Sherpas of Nepal 114, 115, 118, 121, 128, 132, 135, 137, 138, 143, 150, 151, 154, 156, 158, 160, 162, 177, 178, 194
Shipton, Eric 114, 139, 188, 189
Shumshere, Colonel (Kham Shumshere Jung Bahadur Rana) 123, 126
Singha Durbar (Kathmandu) 113
Singing in the mountains 31, 34, 35, 98, 127
Sisagarhi Pass (Nepal) 2, 106
Smith, Annie Peck 69
Smith, Emilie Strong 6–11, 21, 51, 54, 62, 92, 93, 98, 167, 168, 171, 172, 180, 181, 187
Smith, John 2
Smith, Judge Macauley 54, 62, 63, 65, 66, 167, 181
Solu. *See* Khumbu.
Sonam Tensing (Foreign Sportsman) 139
South Teton (Wyoming) 44, 90, 198, 199
St. Mary's College (Kurseong) 117, 118, 191
Standley, Harry 50, 51, 52n7, 96
Stephen, Leslie 42
Stewart, Sarah Cowles ("Aunt Fannie") 16, 18
Stewart, Philip ("Uncle Phil") 16, 18, 103, 167, 168, 174
Stieglitz, Alfred 77
Strong, Augustus Hopkins 6
Strong, Bessie Rockefeller 11

Strong, Charles 10
Strong, Elizabeth Livingston. *See* Partridge, Elizabeth.
Strong, Eliza Livingston McCreery 5–12
Strong, Emilie. *See* Smith, Emilie Strong.
Strong, John Henry 6–9, 12, 21–27, 32–35, 41, 49, 174, 39n26
Strong, William McCreery (Bill) 7, 8, 10, 11, 49, 51, 85
Sun River (Nepal) 118
Swartz, Dorothy Teague 95–98, 101, 171
Sweet, Walter 95
Swift, Jessica 174
Swiss Day 62, 90, 91, 99n3, 181

Tamur River (Nepal) 118, 122, 126, 162
Taweche (Nepal) 151, 155
Teague, Dorothy. *See* Swartz, Dorothy Teague
Tengboche Gompa 1, 121, 139, 143–151, 154–156, 166, 190, 193, 194
Tenzing Norgay 189
Tetons (Wyoming) 53–67, 89–93, 102, 175, 197–199
Thami (Nepal) 138, 189
Thanksgiving in Nepal 160, 161
Thomas, Frank A. C. 115, 116, 160, 162, 163, 164n23
"Three Musketeers" 133, 139, 162
Thyangboche. *See* Tengboche.
Tibet 114, 115, 122, 133, 153, 178, 193
Tibetan …
  bowls 157, 161
  clothes 137, 156
  ponies 106
  rugs 143
  tea 148, 150
  writing/language/books 145, 147

"Tigers" 18
Tihaar festival 123, 158, 160
Tilicho Pass (Nepal) 177, 178
Tilman, H. W. (Bill) 4, 108, 109, 114–118, 120n16, 121, 127–130, 133, 134, 139, 140, 141n18, 143, 151–154, 157, 158, 160–163, 188, 189, 191–193
Tramsurku (Tramusurmu) (Nepal) 155
Tribhuvan, King 107, 161, 162, 164n22, 177, 188
Tuesday Club 20, 102
Tumlingtar (Nepal) 127, 160

Ujueta, Juan 74, 78, 81
"Uncle Phil." *See* Stewart, Philip.
Underhill, Miriam O'Brien 69, 71
Underhill, Robert 42, 71
Untergabelhorn (Switzerland) 34, 197

Vassar College 1, 5, 6, 11, 12, 18, 71, 166, 187
Von Heimendorf, Kristoph Von Furer 151

Warren, Ambassador and Mrs. 103, 104
Webb, Dr. Gerald 16
Webb-Waring Institute 16
Whymper, Edward 36, 103
Woman's Educational Society 170
Wood, Walter 72, 81, 103
Wulsin, Fred 91

Young, Geoffry Winthrop 33, 34

∞